Caravan

BIOGRAPHIES

from the SUFISM SYMPOSIA

1994-2014

Introduction by
Nahid Angha, Ph. D.

**International Association of
Sufism Publications**

Second Edition 2022
Library of Congress Number: 2022933077
ISBN: 978-1-7343151-7-2

This book does not imply any gender bias by the use of feminine or masculine terms, nouns, and/or pronouns.

The biographies represent the individual views of their authors. Individual copyright to their work is retained by the authors. The publication of any article, essay, story, or other material herein constitutes neither an endorsement of, agreement with or validation of the contents of the author's views expressed therein.

Compiled by Sarah Hastings Mullin, Ph. D.

Editors:
Heidi Gilpin, Ph. D.
Sheikha Halima Haymaker
Hamaseh Kianfar, Ed. D.
Sahar Kianfar, JD
Salima Ginny P. Matchette
Sarah Hastings Mullin, Ph. D.
Katherine Preston
Amineh Amelia Pryor, Ph. D.
Ashley Werner, Esq.
Special Thanks to Susan Ferdowsali

Cover Design: Soraya Chase Clow, Ph. D.

For more information address:
International Association of Sufism Publications
PO Box 2382, San Rafael, CA 94912 USA

Printed in Great Britain
By TJ Books Limited, Padstow, Cornwall

Table of Contents

Prologue

International Association of Sufism: Programs and Projects Co-Directors, Coordinators, Editorial Staff

History must be told. Contributions of individuals who have shaped our cultures and will continue shaping our future must be recorded. We are to acknowledge the works of men and women who kept the door of civility and peace open, men and women who have taken it upon themselves to serve humanity and shape the course of civilization towards a better fate for all; men and women who stood strong against human failings of all cultures, of all times. They have shaped more than one nation; they have shaped civilizations. Their contributions must not remain unrecognized or unacknowledged.

This book is dedicated to them: The Teachers of Humanity.

Introduction

History must be told. Contributions of individuals who have shaped our cultures and will continue shaping our future must be recorded. We are to acknowledge the works of men and women who kept the door of civility and peace open, men and women who have taken it upon themselves to serve humanity and shape the course of civilization towards a better fate for all; men and women who stood strong against human failings of all cultures, of all times. They have shaped more than one nation; they have shaped civilizations. Their contributions must not remain unrecognized or unacknowledged.

This book is a history devoted to them, to those who have come together, from every corner of the world, to celebrate in an international forum, and to create a global spiritual family for Sufis, interfaith leaders, scientists, poets, musicians, academics, and others through the annual Sufism Symposium.

If we do not record such history, then we live a life disconnected from the living presence of the past, we remain inattentive to those who have shaped humanity, and we will, necessarily, live in our boxed world designed by the limitation of time.

Life is a wonderful unique journey intended for each individual through the genetics of cultures, time periods, nature and all potentialities and actualities. We each walk our own destiny, and we live in a space in time granted to each by the design of a complex and infinite universe, a universe ruled by abstract and tangible laws, laws of eternal values, never changing, open for our intellectual observation and understanding. This world of great richness offers us enough to live worthwhile lives; this design makes every being worthy of life, of honor, of respect; it grants every being the right to be. The heart of every being beats in gratitude for the breath of life. Divinity breathes through the heart of every cell; it is the knowledge of this truth that teaches us to honor all in peace, and, remain honorable ourselves. It is the manner of Sufis to show respect and maintain honor; it is the manner of Sufis to dwell on a level above that of human calamities and failures. Such qualities are the fruit of personal striving for understanding and its attainment.

I

Sufism is the mystical and inner dimension of Islam, historically originating from a group of people who used to gather on the platform of the Prophet's mosque, in Medina in the 7th century, to listen to his teachings so they might learn the meaning of revelation, attain spiritual truth and understand the meaning of unity, develop practices for spiritual transformation, and ensure that their belief was founded upon knowledge embedded in reality. It is from this group, *Ahle Suffa,* the People of the Platform, that Sufism derives its origin. Their devotion contributed to the establishment of one of the most celebrated human movements of peace in the history of civilization. *Ahle-Suffa* was comprised of a few individuals at the beginning, but their numbers increased as time passed. They came from different nations, cultures, and backgrounds.

History tells us that over time, three major Sufi centers were established: the Center of Baghdad (in Iraq), the Center of Fars (in Persia/Iran), and the Center of Khurasan (in Persia/Iran). Over the centuries, Sufis and their students traveled across many lands, introducing this spiritual practice into the fabric of different cultures and times. Thus, over time, many schools, orders, and *tariqat* of Sufism were established. Each School began to focus on certain principles and practices, and gathered around a teacher. History also tells us that sometimes the surface of Sufism has taken the colors of cultures and times, yet the essence of Sufism remained unchanged in the hearts of its practitioners. The central principles of Sufism, a journey of personal transformation, have remained free from the dimensions of time or place, gender or race, cultures or ceremonies. Passing from the world of multiplicity to discover the essential unity became a key pursuit, in the hope that the walls of limitations fall and the manifestation of the Divine illuminates the heart of the seeker, and that the wayfarer discovers the bounty of Being.

Around the 10th and 11th centuries, Sufi teachers began to explain this inner journey through philosophical terminology. Integrating the Sufi understanding, they developed a language of philosophy explaining the stages of the journey, the stations of the traveler, and the meaning of Divine Reality. As a result, many terms and terminologies we use today are the outcomes of that era. Persian Sufis have made the greatest contributions towards the development of Sufism; Arabic and Persian (Farsi) remain the major languages, and Turkish, Urdu and a few others remain the minor languages in the Sufi literature.

One of the most important elements in the success of a spiritual journey is the presence of a teacher, and the history of Sufism has been sanctified with the richness of its noble and magnificent teachers, who have shared their wisdom with many. Over time, students gathered around these teachers establishing centers. As time passed, those teachings and those centers developed into Sufi Schools, *turuq* (plural of *tariqat*).

There are about twenty major Sufi Schools around the world, extending from the border of Malaysia to the coast of West Africa and many lands and nations in between, there are also many organizations that have devoted their missions, teachings and endeavors to the teachings and study of Sufism. One such organization is the International Association of Sufism, with members from around the world, and with over 300 collections of interviews, presentations and performances by its presenters and participants at the Annual Sufism Symposium

International Association of Sufism:

As I wrote in the wonderful book *Women Creating Change*, a book compiled by Dr. Mijares, Dr. Rafea and myself: "I am not sure if we choose our convictions or the convictions choose us; I am not sure if the story we tell transforms communities or communities plant the seed of transformation that grows into lasting stories; I am not sure if every step we take is predestined or if we freely create our own choosing. It does not matter, what matters is that I am born into this journey, into this "space in time" that I can claim as my own. It is with this realization and acknowledgement that I cultivate a longing to serve humanity, as an offering, an appreciation to this magnificent Being that has given me this "space in time," an irreplaceable chance of life. How can I remain indifferent to it? It is from this view that I would like to tell the story of the International Association of Sufism, a gender balanced organization...."

It was as early as 1979 that Dr. Ali Kianfar and I began cultivating the idea of inviting Sufis from around the world to a forum and to open dialogue amongst Sufi Schools. It was late 1980 when we began by writing letters of invitation to many Sufi masters around the world. The responses were of great encouragement. Our first endeavor was establishing the International Association of Sufism (1983) inviting Sufis and Sufi Schools to join and help to build a global center in order to learn from each other, celebrate our cultures, teachers, diversities, colors, styles and history. To my knowledge, this was the first time in the history of Sufism that an organization was established for this goal: bringing Sufis from around the world into a forum. This was the beginning of a most inspiring journey for Dr. Kianfar and myself.

The establishment of the International Association of Sufism has been a journey of great magnitude that required extensive research to identify, locate, contact, communicate with, invite and also to understand all diversities, personalities, and politics, while ultimately remaining truthful to the goal of coming together in the spirit of harmony and friendship for the sake of education, human rights and equality. It has been one of the most valuable journeys of my life. Remembering my maternal grandmother's advice: "the world is an open forum, to stand for what you think is a worthy pursuit, you must first qualify yourself for the endeavor; otherwise you will be pushed aside." So I began such a journey with extensive research and learning, with each step, my personal world expanded into a universe of deeply valued devotion manifested in many colors and forms: what a magnificent treasure was unlocked by the hand of my destiny. Yet this journey was not without its limitations. Being a woman, taking on such an endeavor was not always appreciated or tolerated. So I faced some small pebbles on the road, which I consider excellent experience for the formation of the IAS, an organization that is founded upon gender equality.

Our next endeavor, in conjunction with translation and book publication, was the publication of *Sufism: An Inquiry:* a journal devoted to Sufi practices and schools. Many Sufis have made great contributions to the establishment of this journal. Sufis have contributed towards human rights, education, art, freedom, literature throughout history, and it was a time to have a forum so we all, as an international and global spiritual family, could exchange information and share our knowledge of practices, history, art, literature, science, and linguistics. This was 1985 and the first publication was produced in 1988. *Sufism Journal* was in paper print format until 2012, when we decided to go green, save trees and paper, and offer immediate global access to the *Journal* through an on line version.

In addition to the journal, our publishing included the translations and original writings on Sufism, its practices, history, literature and poetry, schools and masters, and we have accumulated and continue to accumulate a great number of books. Our many projects and missions required the development of Departments. Being admitted as a United Nations' NGO/

DPI, receiving an award from UNESCO for our global peace work, and becoming an ambassador to the UNICEF were great acknowledgements of our work. The time has come to organize the international forum we hoped for, a forum that brings these teachers of humanity together, in the peaceful spirit of harmony and friendship, and in person.

History was in the making: what a beautiful opportunity. The "Annual Sufism Symposium" was the best appropriate title, the gathering of the drunken wayfarers and wanderers, and this was March 1994, the first Annual Sufism Symposium, in San Rafael (Marin County) California. Many Sufis came from around the globe, from the border of Malaysia to the coasts of West Africa and many lands and cultures in between. We honored Sufis from Asian heritage to Middle Eastern, European, Canadian, American and African. A great variety of cultures, songs, languages, and *zikr* were presented, and that was the first time in the history of Sufism that a woman (myself) sat in the central circle and led a *zikr* together with many Sufi masters of our time. That opened a new door of possibility for my sisters and brothers to stand together and lead side by side.

Since its conception, and through developing its eleven departments, and working with many faith communities and human rights advocacy organizations, the IAS remained truthful to its gender-balanced mission to the present time. The coming together of Sufi masters and scholars, men and women, in a mutual respectful ground, within the Annual Sufism Symposia events, has formed a suitable place for honoring Sufi women's leadership. It has reexamined the historical movements of women in the creation of cultures, cultural identity, history, and politics; it has allowed us to honor women who have established leadership in patriarchal societies. The Annual Sufism Symposium was not only celebrated in the US but also in Spain, Egypt and Scotland.

The IAS remains a valuable participant in international interfaith communities, such as the Council for a Parliament of the World's Religions, and the United Religions Initiative, as well as in local organizations such as the Marin Interfaith Council, the Interfaith Center at the Presidio in San Francisco and many others.

The laws of complex simplicity lead our journey, and on the crossroads of destiny we meet our match in those whose presence makes the difference between intolerance and civility, between savagery and courtesy, between barbarism and respect. It is so remarkable how our lives unfold, how the moments of time lead us towards a destination, and how incredible it is to discover our family, our companions, our relations, our relatives and our friendships from within the multitude of cultures, times, nations, and possibilities. What beautiful connections; what an incredible union.

I have been most fortunate that my road of life has come across such respectful friends and fellow travellers, true sisters and brothers, individuals of great integrity. I am also grateful for my sisters and brothers: Interfaith leaders, academics, artists, psychologists, human rights advocates, poets and musicians who, too, have taken this journey with me and in support of Sufism.

This book is dedicated to all these most noble men and women, as they are my reason for the compilation of this manuscript.

Nahid Angha
February 4th 2015
San Rafael, California

6

Biographies from the Sufism Symposia (1994-2014)

Khalifa Aliyu Ahmed Abulfathi

Khalifa Aliyu Ahmed Abulfathi was born in Maiduguri, Nigeria, on May 30, 1956. He was educated as a child in both Qur'anic recitation and Early Islamic studies. He received a certificate of proficiency in Arabic in 1974. Khalifa Aliyu Ahmed Abulfathi attended the College of Art and Arabic Studies in Sokoto, Nigera and obtained a higher Islamic certificate. He also attended the Al-Azahar University in Cairo for History and Civilization studies, the British Career Training College, and the Transworld Tutorial College.

Khalifa Aliyu Ahmed Abulfathi began his working experience as a teacher of Arabic and Islamic Studies and taught at a primary school and teacher's college. He was a publisher at *Trends Magazine* from 1986 to 1989. He also served as chairman of various organizations including, but not limited to: Himayah Ventures, ACC Nigeria, and Netlinc Communication Systems LTD. Khalifa Aliyu Ahmed Abulfathi has also been a member of various boards and organizations such as: the Borno State Preaching Board (2006), the International Association of Sufism (2006-present), and the Network of World Interfaith (2008-present).

Khalifa Aliyu Ahmed Abulfathi has received many awards, including "fellow member of the Institute of Administrative Management of Nigeria" (1989), Sports Writer's Association of Nigeria (SWAN), Borno State Chapter and Sharia Students Association (SHASA) Faculty of Law, University of Maiduguri. He has attended many conferences including: the Conference on Gender-Based Violence and Role of Women in Islam, Nairobi, Kenya (2006); the Conference on HIV Prevention, Kampala, Uganda (2007); the International Association of Sufism Symposium in California, United States (2008, 2010, 2011); and the Conference on the Formation of World Interfaith, Istanbul, Turkey (2008). He has served as Secretary General of the Network of African Islamic Organizations for Population and Development (under UNPFA) 2005-2010, and as a member of the Board of Trustees for the International Tijjaniyya Brotherhood Organization.

In 1970, Khalifa Aliyu Ahmed Abulfathi was initiated into the Tijjaniya Sufi order by Sheikh Al-Hadi and in 1979 was given permission to initiate others into the order. He was appointed the Khalifa of Sheikh Ahmad Abulfathi on April 23, 2003. His disciples are estimated to be in the millions.

Nahid Angha, Ph. D.

I was born in Iran in a family from scholarly and aristocratic backgrounds. My father, Moulana Shah Maghsoud Sadegh Angha, came from a scholarly Sufi family. His father, Mir Ghotbeddin Muhammad Angha, was among the greatest masters of Sufism, an Uwaiysi (also spelled Oveysi). His grandfather, Moulana Jalalleddin Abulfazl Angha, was also a Sufi master. Thus my father's family embraced generations of Sufis who traced their lineage back to the Prophet of Islam.

My mother, Mah Talat Etemad Moghadam Angha, came from an aristocratic family with a rich history of influential individuals accorded great authority and prestige. She became my father's sole partner in life, his long standing supporter and dearest friend. My father respected and honored her greatly, always treating her with reverence and compassion. He made it his final wish for all of us, his physical and spiritual children, to respect, honor, and serve her to the best of our abilities. My mother's paternal and maternal mothers were of Ghajar Dynasty. My maternal grandmother, Inbesat Douleh, was a niece of one of the kings of that Dynasty, a Dynasty that ruled Iran from the eighteenth to the early twentieth centuries. She was a wonderful woman, whose kindness and strength of character touched all who met her. It was her wisdom and support that smoothed the road of life for my parents, and her selfless generosity greatly contributed of building the Sufi school of Oveysi Shah Maghsoudi. She was strong, wealthy, educated, and forward-thinking for her times. Though not formally a Sufi, she supported, understood, respected and honored Sufism. She was among my father's greatest supporters, and her mansion remained a center for Sufi gatherings for many years. In history we come across individuals who advocate and build key bricks in the foundations of human civilization. Many of these individuals might have remained unknown to the majority or forgotten through time, despite the vital roles they play in opening and supporting cultural, historical, and intellectual possibilities; they are the architects behind history. Inbesat Douleh was one of those individuals.

When I was born my parents were in their twenties, and my birth coincided with the advent of my father's quest for inner traveling. I was not only his first child but also his first student. My earliest childhood memories are of exploring the Sufi path together with my father. He taught me how to be, how to meditate, how to stand for and honor my being. From infancy, he held my hand and lovingly guided me along the most fascinating and beautiful roads towards achieving self  knowledge towards the doorway to divine understanding. It seems as if we grew up together in this spiritual path. In his later years, he would call on me as his closest confidant, his friend, and sometimes even as a mother. This spiritual connection between the two of us created animosity among a few and became even stronger after his physical passing. The bitter sweet journey of becoming is a worthy journey nonetheless.

My father made it his responsibility to guide me towards the most favorable destination, the study of self. At his instruction, I used to meditate for hours, reading numerous books and studying different disciplines, from philosophy to literature, from theology to poetry. I studied as much as there was to study. I was especially fascinated by the life stories of philosophers, Sufis, and mystics and their teachings. Whether it was the life story of Socrates or Einstein, Ba Yazid or St. Augustine; whether it was the Upanishad or the sacred teachings of Zoroaster; quatrains of Khayyam or sonnets of Hafiz, I read and meditated upon all of them. I gave myself an opportunity to learn from each, and, in turn, each taught me to better understand my own path - Sufism: Islam in its purest practice.

Throughout the course of my studies, none affected me more than the life story of the Prophet. The effects of his story on my life still remain beyond measure. I began studying the life and the teachings of the Prophet when I was in my early teens and still continue to the present time. I remain in awe when thinking of the depth of his teachings, and my admiration for his invaluable service to human civilization increases as I learn more. Studying his life taught me the art of becoming. I searched for meaning, and I was granted such a request.

I was eighteen when Moulana Shah Maghsoud honored me and approved my spiritual advancement by giving me a woolen robe. The robe, itself, was his own. It was a camel color, with delicate brown embroideries. This was my first robe, and with it my heart opened towards the knowledge of the inner journey, I was granted eyes to see, ears to hear, and a heart to recognize such everlasting Beauty. He asked me to teach when I was in my mid twenties and I taught under his supervision and in his presence for many years. I received another robe of honor in 1980, the year he passed away. He entrusted that Robe to my mother to give to me. It was a black woolen robe. These robes have remained among my valuable possessions to this day. He entrusted me with many of his writings, and at his instructions I have translated and publised many of his works.

My academic life was also focused. I studied philosophy, psychology, literature and education, and graduated from universities in Iran, the United Kingdom, and the United States, with masters and doctorate degrees. I studied Persian literature in depth, as well as English literature, to hone my abilities to translate my father's and other's worthy works. Next to Sufism, philosophy was my greatest academic passion.

I have traveled extensively to speak to varied audiences on a range of topics regarding human rights, global peace, Sufi literature, Sufism and Islam - in America, Africa, the Middle East, Europe, Asia. I have been honored to be invited by many humanitarian and educational organizations to participate in their works and contribute to their worthy causes - from global to grassroots, from interfaith to social justice, from poets to politicians. I have worked with many people from numerous countries with wide ranging passions, where I have built lifelong friendships with individuals who led me to learn not only more about myself, but also about the world around me. I was inducted to the Marin Women's Hall of Fame, the first Muslim woman given that honor; I have received numerous awards for my global peace works as well as for my advocacy for human rights, and was also recognized by international agencies as among the most influential women in religion globally.

Remembering that on the path of religion guidance remains in the hands of the Divine and not of people gives me great assurance and hope for the hearts of the seekers. I have offered my heart to the Reality and I have received my share from this everlasting treasure. My being has absorbed the richness of the Infinite; my inner quality has found its way into the wealth of *faghr* (poverty). My share of attunement to the Divine was richness; honesty was my wealth. It was this richness that saved me from the pain of hardships, bitter realization, and envious acquaintances after the physical passing of my father. That was a hard time. My father wrote in the Introduction to *Anvare-Gholub-e-Salekin*, a book written by his grandfather Hazrat Jalalleddin Abulfazl, of the same experience of disillusion after losing his own father to the hands of time. "When the time of the journey arrived, and the essence of truth [referring to his father and teacher] took the journey from the world of possibilities into the hidden realm of the essence — it was then that disagreeable accompanies revealed their corrupt intentions. But what they have revealed was not the voice of wisdom but the harsh sound of the empty drum. Yet since there is a truth in each message, and every story teaches a moral principle, the share for the false friends took the suffering of the distance of the friend [referring to his father] away and added to my eternal love for the Beloved. All became a wealth added to my treasure. And so I chose seclusion, reaching into the treasure of the heart, and there found my portion of the eternal richness of Being, and my words found truth of their meaning."

His life story after the passing of his father resembles my life story after his passing. The deceit of individuals was a painful realization for me. I kept the door closed to those false friends, and left the mirage to the sandy desert, and rid my road from such chaos.

My inexpressible gratitude is to the Eternal sacred - who has granted me many trustworthy and respectful friends, true sisters and brothers; a wonderful physical and spiritual sister, Tannaz Angha, whose endless devotion is manifested in her beautiful daughter, Avazeh; a knowledgeable and honorable partner in life, Shah Nazar Dr. Ali Kianfar, whose friendship has helped me walk safely on this road of life; my two daughters, Hamaseh and Sahar, who are devoted to this path of self knowledge and whose merit and friendship are my life's treasures; my grandson Kian, whose joyous quest for knowledge is inspiring; and above all for the honor and the opportunity to serve my beloved mother, Mah Talat Etemad Moghadam Angha, for the last twenty eight years of her physical life, during her most precious time.

Life is a gift of beauty, thank God for such a beautiful journey.

Shaykh Taner Ansari

Es-Seyyid Es-Shaykh Taner Mustafa Ansari Tarsusi er Rifai el Qadiri was born in Tarsus, Turkey, to a devout Muslim family of *Seyyids* (descendants of Prophet Muhammad). He completed his university studies in Michigan, where he helped found the Muslim Students Association of the United States and Canada. He was initiated into the Qadiri Rifai Tariqa in Istanbul under Es-Seyyid Es-Shaykh Muhyiddin Ansari, from whom he received his license to teach Sufism. His spiritual lineage also includes the Naqshbandi, Mevlevi, and Bektashi orders. Under his Shaykh's orders, Shaykh Taner founded a new order of the Ansari Tariqa of the Qadiri Rifai Tariqa. Shaykh Taner and his wife Es-Sharifa Es-Shaykha Muzeyyen Ansari travel to and have established centers of the order in the United States, Canada, Mexico, South Africa, Tanzania, Mauritius, Germany, Australia, and the United Kingdom.

Shaykh Taner teaches Sufism and the Holy Qur'an and gives weekly talks internationally through live classes on the Internet. He also holds regular lectures and congregational *zikr* (*dhikr*). He has spoken and written about Islam and Sufism, alternative healing, and sustainable living in television and radio interviews, at churches, synagogues, schools and universities, among them Harvard University, Humboldt State University, Napa Valley College, and Boston University, and has given several presentations at the annual Sufism Symposium. Many of his talks are published in a periodical entitled *Call of the Divine.* He and his wife publish a blog called *A Sufi Point of View: Messages from the Heart* (http://www.sufiview.com). Shaykh Taner is a healing practitioner who sees patients in person and also does remote healing. He and his wife founded the Ansari Institute of Sufi Healing (AISH) to teach healing arts. Along with his wife Shaykha Muzeyyen Ansari, he has presented healing workshops worldwide for healers and health professionals and anyone else interested in the healing arts.

He is the author of several books in print and e-books including: *The Sun Will Rise in the West: The Holy Trail,* a book on Islam from the Sufi perspective (Ansari Publications, October 2000); *What About My Wood: 101 Sufi Stories,* a collection of Sufi teaching stories, many of which are based on the real life experiences of his students and former shaykhs (Ansari Publications, 2003); *Grand Masters of Sufism*, translations of Abdul Qadir Geylani's *Secret of Secrets* and Ahmed er Rifai's *Guidance to Mysticism* (Ansari Publications, 2008; e-book, 2013); *Alternative Healing: The Sufi Way*, prayers and remedies from the Holy Qur'an, and health tips for those interested in healing (Ansari Publications, 2007, revised second edition, 2012; e-book of second edition, 2012); *Surviving 2012 & Beyond: A Must Have Survival Book*, a book on sustainable living (Ansari Publications, 2010); *Ya Sin: Sura 36 of the Holy Quran,* a booklet (Ansari Publications, 2013).

Shaykh Taner is currently translating the Holy Qur'an into modern English from the Sufi perspective. He and his wife Shaykha Muzeyyen Ansari personally supervised and engaged in the building of the main center of the Tariqa in upstate New York. Plans are for the center to be an environmentally friendly model of sustainability. He and his wife reside at the main center in upstate New York.

Shaykha Muzeyyen Ansari

Es-Sharifa Es-Shaykha Muzeyyen Ansari is the Shaykha of the Islamic Sufi Order of Qadiri Rifai Tariqa. Shaykha Muzeyyen gives lectures and leads congregational *zikr* (*dhikr*) both locally and on the Internet. She and her husband Shaykh Taner Ansari founded the Ansari Institute of Sufi Healing (AISH) to teach healing arts. Along with her husband, she has presented healing workshops in the United States and abroad and has been interviewed on television and radio about women's role in Islam, Sufism, spiritual healing and sustainable living. As a healing practitioner, Shaykha Muzeyyen works together with her husband, seeing patients and providing remote healing.

Shaykha Muzeyyen has edited and written many articles on Sufism and alternative healing, Islam and sustainable living. She is an editor of all of Shaykh Taner Ansari's books. She and her husband also publish a blog that is called *A Sufi Point of View: Messages from the Heart* (http://www.sufiview.com). She served as Secretary of the Sufi Women Organization for one year.

She was on the board of Ansari Sustainable Living (2009 to 2012), a company dedicated to building eco-friendly structures and to education on how to live sustainably. She and her husband are currently overseeing and personally supervising the building of the spiritual center in upstate New York, which is eco-friendly.

Sufi Mystics Ayshegul Ashki and Kaan Kamil

Sufi Mystics Ayshegul Ashki and Kaan Kamil started the search for Truth in their teenage years and soon came upon the Transcendental Meditation (TM) Program. They practiced TM, TM-Siddhis and their associated precepts diligently and dedicatedly, always communally, and for many years within the largest TM intentional community in Iowa, with the intention of promoting World Peace. There they also earned academic degrees, at Maharishi International University.

Upon meeting their late teacher Dr. Lex Hixon—Sheikh Nur al-Jerrahi, their journey through the first-hand appreciation of the world's other mystical traditions began with intensity. Within a core Sufi practice, with the prompting of their teacher, they also took initiations with Vedanta, Mystical Christianity, and Buddhism, and deepened their vision and experience of Unity at the core of their being and in the expressions of life. Through the prompting of their mystic guide who appointed them as his successors in 1993, they started sharing the universal Sufi teachings, and continued on with this mission and natural inclination for the last two decades.

While their non-dual wisdom teachings and devotional practices are deeply rooted in Sufism, they universalize these on the shared basis of human experiences from mundane to mystical spectrums. Ashki and Kaan lead monthly interfaith peace retreats, participate in and lead interfaith and trans-traditional councils, environmental coalitions, community service groups, and present in science and non-duality, international Sufism, interreligious conferences and spiritual centers. Ashki holds a B.A. in Education and an M.A. in Science of Creative Intelligence, and an H.H.P. in Healing Arts. Kaan has a bachelor's degree in Computer Science, and has been in the IT industry for nearly three decades. They have been married for 25 years and have three children. They reside and share mystical teachings in Tustin, California.

Shahid Athar, M.D., F.A.C.P., F.A.C.E.

Shahid Athar is a Clinical Associate Professor and a physician in private practice in Indianapolis, Indiana. A United States citizen, Dr. Athar was born in India and educated at Patna University (India), the University of Karachi (Pakistan), and the Indiana University School of Medicine. He is an endocrinologist by specialty. He is a Fellow of the American College of Physicians and American College of Endocrinology and a past president of the Islamic Medical Association of North America.

He was Co-Founder and Chairman of the Islamic Society of Greater Indianapolis (ISGI) and the Interfaith Alliance of Indiana (IAI). He is an author of several books (including *Islamic Perspective in Medicine, Health Concerns for Believers* and *Healing the Wounds of 9/11*) and has over 120 published articles on medical and Islamic topics. He has spoken to many churches, civic organizations, universities and colleges on various topics including Islam, interfaith, spirituality and medical ethics. His affiliations include the Islamic Society of North America (ISNA), the Islamic Medical Association of North America (past president and chair, medical ethics) and the International Association of Sufism. He serves on the board of advisors for the Protection of Consciousness Project, an international human rights organization. He is not affiliated with any political or religious party. For his interfaith activities, The Indianapolis Medical Society in 2002 awarded him the Gov. Otis Bowen Award for Community Service. In 2008, the American College of Physicians named him as "The Laureate Physician of the Year" and in 2009 the St. Vincent Hospital in Indiana named him as a "Distinguished Physician." In 2011, the Islamic Medical Association of North America (IMAN) bestowed on him the Dr. Ahmed El-Kadi award for service to IMAN. Dr. Athar has been associated with the International Association of Sufism for the last ten years and has contributed to IAS symposia and to its journal, *Sufism: An Inquiry*. The web page for his writings is http://www.islam-usa.com.

Joseph Bobrow Roshi, Ph. D.

Dr. Joseph Bobrow Roshi is a Zen master and the founder and director of Deep Streams Zen Institute. A Dharma successor of Robert Aitken Roshi in the Diamond Sangha tradition of Zen, he also studied with Yamada Koun Roshi of the Sanbo Kyodan, with headquarters in Kamakura, Japan. In the early 1980's he lived and studied with Thich Nhat Hanh in Plum Village, where he co-translated his *Guide to Walking Meditation.* He is also the founder and president of the Coming Home Project, a service of Deep Streams that creates community for veterans, their families, and their providers while providing a range of integrative services that transform trauma and enhance well-being.

Arthur F. Buehler, Ph.D.

I have been asked by Dr. Nahid Angha for my biography, but much more important than any biography is communicating to you the privilege of being friends with Dr. Angha and Dr. Ali Kianfar for two decades. It is they who continually opened the door for us to the privilege of meeting Sufis from all over the world. Many of these beautiful souls have become friends, flowering in the garden of our hearts. By the grace of God, what a gift!

Here are some non-linear pieces of my life. The first conscious transformative experience I had that I still remember happened in my third year of studying Chemical Engineering. It was the result of spending three days ill in a high-temperature delirium. When my body returned to 98.6 degrees Fahrenheit, it was clear to me that I was no longer going to study Chemical Engineering. Literally at the same time, a new interdisciplinary undergraduate studies program was created at my university. I ended up studying gestalt therapy and organizational behaviour and learning how to conduct sensitivity and encounter groups, extending my undergraduate program one year. To pay off my student loans, I decided to obtain a secondary teaching credential in physics, chemistry, and math. This required some education courses and student-teaching experience.

The summer before graduating from university, I began teaching chemistry at George Washington High School in San Francisco, California.

My master-teacher was the head of all of the science teachers in San Francisco and wanted me to teach in her department at Mission High School, since she needed a bilingual (English-Spanish) chemistry teacher the next year and I spoke both English and Spanish. Everything was arranged – she was on the same bowling team as the person who made the hiring decisions and she had a friend with a studio apartment a few blocks away from Mission High who would give me a great deal. The job interview  was only supposed to be a formality, since I had all of the boxes checked off and her approval. It ended up being a formality since the gentleman hiring was required to hire minority teachers. Since I did not fall in a recognized minority, the possibility for me to teach in San Francisco ended.

The story picks up in Merced, California, a very conservative farm town in the San Joaquin Valley. A school there needed a physics teacher, so I interviewed and reluctantly, they offered me a job. They considered San Francisco State University, where I had done my student teaching, to be a very radical place. Later I discovered that they really did not want to hire me at all but had to because they couldn't find anyone to teach physics. How lucky was I to have such a dramatic demonstration of how little each of us on this speck orbiting the sun really can control the important things in life!

Indeed, considering the next stage of my life, living in Merced was the perfect preparation. Since having graduated from university, I had told everyone that I was preparing for a ten-year trip around the world, the first ten thousand or so kilometres by foot in the mountains. The five previous summers I had spent walking in the Sierra Nevada or in the various mountain ranges in Mexico in preparation for walking the Andes from Columbia to Tierra del Fuego. I first walked in the U.S. national parks that I had not visited (in the winter I became a ski bum in Utah). Then I hitchhiked to Panama, crossed the Darian Gap by air and arrived in Bogota. I spent the next 16 months hiking every trail in the Andes above 4,000 meters, except some areas between Chile and Argentina because of a war between the two countries that made border crossings on the Argentine side a problem. My first childhood aspiration, to hike the "Inca Trail," had been fulfilled.

My next aspiration was to see where African-Americans had come from. I spent the summer in Paris learning French and getting my visas. That September I arrived in Algeria and hitchhiked across the Sahara and into Niger. Hitchhiking was not so viable there due to the lack of traffic, so I took buses or trucks. After arriving in Mali, I hiked into the Dogon lands and then went overland until reaching Cameroon. By that time four months had elapsed and I had contracted malaria and then dengue fever back to back and endured considerable physical pain. During that time I had seen where many African-Americans had originated, and my second aspiration had been fulfilled. Although I had planned to travel all the way to South Africa, I realized that it was time to stop. It was a good lesson in travelling: without a meaningful reason to be in a place, it is better to stay at home.

Originally I had planned to fulfill my third aspiration, that is, to spend a few years in Iran learning Farsi and studying Sufism. I received this aspiration after reading Idries Shah's books on Sufism and realizing that much of his writing was an amalgamation of half-truths. The only way to discern the truth was through personal experience. The revolution in Iran and the Russian invasion of Afghanistan precluded my realization of my third aspiration, but another had emerged. After arriving in Cameroon, I finally realized that while I had been in West Africa, most of the time Muslims had been kindly assisting me. I decided to learn Arabic to find out more about Islam and started teaching English in Cairo while spending most of my free time learning colloquial Egyptian Arabic. On a vacation trip in the mountains of Yemen, I was offered a well-paying position in Sanaa teaching English in the mornings and Arabic in the afternoons.

North Yemen at that time was another world. It was more isolated than Tibet until the middle of the 1970s. Yemen was my first experience travelling back into time. Before leaving Egypt, I purchased a copy of al-Hamdani's *Sifat jazirat al-'arab*, a tenth-century Lonely Planet Guide to Yemen. In my free time I went out with my friends and visited some of the places mentioned in the book. We would arrive around noon after a grueling drive on 4-wheel-drive roads and be invited for tea and lunch. After lunch just about every Yemeni chewed qat leaves, an intellectual stimulant, and we were expected to do so also. When everyone was comfortably seated in the top-floor windowed room looking out over the beautiful countryside, our host would ask me, "What are you doing here?" I explained that I had read about his village in al-Hamdani's book and came to see for myself. Almost always I had to go down and fetch the book and haltingly read the paragraphs dealing with their village. The next few hours we would discuss the history of the area. It was fascinating.

At the same time I had been teaching myself to read Arabic and after a year needed a teacher. Dr. Gerd Puin, the head of the Yemeni Qur'an project, kindly agreed to teach me the finer points of Arabic grammar in addition to Arabic calligraphy, the prerequisite for reading unpointed manuscripts. He also informed me that what I had been doing informally in my travels around Yemen was something called "research," but that I would need a Ph. D. to get paid for doing it.

When my contract teaching English and Arabic was finished, I applied to graduate school and ended up learning from his mentor, the late Annemarie Schimmel, earning a Ph.D. in 1993. Instead of focusing my work on Yemen, I decided to work on South Asian Sufism. My last childhood aspiration had been to go to India and learn Hindi/Urdu and to hike in the Himalayas, which I accomplished during graduate school. In addition, I learned Persian and Turkish, though it was not until 1994 that I was able to visit Iran, as one of the first American scholars officially invited to Iran after the revolution in 1979. Needless to say, the non-linear path of this short life has been punctuated with some intriguing synchronicities.

After eleven years getting bounced around in American academia, I received tenure and promptly left for a very satisfying job in New Zealand. I teach at Victoria University in a wonderfully harmonious work environment and live in a house overlooking the ocean facing the South Island. Soon this too will change as we move to Amman. The last four years this life has been crowned with joy by being married with the woman for whom my soul has long yearned. Adventure and learning have their place but without love there is no fragrance of the One.

Rev. Paul Chaffee

Paul Chaffee spent 13 years growing up in Asia, the son of American Presbyterian missionaries. He left college teaching in the humanities to pursue a divinity degree from Pacific School of Religion and was ordained in the United Church of Christ in 1977. His first parish was Church for the Fellowship of All Peoples, founded in San Francisco in 1944 as an intentional

interracial, interfaith congregation.

In 1993 he went to work for the group that subsequently incorporated as the Interfaith Center at the Presidio, and was named executive director in 1995. In 1996 the Center was invited to take care and custody of the Interfaith Chapel in the Presidio of San Francisco. Under his direction, the Center has hosted hundreds of interfaith programs. It published *One World, Many Voices* (2002), a pioneering interfaith songbook, and sponsored an international sacred space design competition that drew 160 submissions from 17 countries. It sent a video team to the 2009 Melbourne Parliament of the World's Religions that webcast 24 interviews live from the site. He retired from the Center in January 2011, and the following September launched *The Interfaith Observer*(TIO), a free monthly internet publication exploring the interfaith culture growing in our midst.

Rev. Chaffee served on United Religions Initiative's original board of directors for six years and led the team that planned the initial URI-North America summit in 2001. He served on the board of San Francisco Interfaith Council from 1995 through 2010. He is a trustee of the North American Interfaith Network and led in planning *Embracing an Interfaith Future,* its 20th anniversary conference in San Francisco in 2008. His publications include: *Accountable Leadership* (1997); *Shared Wisdom* (2004); and *Remembered Light* (2007).

Paul lives with his wife and partner, Jan, in San Francisco.

Sheikh Hassan Cissé

Shaykh Hassan Ali Cissé was the Chief Imam of the Grand Mosque in Medina Kaolack, Senegal, and one of the leaders of the Tariqa Tijaniyya, a Sufi order based exclusively on the Qur'an and the Hadith. A respected Islamic scholar and leader, Shaykh Hassan Cissé has been appointed to the Ulaama of the Islamic Republic of Mauritania and Special Advisor on Islamic Affairs to the Republic of Ghana. He was the founder and president of the African American Islamic Institute (AAII), an international non-governmental organization (NGO) of the United Nations headquartered in Senegal, West Africa, with affiliates throughout Africa, Europe and North America. Eleven of AAII's sixteen affiliates are located in Sub-Saharan Africa.

Shaykh Hassan was born in Kaolack, Senegal in December 1945, as the first grandson of *Shaykh–al-Islam*, Al Hajj Ibrahima Niass (RA), the latter who illuminated the essence of Islam throughout West Africa. After memorizing the Holy Qu'ran at age ten, Shaykh Hassan completed his elementary and secondary education in Senegal.

Educated in Senegal, Mauritania, Egypt, England and the United States, the Shaykh holds a B.A. in Islamic Studies and Islamic Literature from Ain Shams University of Cairo, Egypt and a Master of Philosophy degree and Diplomas in French and English from the University of London. While engaged in research for a Ph.D. in Islamic Studies from Northwestern University in Chicago, Illinois, his father, Shaykh Ali Cissé (RA) passed away and he was recalled to Senegal to assume the inspired work that has given direction and meaning to millions of seekers of Truth in Africa, Europe and, especially, the United States.

Shaykh Hassan traveled to the United States in 1976, where he introduced the Tariqa Tijaniyya to Muslims in America for the very first time. Since then, he has been teaching, guiding, and inspiring Muslims to fear Allah and love Prophet Muhammad (*SAW*), always reminding them to do what Allah says to do and stop where Allah says stop.

Up to his leaving the corporal world, the Shaykh traveled to numerous U.S. cities, where he was honored as a distinguished Islamic scholar and religious leader and for the work of the African American Islamic Institute (AAII). Shaykh Hassan Cissé has been awarded the Keys to the City of Cleveland, Ohio. In Washington, D.C., June 16, 1986 was proclaimed Shaykh Hassan Cissé Day. Detroit, Michigan and Memphis, Tennessee, respectively named him an Honorary Member of the City Council and an Honorary Citizen of Memphis. The City of New Orleans, Louisiana proclaimed October 2, 1996 as Shaykh Hassan Cissé Day. Internationally, Shaykh Hassan has been recognized by the United Nations Population Fund (UNFPA) as a respected Islamic scholar and leader for his outstanding work and cooperation with the UNFPA towards achieving goals set forth during the Bejing and Cairo conferences that include family planning, the status of women and the education of girls. He has been recognized by the United Nations Children's Fund (UNICEF) for his scholarship, leadership, cooperation and advocacy regarding the protection of children, the prevention of drug abuse and other issues vital to the health, education and well-being of children. The Shaykh has spoken extensively on these issues during AAII's annual International Islamic Conferences in Senegal and the Gambia. In 1998, Shaykh Hassan Cissé was awarded the Key to the City of Banjul. As a key speaker during major international conferences held in Indonesia, Europe, Africa and the United States, Shaykh Hassan Cissé works tirelessly to spread the word of Islam and promote cooperation with different religious groups to improve living conditions and promote peace.

In 2002, the Shaykh met with the President of South Africa during a meeting with twenty-one NGOs chosen from among the 2,600 NGOs that attended the United Nations World Summit on Sustainable Development. During this three-hour meeting, Shaykh Hassan Cissé reaffirmed AAII's commitment to lifting the barriers of ignorance and poverty, especially as they affect women and children, through access to health care, socio-economic development, income-generating activities for women, access to education and adult literacy. In the same year, the Shaykh participated in the Interreligious and International Federation of World Peace Summit of World Muslim Leaders in London and the Governance and the Role of Religion in Peace and Security Symposium in New York. The Shaykh accepted the World Association of Non-Governmental Organizations (WANGO) 2002 Education Award presented to AAII on October 19th at an International Awards Ceremony held in Washington, D.C.

As the founder and president of the African American Islamic Institute (AAII) (an institute of *Nasrul Ilm* or Assisting Knowledge), Shaykh Hassan Cissé established the guidelines for AAII's humanitarian activities in keeping with the teachings of Islam: feed the hungry, care for the sick, teach the unlettered, protect the interests of women and children, pursue knowledge and foster understanding and peace among mankind.

Shaykh Hassan Cissé has spearheaded the development of AAII's Qur'anic School in Medina Kaolack, Senegal, where an international faculty and student body teach and learn the Qur'an within an Islamic environment and are immersed in a rich and meaningful cross-cultural experience. Students receive support in their study of secular subjects for which they receive academic credit to facilitate their successful re-entry into educational systems upon their return home. The Qur'anic School includes a Literacy Center where adults and children learn to read and a Computer Literacy Center to teach academic and marketable computer skills.

Shaykh Hassan Cissé's vision and determination to make health care accessible to children and adults in rural communities where medical facilities are lacking resulted in the establishment of the Shifa-as-Asqam Socio-Medical Center in Medina Kaolack, in collaboration with UNFPA. As a direct result of the pre-natal care provided by the Center, infant and maternal morbidity and mortality in the area have been significantly reduced. In 1999, this health-care facility became the first in Senegal to receive the prestigious UNICEF designation, "Baby Friendly." AAII is developing residency and continuing medical education programs with the Shaykh Ibrahim Niass Medical School in Dakar, Senegal. Volunteer physicians, nurses, midwives, dentists and other health-care professionals form an interdisciplinary medical team to provide uninterrupted primary and reproductive health care throughout the year and provide training to community health workers.

Shaykh Hassan is highly respected internationally. At The Abuja Declaration of the Network of African Islamic Faith-Based Organizations in Abuja, Nigeria, Shaykh Hassan was chosen as president of the new organization, which focuses on population and development issues in 45 African countries. The conference was organized and convened by the United Nations Population Fund on March 17, 2005. Shaykh Hassan keeps a very busy schedule providing international service to humanity. In his capacity as President of the Network of African Islamic Organizations for Population and Development, he was a lead advocate at the UNICEF Conference on Violence Against Children that served as a regional consultation for West and Central Africa and was held in Bamako, Mali from May 23 to 25, 2005.

Shaykh Hassan Cissé's commitment to serving Allah through service to humanity and protection of Allah's creation is transparent through his leadership of the African American Islamic Institute and the generous use of his life for the benefit of mankind.

Leslie Davenport M.S., M.F.T.

Leslie Davenport has unique qualifications in the Body-Mind-Spirit field. Dance critic Allan Ulrich reviewed Leslie as a professional dancer endowed with "a superior sense of balance … and powers of communication that set her apart from the herd." As a licensed Marriage and Family Therapist in practice for more than fifteen years, Leslie understands the health impact of thoughts and emotions. Her passion for the mystery of the human spirit drew her to become an ordained interfaith Sufi minister in 1984. As a pioneer in the role of guided imagery in psychotherapy and integrative medicine, Leslie has braided her expertise with body-mind-spirit into a health-care revolution that recognizes the role of meaning and the spiritual dimensions of life as an integral part of health and healing.

In the late 1980's Leslie was a founder of the Humanities Program at Marin General Hospital, which evolved into the Institute for Health and Healing in collaboration with California Pacific Medical Center in San Francisco. Her years of clinical experience culminated in the publication of *Healing and Transformation through Self-Guided Imagery* (Celestial Arts/ Random House). She has also served as Editorial Consultant to Aspen Publishers for their book, *Holistic Health Promotion and Complementary Therapies: A Resource for Integrative Practice.*

Leslie has more than ten years teaching experience at universities including Mills College, University of San Francisco, California State University Hayward, and Holy Names University. She served as core faculty at the Transpersonal Psychology Graduate Program at John F. Kennedy University.

Her expert advice has been published in various magazines and journals, including *Spa, Yoga Journal, Women's Day, Family Circle, Natural Health, Great Health, Body + Soul, Shift* and *San Francisco Medicine.* A sought after speaker, she lectures in a broad range of settings that have included KRON Television, the National Wellness Conference, Rancho La Puerta, the Commonwealth Club, Uncovering the Heart of Higher Education Conference hosted by the California Institute of Integral Studies and the Fetzer Institute, to name just a few. She was honored in her home county with the Marin Breast Cancer Council's "Honor Thy Healer" award in 2003.

Leslie is currently in practice at the Health & Healing Clinic at California Pacific Medical Center in San Francisco and Marin. She is also clinical faculty with the Institute for Health and Healing's Integrative Medicine Program, faculty with John F. Kennedy University, and a clinical supervisor for the California Institute of Integral Studies.

Sheikh Vasheest Davenport

Although Vasheest was an avid traveler, he lived the majority of his life in Northern California. Raised as a Christian from birth, in the mid-1960's, Vasheest embraced the Sufi movement and was a *mureed* of the late Murshid Samuel L. Lewis. He founded the non-profit Sufi center, Sami Mahal, in San Rafael, which thrived from the late 1970's through the early 1990's. With a passion for music and a beautiful singing voice, Vasheest was a founding member of the Sami Mahal Sufi Choir and his life-long devotion to Sufism never wavered.

Seido Lee de Barros

Seido Lee de Barros is a Dharma teacher in the Suzuki Roshi Soto Zen lineage. His home temple is the Green Gulch Farm Zen Center in Marin County, California. He also serves as the Buddhist Volunteer Chaplain at the San Quentin prison, is a minister to the homeless and serves on the Zen Hospice Project Board of Directors. He is active in the interfaith community and is an associate teacher for the Dharma Eye Zen Center.

Sister Chandru Desai

Brahma Kumari Sister Chandru Desai was born in August 1948, in the city of Mumbai, India. Her family was of the Brahmin caste and her father was proprietor of a confectionery. In 1963, she began to study Raja Yoga Meditation as it is taught by the Brahma Kumaris World Spiritual University (BKWSU), an international organization that has centers in over 90 countries and is headed in Rajasthan, India.

Sister Chandru became an instrumental teacher for the Brahma Kumaris in 1964 and has been teaching and practicing Raja Yoga Meditation for nearly four decades. During her early years as a yogi, she traveled extensively in India, arranging and attending spiritual conferences and teaching meditation. From 1972 to 1975, she lived in Africa and was instrumental in helping to set up centers of the university in many African nations, including Zambia, Zimbabwe and Kenya. In 1975, interest in spiritual service led her to Canada, where centers were established in Vancouver and Toronto. (There are now ten centers in Canada.) In 1977, she was instrumental in starting the first U.S. center in San Antonio, Texas. Since that time, 31 centers have been established throughout the United States.

Currently, Sister Chandru is the Director of the San Francisco Brahma Kumaris Meditation Center and the Anubhuti Meditation & Retreat Center. She is Vice President of the Brahma Kumaris World Spiritual Organization (the American arm of the BKWSU). As such, she administers Brahma Kumaris centers in the Western region of the United States and Hawaii. From 1988 to 1990, Sister Chandru acted as Regional Coordinator for North America in the worldwide Global Cooperation for a Better World project. The project, a Peace Messenger Initiative dedicated to the United Nations, was conducted by the Brahma Kumaris in close affiliation with the UN's Peace Studies Unit.

Locally, Sister Chandru is a founding member of United Religions Initiative, the San Francisco Interfaith Council, and the Interfaith Center at the Presidio, and active in many interfaith programs. In 2004, she started the construction for a new Meditation and Retreat Center in Novato, California, which opened in June 2007. In addition to her administrative and teaching duties at the San Francisco Meditation Center, Sister Chandru conducts meditation classes at community gatherings around the San Francisco Bay Area.

Musa Dieng Kala

Native to Senegal where he lived until the age of 30, Musa Dieng Kala is more well-known in the world of music than within the world of cinema. He is an author-composer-singer recognized internationally for the quality and the depth of his works. He first involved himself in the promotion of Africain music before turning to focus on production.

From 1991 till 1993, he managed the recording studio of Youssou N' Dour in Dakar, and produced several video-clips. He then established himself in Quebec where he discovered his hidden talent as a singer. He has been inspired by Sufi poems and the teaching of his spiritual master, Sheikh Amadou Bamba, the first peaceful resistance fighter who broadcasted the message of non-violence before Gandhi and Martin Luther King. With this inspiration, Musa Dieng Kala produced his first album in 1996. The media nicknamed him the "Nusrat Fateh Ali Khan of Black Africa". Praised for his warm voice and the expression of his extraordinary creativity in an unprecedented synthesis of world music, he travelled the world from Quebec to Africa by way of Europe and the United States, sharing the stage with big names such as: Myriam Makéba, Cheb Mami, Noa and Manu Dibango. In 2001, his second album gave him nominations in four galas, including ADISQ. In addition to creating his third album, which has just been launched, he has also participated in various compilations and sang solos for Rock Voisine.

In 1996 Musa Dieng Kala obtained a Bachelor of Arts in option cinema, at the University of Quebec in Chicoutimi. Eager to translate the topics which he develops in his albums and shows into picture, he registered at the University of Quebec in Montreal for a Masters degree. Here he spent a period of training under the direction of Spike Lee for the creation of the film Clockers. Earlier in life, as a 10-year-old, he created westerns with whatever was available, offering his small neighbours performance of Chinese shadows with direct sound effects.

A communicator with multiple talents, Musa Dieng Kala also participated in theatre production and animated two television programs: Free Expression, in Channel Vox, and Mosaic, which he directed. An engaged artist, he was the director of the committee of cogitation on the African cinema within GRA7, including artistic research on the 7th Century African art. In 2003 and in 2007, he was a member of the jury of the Council of Arts and Letters of Quebec for the attribution of grants.

To date, Musa Dieng Kala made several video-clips for his compatriot Youssou N dour and is preparing Borom Touba, a feature-length film on the life and work of Sheikh Ahmadou Bamba, founder of the Muslim brotherhood of the Mourides. Dedicated to the condition of African youth, the documentary *Dieu a-t-il quitté l'Afrique?* (Has God left Africa?) is the result of the first collaboration with the National Film Board (NFB).

Discography: 1996: *Shakawtu – Faith*; 1997: Compilation *African Tranquillity*; 1997: Compilation *Soufi Soul*; 1998: Compilation *Prayer*; 2001: *Salimto*; 2003: Album 18 Safar; 2008: *Exil*

Sheikh Abdoulaye Dieye

Sheikh Abdoulaye Dieye was born in the town of Saint Louis in Senegal in 1938. By profession, he was a town planner and a landscape architect, but above all he was a man of God, a searcher, a writer and a lecturer of international fame. He was a Deputy Mayor and a member of the Legislative Assembly, for he believed in serving the people and moralizing politics for the welfare of man. Sheikh Abdoulaye belonged to the Sufi Order of Muridiyya and was the disciple of the great Deymani Mauritanian Saint Sheikh Sidy Ahmed Ibn Ismouhou who was one of the first disciples of Sheikh Ahmadou Bamba.

As the spiritual Sufi master of Muridiyya, Sheikh Abdoulaye travelled the world, bringing the message of truth, love and peace to people of all creeds. He was a member of the organization Islam and the West and a staunch believer of interfaith dialogue that he promoted for building bridges of tolerance and harmony among people.

He disseminated the seeds of the Khidmatul Khadim, the school of Peace and Service in the *daaras*, or centers of learning, which he created in Reunion Island, in Mauritius, England, France, South Africa, Italy, the USA and India. Old and young are trained in these centers for discovering their inner selves, finding harmony between the spiritual and the temporal, and serving humanity as agents of peace.

Sheikh Abdoulaye laid the foundation of the Humanitarian Organization Third World Family Humanitarian (TFH) that aims at restoring human dignity in the world. Members of this organization are active in giving solace to the underprivileged and implementing social projects for the well-being of needy people in different parts of the world by empowering communities to play an active role in shaping their futures.

All the actions of Sheikh Abdoulaye Dieye were guided by his love for humanity, and he endeavored to sow love and compassion within the hearts of man. For him, true religion is the religion of love. All men, he believed, are flowers in the garden of God and must be nurtured with love and compassion. Each one of us has the potential to be a peace being and a peace builder after rediscovering the treasure in our inner most being.

Neil Douglas-Klotz (Saadi Shakur Chishti), Ph.D.

Neil Douglas-Klotz (Saadi Shakur Chishti) is the student of Hazrat Pir Moineddin Jablonski Chishti, who was the student and successor of Hazrat Pir Sufi Ahmed Murad Chishti (Samuel L. Lewis), who was the student of Hazrat Pir-o-Murshid Hazrat Inayat Khan Chishti. His other teachers in the Chishti lineage have included Pir Hidayat Inayat Khan, Murshid Shamcher Beorse, Pir Vilayat Inayat Khan, Murshida Fatima Lassar and Murshid Saul Barodofsky. The Chishtia lineage, one of the oldest Sufi families, uses music, art, poetry and sacred movement as practices to help "remember" our original relationship to the Source and Ground of all Being. As a branch of this lineage, the Sufi Ruhaniat International follows in the footsteps of its teachers and is currently guided by Pir Shabda Kahn.

Klotz is the author of several books of translation on the Aramaic words of Jesus, including *Prayers of the Cosmos*, *The Hidden Gospel*, and *Blessings of the Cosmos*. He has also authored a number of books of translation and

commentary on the mysticism of the Middle East, including *Desert Wisdom, The Genesis Meditations* and *The Tent of Abraham* (with Rabbi Arthur Waskow and Sr. Joan Chittister). His main work in the area of Sufism is *The Sufi Book of Life,* published in 2006, a new translation and commentary on the practice of the *Asma ul Husna* (99 Most Beautiful Names), comparing the origins and use of these sacred words across the major ancient Semitic languages. He founded the annual European Summer School of the Sufi Ruhaniat International, now in its 11th year (http://www.ruhaniateurope.org).

He is the past chair of the Mysticism Group of the American Academy of Religion and active in various international colloquia and conferences dedicated to peace and spirituality. He directs the Edinburgh Institute for Advanced Learning (http://www.eial.org) in Edinburgh, Scotland and co-founded the Edinburgh International Festival of Middle Eastern Spirituality and Peace, now in its 11th year (http://www.mesp.org.uk). In 2005, he was awarded the Kessler-Keener Foundation Peacemaker of the Year award for his work in Middle Eastern peacemaking. Information about his work may also be found at the website of the Abwoon Resource Center (http://www.abwoon.com).

Some personal details follow: Neil Douglas-Klotz grew up in a multicultural family. His grandparents (on both sides) were refugees from Europe with German, Jewish, Russian, and Polish blood in their veins. Klotz was raised by Christian parents who were both devout and free-thinking. They brought into his early life the impulse to worship and praise, as well as to question everything that constricted and opposed the injunction "love your neighbour as yourself." His father was a chiropractor, his mother a student of the health education of Edgar Cayce. They raised Klotz with a respect for the body and the wonders of nature found therein, as well as a disdain for the superficial innovations of humanity that polluted both body and nature. Hearing from childhood German, Yiddish and Polish in his home, raised on the stories and miracles of Jesus, taught the practical truth of Rachel Carson's *Silent Spring*, Klotz formed an interest in language, spirituality, the body, and ecological justice early in life. In many ways, he has been pursuing these interests ever since.

After graduation from university in 1973, Klotz pursued a career as a journalist in the fields of social justice, environmentalism, and consumer protection for several years before turning to the following questions: Why do people change? What causes me to change? Is there a more powerful level of motivating change than that of ideas? In pursuing these questions, Klotz returned to interests he had developed in college, which centered on the body and changes of attitude and behavior, mystical and "expanded" states of consciousness, and the early roots of the spirituality of Judaism, Christianity and Islam.

Neil Douglas-Klotz pursued some of this study academically but most of it found him seeking out teachers from the native traditions of the Middle East, Pakistan and India who introduced him to other modes and methods of learning (and unlearning) as well as the body-oriented spiritual practices that accompanied this study. Beginning in 1976, Klotz was very privileged to study with the early students of the American Hebrew/Sufi mystic Samuel L. Lewis, who introduced him to the body prayer meditations called the Dances of Universal Peace. One phase of this intense period of study led Klotz on a pilgrimage with twelve other Sufi *mureeds* in 1978-9 to visit sacred sites and teachers in Turkey, Pakistan, and India, including the still-living teachers and colleagues of Murshid Samuel Lewis. This trip included visits with and blessings from Hazrat Sheikh Muzzafer Effendi of the Jerahis in Istanbul, Hazrat Sheikh Suleiman Dede of Konya, Pir Sufi Barkat Ali of Salarwala, Shemseddin Ahmed of Lahore, Mother Krishnabai of Anandashram in Kanhangad, India, the Dalai Lama in Dharmsala and many others.

In 1982, Neil Douglas-Klotz co-founded the International Network for the Dances of Universal Peace, a multicultural resource center for those who chose this form of peacemaking through the arts as their form of peace "demonstration" as well as spiritual practice. In the intervening years, Klotz has been actively involved in leading educational exchanges and citizen diplomacy trips with the Dances to Eastern Europe, the former Soviet Union and to the Middle East. Shortly thereafter, he had the grace to meet, learn from and work with Dr. Ali Kianfar and Dr. Nahid Angha of the Uwaisi *tariqa* as part of the International Association of Sufism.

From 1986 until 1996, Klotz worked as a colleague of Dr. Matthew

Fox, as a faculty member of the Institute in Culture and Creation Spirituality (ICCS). During its "golden age," the ICCS was a gathering place for scientists, artists, educators and learners from many different cultural and racial backgrounds. Many of the students were non-U.S. citizens, and Klotz enjoyed the opportunity to teach and learn across the differences and within a rich field of diversity. During this time, he had the good fortune to work with Dr. Brian Swimme, Thomas Berry, Starhawk, Sr. Marlene DeNardo, Luisa Teish, Jeremy Taylor, Robert Rice, James Conlon and other artists, scientists and mystics who served on the core faculty at the time.

Following several citizen diplomacy trips to the former Soviet Union beginning in 1988, Klotz co-led a group of students from Europe, Australia, the U.S. and Canada on a citizen diplomacy/educational trip to Jordan, Israel and Syria in September 1993. He has since visited and led groups to the Middle East, India and North Africa a number of times on pilgrimage and citizen diplomacy trips.

Since 1994, he has lived in the UK and since 1999 in Edinburgh, Scotland. Since 2006, he has been married to Natalia Lapteva, a Russian therapist and coach. In 2013, they moved north of Edinburgh to the district of Fife to set up a Sufi healing and meditation center. He continues to travel and teach throughout Europe and the rest of the world. For his schedule, please see http://www.abwoon.com or http://www.eial.org.

Hajjah Noura Durkee

Hajjah Noura Durkee is an author, editor, illustrator, and lecturer on subjects ranging from the Qur'an and the Seerah, particularly (but not exclusively) as they relate to women, children and families. She has *idhn* to teach from her Shaykh, Dr. Ibrahim al Batawi (Allah Yarhamhu) of al-Azhar, Cairo, and from Shaykh Muhammad al Jamal ash-Shadhdhuli ar-Rafai of al Quds ash-Sharif. In addition she has studied with Shaykh Ali Ashraf, who taught at Cambridge University and instructed her specifically in the education of Muslim children; Shaykh Umar Abdullah; and her husband, Shaykh Nooruddeen Durkee. She is the mother of five children.

As a young person, Hajjah Noura Durkee was very interested in religion, but could find no satisfaction in the explanations given. After receiving a Bachelor of Arts in Humanities and a Master of Arts in Fine Arts from Stanford University, she concentrated on teaching children and on museum work regarding art history, until giving up academic life and moving to the mountains of New Mexico in the 1960's. The Lama Foundation was most valuable for the community and teachers in the mountains living without electricity and living close to the natural environment. She helped illustrate Ram Dass and Shaykh Nooruddeen's book, *Be Here Now*; Shaykh Nooruddeen's *Seed*; and *In the Garden*, by Murshid Sam Lewis, who directed her toward Islam. She left Lama to work with Pir Vilayat Khan at his camps in France and was art editor for his book, *Toward the One*.

In al Quds ash-Sharif, working on another book on the confluence of the three great monotheisms, Hajjah Noura became convinced by the quality of life of the Palestinians and by the teachings of the Shaykhs, particularly Shaykh Muhammad al-Jamal, who explained the continuity of the Prophetic message. Returning to America, she helped to build the Islamic Study Center at Lama, where she took formal *shahadah*, and then left for three years to study in Makkah at Um ul Qura University. Assisting Shaykh Nooruddeen Durkee, she raised funds and upon returning to America, searched for land to build the Dar al-Islam Foundation.

In the early 1980's she met Shaykh Ibrahim Muhammad al-Battawi and became his *mureed*. Aside from providing Hajjah Noura a beautiful example of an Islamic life, and advising her on personal and spiritual matters, he encouraged her to read the work of Abu Hamid al Ghazzali, a lifelong study and influence. He also advised her, as every shaykh she has met has done, to "Take care of Shaykh Nooruddeen!"

Dar al-Islam was a vast project. Hajjah Noura concentrated on the school and summer programs for teachers, which she developed under the direction of Syed Ali Ashraf, who had spearheaded five world conferences on Islamic Education, one of which the Durkees attended. His teaching involved bringing the principles and morals, stories and examples and language of the Qur'an into children's daily lives, so that they did not become confused between "western" sciences and "eastern" religious knowledge. Hajjah and a team of others composed a series of early readers along these lines, called the *Gazelle Books*, based on the lives of the children at Dar al-Islam.

After Dar al-Islam, Hajjah Noura moved with the Shaykh to Egypt where she taught English and studied the Qur'an and calligraphy while raising her family and beginning the serious writing of children's books. She met the Ghazis of Iqra Books, and began to write and edit for them as well as to work with Syed Ali Ashraf on an international Muslim curriculum.

After five years in Egypt, the Durkees returned to America and Shaykh Nooruddeen continued intensive work on translation and transliteration, which ten years later culminated in the publishing of the *Tajwidi Qur'an*. Hajjah compiled a series of five books on the *Sahaba* and a book of Islamic History. Her major focus, however, was in assisting with the Qur'an in all of the visual, layout, and publishing details as well as a thorough reworking of the translation. Since then, most of her attention has been on the Islamic Study Center, on proofing and editing the books of the Shaykh and lecturing. She lectured in England at the Islamic Foundation on the subject of marriage; in Turkey on serving the husband as a means of serving Allah; in Pakistan on the four perfect women; at the summer schools in America of Shaykh Muhammad Jamal working with reverts to Islam explaining the many aspects of how Islam works to change and develop our lives; at the ISRA conferences on love of the Rasul, peace and blessings be upon him and his family. She also worked for many years in the women's prison, teaching Islam.

Hajjah Noura Durkee has written three books for Tahrike Tarsile Qur'an on stories from the Qur'an, on Sulayman, Dawud, and Yunus, *'alayhum as-salaam*. More books are currently being planned. She has also continued work with Iqra on many workbooks in their education series, most recently regarding high school level books on the *hadith, fiqh* and *seerah*. Additionally, Hajjah Noura Durkee wrote a number of books for very early readers on the Prophets for Hood Books: the *Three Shirts of Yusuf*, a book on Musa, another on ibn Battuta, and a big book called *The Animals of Paradise*, stories of all the animals in the Qur'an told from *their* point of view. She has also edited for The Islamic Foundation.

Along with Shaykh Nooruddeen, Hajjah Noura is deeply interested in finding ways to express the love and mercy of Islam to audiences in both east and west, and to counter the false impressions fed by hysteria and the violent minority. To this end, the Durkees run the an-Noor Educational Foundation, dedicated to the propagation of the Qur'an and its message of peace, justice, mercy, love and freedom. The Foundation sponsors talks by prominent shaykhs on this and similar subjects, runs the Green Mountain School that hosts students of all ages from Universities in Virginia and from refugee populations, makes, sells and distributes the books and essays of Shaykh Nooruddeen and others, and supports the mission of the Shaykh to give *khutbas* on a weekly basis in many different places.

Hajjah Noura continues to write and to proofread and edit the Shaykh's prolific output. A large concentration in the past few years has been on early Shaykhs of the Shadhdhuliyyah, editing and preparing for publication Shaykh Nooruddeen's *Origins of the Shadhuliyyah* and the an-Noor publication of Ibn 'Ata 'lillah's *Illuminating Guidance on the Ceasing of Self Direction*. A fitting conclusion to the work on the *sahabah* was the preparation of *In Defense of the Sunnah*, by Ibrahim Hakim, which is an explanation of the original practices of the Sunnah by the companions and includes a thorough defense of Sufic practices.

Shaykh Abdullah Nooruddeen Durkee

Shaykh Abdullah Nooruddeen Durkee is a Muslim scholar, author, translator, teacher and builder. He is the *Khalifah* (successor) for the Western Hemisphere of the Shadhdhuli School for Tranquility of Being and the Illumination of Hearts, Green Mountain Branch. He was granted *Khilafa* by Shaykh Dr. Ibrahim Muhammad al-Battawi, Allah Yarhamhu, of al-Azhar, Cairo in 1986.

Shaykh Nooruddeen is the founder of the Lama Foundation, the Islamic Studies Center, the Dar al-Islam Foundation, and the Green Mountain School: all educational institutions. He is specifically interested in the teaching of reading, writing, and recitation of the Qur'an. One of his great contributions is the transliteration and translation of *The Transliterated Tajwidi Qur'an*. With the addition of a clear Roman transliteration system, shown alongside the Arabic text, he has enabled non-Arabic speakers and learners to understand and recite the Qur'an.

Shaykh Nooruddeen lectures both nationally and internationally. In Charlottesville and Greater Richmond, Virginia and Washington D.C., he has delivered the weekly *khutbah* for more than ten years at a number of different community *masajid*, where he serves prisoners, students, immigrants and refugees, including both African-Americans and Euro-Americans. He works with several other shaykhs and Islamic organizations including the Islamic Studies and Research Association, the North American Islamic Foundation, the Naqsbandiya Foundation for Islamic Education, and the International Association of Sufism, to share the true *sunnah* of Islam, a message of peace, justice, mercy, love, and freedom. He speaks at a large number of *mawaalid* on the East coast, in Arizona, in Chicago, Illinois and in England at the yearly Gateway conferences and other sites.

Some of Shaykh Nooruddeen's other international appearances include inter-faith and intra-faith dialogues sponsored by the World Council of Religions, which named him an "Ambassador for Peace," and has sent him from Istanbul to Jakarta to Seoul to speak on such subjects as "Spirituality and Practice," "Making Peace with the Earth," and "Islam and the Family."

In addition to studying all aspects of Islam with Shaykh al-Battawi for many years, Shaykh Nooruddeen also studied with the Mujaddidi Naqshabandi Shaykh, Dr. Seyed 'Ali Ashraf, professor of Islamic Education at King Abdu-l-Aziz University in Jeddah and later at Cambridge. Dr. Seyed 'Ali Ashraf granted Shaykh Nooruddeen an *'Ijaza* in the science of *Muraqabah* (inner contemplation). In 1983, he received an *'Ijaza* in Islamic Calling (*da'wa*) from Shaykh Ambassador Umar Abdullaah, a Ba'Alawi shaykh from the Commoro Islands. In 1999 Shaykh Nooruddeen was granted an *'Ijaza* and given *'Idhn* to teach from Shaykh Muhammad al-Jamal, of the High Council of Sufism in al-Quds ash-Sharif, in occupied Palestine. He was also granted *Khilafah* by Hazrat Quttubuddin Yar Faridi of the Nizamiyya/Chistiyyah in Rahim Yar Khan in Pakistan, after a series of lectures he gave there in 2004.

Within the professional world, Shaykh Nooruddeen has also studied with world-renowned Islamic architect Dr. Hasan Fathy, and was awarded the degree of Master of Islamic Architecture by the al-Sabbah Institute of Appropriate Technology in Kuwait. He also built Dar al-Islam in Northern New Mexico, an outstanding example of Islamic art, which has served for many years as a teaching and retreat center.

Abdullah Nooruddeen Durkee was born in 1938 in Warwick, New York, USA as Stephen Durkee. He grew up with his grandmother, a devout Catholic and herbalist, at Greenwood Lake, New York. He attended

Roman Catholic schools in New York City and developed a broad interest in religious and spiritual knowledge. From 1957-1960, he studied with Dr. Robert Lowe, Professor of the Fine and Applied Arts, Teachers' College at Columbia University. From 1960-1966, he worked as an artist and creator of environments in New York City and San Francisco. His paintings are in various private collections as well as at the Guggenheim and the Museum of Modern Art in New York. Shaykh Nooruddeen was one of the founders of USCO, and created the first multimedia lightshows, traveling and exhibiting at universities and museums throughout the northeast. Articles on his work have been published in various publications including *ArtNews* and *Life* magazine.

In the mid-1960s, Shaykh Nooruddeen moved his family West in search of a more inclusive art-form and a more natural lifestyle and more conscious environment. From 1965-1967, he lived in California with Richard Alpert (later known as Ram Dass) and lectured with him throughout the West. From 1967-1970, he initiated the Lama Foundation in New Mexico, one of the first centers in North America for Spiritual Realization and Interfaith Studies. He initiated contacts with teachers of many traditions, including Kalu Rinpoche and Zalman Schachter-Shalomi, Murshid Samuel Lewis and Pir Vilayat Inayat Khan. He organized, edited and produced Ram Dass' book *Be Here Now*.

From 1970-1971, Shaykh Nooruddeen coordinated the International Work Camps in the Alps conducted by Pir Vilayat Khan and also began travelling in the desert regions of North Africa including visits to the Subcontinent and Middle East. Here he first came into contact with Muslims and also edited Pir Vilayat's book *Toward the One*.

In 1972, Shaykh Nooruddeen lived on Jabal Zaytun, outside of al-Quds ash-Sharif in occupied Palestine, where he embraced Islam at the Madrasah of the Masjid al-'Aqsah and studied *Tasawwuf* with Shadhdhuli Shaykh Muhammad al-Jamal and Shaykh Abdur Rahman ash-Sharif of al-Khalil. He also received benefit from the teaching of Shaykh Noor-i-Muhammad, a Naqshbandi from Bokharah.

From 1973-1976, he designed and built the Intensive Studies Center (also known as the I.S.C. or Islamic Sufi Center) in the mountains above San Cristobal, New Mexico. It contained the first mosque in Northern New Mexico, and at this center, many young American people came to hear about

Islam for the first time from the perspective of *Tasawwuf* and began to practice as Muslims.

During 1976-1979, he lived and studied in Makkah al-Mukarramah and attended the Markaz al-Lugaht-al-Arabiyyah, Kulliyat ash-Shari'ah, at Jami'at Malik 'Abdu-l-'Aziz (now known as Jami'at Ummu-l-Qurra). During this time he developed the idea of an artistic, educational, social and cultural center for Islam in America, and began raising funds for the project. On the first day of the new *Hijri* 1400 century, Shaykh Nooruddeen was the sole signatory on incorporation papers for the Dar al-Islam Foundation in Abiquiu, New Mexico. He served for eight years from 1980-1988 as President, during which time the Foundation grew from an idea to a physical reality. At the time of leaving his office as President, the foundation had assets of $7 million, was debt-free, in full operation, and included a mosque, a school, a number of residences, and small businesses. It drew visitors and residents from all over the world, particularly, but not exclusively, from among Muslim reverts from America. At the end of his period as President of Dar al-Islam Foundation, he returned to Egypt, where he continued his studies with his Shaykh Dr. Ibrahim al-Batawi of al-Azhar Sharif and began teaching in Alexandria, Egypt under the guidance of his Shaykh. Shaykh Nooruddeen was a National Delegate to the Fifth International Conference on Muslim Education, Cairo, 1988, and then moved with his family to Alexandria, Egypt. There he studied the Shadhdhuliyyah Shari'ah Way for Lovers of Qur'an and Sunnah with Shaykh al-Batawi. They developed a circle of students deeply involved in the Shadhdhuliyyah, produced volume one, *Orisons of the Shadhdhuliyyah,* and collected volume two, *Origins of the Shadhdhuliyyah*. He also began the first work on the *Tajwidi Qur'an*.

In 1994, Shaykh Nooruddeen returned to America and settled in Virginia, working full time on the *Tajwidi Qur'an* that was published in 2003. During this time, he founded the Green Mountain School as a conduit for teaching the Qur'an and the publishing of other books and lectures. He also established the an-Noor Foundation, a non-profit 501(c)(3), specifically for the publication of the *Tajwidi Qur'an* and for the propagation of traditional, moderate Islam. He has written numerous articles and essays to this effect, as well as editing books written or translated by his students including *Illuminating Guidance on the Dropping of Self Direction* by 'Ibn 'Ata'illah, and *Defense of the Sunnah* by Ibrahim Hakim. He is emphasizing tassawuf as the only moderating influence between the extremes of contemporary Islam; the great need for the shaykh and the community of believers; and the fact that we who follow this path are all of us on some level refugees and strangers.

The Foundation runs a daily school for the mentoring of refugee children, the teaching of the Qur'an, and for the weekly meetings for students and friends of the Shaykh and monthly all-day events on specific subjects. The first five were: Peace, Justice, Mercy, Love and Freedom, followed by various other topics. In 2012-13 the subject was the lectures on the six Resolute Prophets, peace and blessings on them all, and in 2013-14 it is "The Unseen."

Many of his speeches and *Khutbahs* are available as videos and mp3 files, as are all his publications, at http://www.GreenMountainSchool.org. The monthly talks can be watched live online, and all talks and khutbahs are viewable on YouTube, the greenmountain channel.

Jeffrey Eaton, M.A.

Jeffrey Eaton M.A. is a graduate and faculty mem— ber of the Northwestern Psychoanalytic Society and Institute and a Fellow of the International Psycho— analytic Association. He is in private practice in Seattle, Washington where he provides psychoanalysis and psychotherapy to children and adults. He speaks, teaches, and consults internationally. Eaton is winner of the 10th International Frances Tustin Memorial Lecture Prize for his paper "The Permanent Earthquake: Notes on the Treatment of a Young Boy"  forthcoming in *Francis Tustin Today,* published by the Library of Psychoanalysis. His first book *A Fruitful Harvest: Essays after Bion* was published in 2011 by The Alliance Press, Seattle and is available at www.amazon.com.

Eaton co-founded of The Alliance Community Psychotherapy Clinic where he served as Chair of the Steering Committee and on the board of the NW Alliance for Psychoanalytic Study from 1996-2008. His special interest is the treatment of autistic states and he is a founding member of INSPIRA, the International Seminar on Psychoanalytic Intervention and Research into Autism. He is also a Trustee of the Frances Tustin Memorial Trust.

Eaton has studied Buddhism and practiced meditation since the early 1990s. He took refuge in the Tibetan tradition under the guidance of Lama Yeshe Wangmo and Lama Tharchin Rinpoche. Recently he also became a student of Qi-gong which adds another energetic and movement dimension to his deepening spiritual path.

He can be reached through his website www.jleaton.com

Dr. Nevit O. Ergin

 Dr. Nevit O. Ergin, a Turkish-born surgeon, is the original translator of Rumi's 44,829 verses of the *Divan-i Kebir* into English. He has been a student of Sufism and the poetry of Rumi since 1955. Dr. Nevit spent 35 years translating the *divan* (or anthology) from the Turkish version prepared by Golpinarli, one of the most important Turkish scholars and an admirer of Rumi. Dr. Ergin emigrated first to Canada and later to the United States to pursue post-graduate medical work. He founded The Society for Understanding Mevlana in 1992. Dr. Ergin currently resides in San Mateo, California, in a little house called a Rumi Sanctuary.

Dr. Julie Jilani Esterly

Recently, I was looking at a photograph of the presenters from a Sufism Symposium. I was privileged to be among those in the photo, sharing in the atmosphere created by practicing with companions on the path. Struck by the light shining from the eyes of each being, I was reminded of some lines from the poet Kabir (translation by Robert Bly):

There is a Secret One inside
The stars and all the galaxies
Pass through his/her hands like beads
That is a string of beads one should look at with luminous eyes.

My path to meeting with mystics from around the world at the Sufism Symposium began with experiences as a youth in Ohio (USA). Although raised in a family that attended the Methodist church, it was a cultural rather than a spiritual experience. As a teenager, I began to have a deep interest in the world's religious traditions. I recall asking my parents if the Mormon missionaries who knocked on our door could come in to tell us about their religious beliefs. Soon after leaving home for college, I had the fortune of

40

being introduced to meditation. Primarily informed by *Vipassana*, with influences from Sufi and Hindu meditative traditions, my practice has grown over the last four decades. I am ever more grateful for the touchstone of quiet, unity and knowledge that meditation provides. When I relocated to Portland to attend Chiropractic college in 1973, my spiritual horizon expanded even further. A few days after arriving, I met Nuria Julia Hanfling, who remains a

close friend. She introduced me to the Dances of Universal Peace, originally created by Murshid Samuel Lewis (SAM).

In the dances, I felt the flow of life, an expanded heart, and experienced embodied, light-filled, unity. Chanting the sacred words from many of the world's traditions satisfied a deep need in me to attune to what they had in common. After a period of practice and study, in 1976 I was initiated into the Sufi Ruhaniat International, a *tariqa* of pir-o-Murshid Hazrat Inayat Khan and his student Murshid SAM. For the last 37 years, I have been blessed by kind, wise teachers from the Sufi stream and other mystical traditions and nourished by profound practices and the companionship of others on the path. My primary guide, Murshid Wali Ali Meyer, graciously bestowed his wisdom and compassion, as did Pir Moineddin Jablonski before his passing. Early on, I began to take retreats (*khilvat*) and established a rhythm of retreat that renews me in the midst of life's busyness. Eventually I started helping *mureeds*, teaching classes and workshops, and speaking to groups about Sufism.

Attracted by a gathering of Sufis from a variety of orders, I attended the first Sufism Symposium as a guest. What stands out from those early years is an extraordinary generosity, i.e., the hospitality suite hosted by Maryam (with Bawa Muhaiyaddeen's transporting tapes playing in the background) and Sheikh Ragip Frager inviting me to have a cup of tea on the sidewalk with his community. In 2004, the Symposium organizers were interested in adding practice-oriented presentations. My friend Dr. Sharon Mijares suggested that I offer the Dances of Universal Peace. From the years that I led workshops and spoke on panels, many sweet memories are strung like beads:

the mysticism of the human experience transmitted with dignity and great depth in Dr. Kianfar; Dr. Angha's impeccable decorum flavored with a sense of humor and her profound dedication to the message of Unity; the longing and beauty of Taneen's music; Sheikh Ahmad Tijani's booming voice and heart; the broad interfaith perspective of Rev. Paul Chaffee; the pleasure of developing friendships with Sheikh Kabir and Camille Helminski; the joy of crossing paths with Sufi Ruhaniat companions like Dr. Saadi Neil Douglas-Klotz, Pir Shabda Kahn, and the Rev. Azima Lila Forest; and the tears that arose on first hearing Sheikha Tamam Kahn's poetry about the wives of Mohammed (PBUH). In addition to creating a family of light, the Sufism Symposium created connections that led to unexpected places. I had been receiving guidance to go to Africa. At the Symposium, I was asked by Sheikh Tijani to speak at a conference in Ghana. Among the strong memories of that trip are speaking on a panel with African women who had never been permitted to share their voices in that capacity before, doing *zikr (dhikr)* with 5,000 people, and visiting a major slave trading fort. The dedication of Dr. Angha, the Sufi Youth International, and the Sufi Women's Organization strengthened my commitment to spiritual activism. On the return from the Africa conference, I stopped in Amsterdam and visited the Holocaust Museum. It was a moving experience that culminated with walking through the flags of the United Nations. I was inspired to join the local United Nations Association and hosted a TV show for the group. For a number of years, I have been on the Board of Directors for Capacitar International (http://www. capacitar.org), a profoundly effective group working with war, post-traumatic stress, and AIDS around the globe.

Recently my daughter graduated from college with a double major in Middle Eastern and Religious Studies. She is a radiant being, one among the next generation of those capable and willing to look with luminous eyes. While she was in school, I was asked by her Arabic teacher to speak to the students at Claremont McKenna College. I spoke about Sufism, answered questions, and then led them in *zikr (dhikr)* so they might have their own experience of the Secret One inside.

Mah Talat Etemad Moghadam (Angha)*

Everyone is born into a destiny and I was born into an aristocrat family, and my destiny opened the door towards spiritual seeking so I continued my life as a Sufi, at the very heart of aristocracy, an interesting turn.

It was the twentieth day of March, one day before the celebration of the Persian New Year; the first day of Spring when I was born, at dawn, in Teheran, the capital city of Iran, and I was named Mah Talat (Rising Moon). My parents were elite, educated, open-minded and very supportive through my entire life. Princesses Amir Aghdas (from my father's side) and Inbesat Saltane (from my mother's side), from the Ghajar Dynasty, were my dear grandmothers. Born into this wealthy and aristocratic family, our childhood, my sister's and mine, was filled with richness, great fortune and happiness.

When I was twenty years old I married into a family with a background very different from that to which I was accustomed. With this marriage a new chapter was beginning to unfold in my life. As the hand of destiny was creating new moments and tests of endurance, I was being led towards a magnificent new beginning: to Sufism, a religious system far from my traditional up bringing. My husband, Shah Maghsoud Sadegh Angha, was in his mid twenties, had just completed his education in law and was a devoted student of his father, Moulana Mir Ghotbeddin Mohammad Angha, a great Sufi master of the Uwaiysi/Oveysi Tariqat.

Moulana Mir Ghotbeddin, a highly prominent Sufi Master of his time, held gatherings every Thursday evening with many students. Accompanying my husband, I began to attend his sessions on a steady basis. His teachings were interesting and intriguing. This great Sufi Master opened a new door of understanding for me and my heart became illuminated by the sacred words of the Qur'an. He helped to change the face of religion in my mind. Seeing my husband, Shah Maghsoud, spending countless hours studying in our library and by the encouragement of my mother, who was a great influence in my life, I was guided to take the journey of the heart.

I had a busy schedule working full-time as a high school vice principal and caring for our three children, yet I would set aside time every evening to study Sufism. In later years I wrote a history book on Sufi Poets called: *Tazkereh Talat*, and a history of Sufism called: *From Prophet Mohammad (swa) to (Mir Ghotbeddin) Mohammad*. I began the book with the biography of the Prophet Mohammad (swa) and concluded the final chapter with the biography of Mir

Ghotbeddin, who was a student of his father, Hazrat Jalalleddin Mir Abulfazl, who was also a well-known Sufi of his time. He was a true teacher for me, in fact, a true friend, who creates worthy and essential chapters in the book of life. True teachers instruct us to remain truthful to ourselves and to others. Such teachers of humanity guide us and show us how to avoid prejudice, ignorance and imitation. They instruct us not to follow whatever we have no knowledge of. All is favorable if the student is also deserving and qualified to receive. Perhaps, the more knowledgeable we become, the more we discover the value of the hidden universe within our being, and we become immersed into the spiritual universe, the inner treasure. When I reflect back on my life, I see that I learned many principles from Mir Ghotbeddin, who was a true friend not only to me but also to many others. His book, *az janin ta janan* (*Destination: Eternity*), was translated into English by my daughter and his granddaughter, Nahid Angha, a great book among a few which remained from him. He passed away in 1962 and this incident caused great suffering for Shah Maghsoud. He chose seclusion and solitude for a long time.

My mother's unconditional love and support played an important role in our lives, especially during that time when his father passed away. She truly was a mother to him as well as to his people. If it were not for her exceptional generosity, dedication and understanding, possibly the school we know today as Oveysi Shah Maghsoudi never would have materialized. She opened her grand mansion to the students of Hazrat Shah Maghsoud. We had gatherings every Monday night (for women) and Thursday night (for men), and Hazrat Shah Maghsoud would teach everyday. Early sixties he gave permission to a few of his students to teach. These students were among the ones who had passed the stages of heart, they held gatherings under his supervision.

As destiny followed its course, my mother passed away in 1976 and once again I saw Hazrat Shah Maghsoud suffer deep sadness.

Over time we moved to Karaj, northern part of Teheran and stayed in the estate of Sufi Abad where Hazrat Shah Maghsoud began to build a two story

44

Khaneghah with a museum, library, an observatory and guesthouse. We built our own house in the village, at the same time. Our three children moved in that estate and they also built their own places. The estate of Sufi Abad began its life and a new chapter was opened. Gradually, other people bought land nearby and built houses for themselves. Hazrat Shah Maghsoud designed and supervised every aspect of the Khaneghah, including the establishment of all of the buildings and the creation of a beautiful garden. All of his students, men and women, participated in building the facilities. With celebration and joy the Khaneghah formally opened on the day of Amir al Momenin Ali's birth.

We met every Monday, every Thursday and every first Friday of each month which was known as the Night of *Niaz*. Many men and women would come to the Khaneghah to participate and to hear the teachings of Hazrat Shah Maghsoud. Wearing white clothing with gold and black silk *zona'ar* (belts) they would all sit in his presence and take part in the *zikr*. In one of the gatherings, Hazrat Shah Maghsoud presented the Robe of *faghr* to over three hundred men and women. After each *zikr*, dinner, tea and sweets were served. There was an abundance of food for everyone and meals were always provided for those in need who lived nearby the Khaneghah. The serving of food in the neighborhood is just an example of the generous manners of the Sufis.

Our female Sufi students were in charge of organizing the library, and our male students usually prepared the meals. On Fridays, many followers would gather together to discuss building plans, organize projects, talk about important matters and to enjoy companionship. We would hear the sound of *aza'an* at dawn, noon, and in the evening from the Khaneghah. Those were wonderful days, simple times, glorious and meaningful. It was a time of service, friendship, family and honesty. Hazrat Shah Maghsoud was the strong pole in the center of all that beauty, the center of truthful service.

In 1978, we traveled to the United States with our children and their spouses. When we returned to Iran in 1979, Hazrat Shah Maghsoud, who was sixty-three years old, began to show signs of illness, but still would teach and accept a few students. In the summer of 1980 he wrote his final book, a masterpiece, a book of love poems, *Diwan-e-ghazal*, most beautiful sonnets and quatrains, for our daughter, Nahid. This book holds great values; as it is also his final handwritten masterpiece. He dedicated this book of poetic treasures, his personal autobiography and many of his handwritten notes collected over forty years directly to her, and asked her to devote time to translating his books into English and writing commentaries on them.

Moulana Shah Maghsoud taught for over forty years to introduce the meaning of the holy religion of Islam and free from the hands of superstition. He opened the road for many to learn the true meaning of Islam and become knowledgeable of the teachings of the Prophet. He instructed his students to teach what they had learned and be useful to humanity.

When we returned to the United States in the fall of 1980 his health had worsened and his illness had become more severe. He began to express his final advice and make final requests to his family members, students, asking them to honor his family, to honor one another, and to always remain good friends. Yet life has a turn of its own, not everyone kept their promises and not all remained faithful. Some changed their tunes and donned their masks. Two years before his passing he made an announcement. He said: I will be among you for another two years, ask me before you lose me. He knew of the date of his passing, and when the time came, November 17, 1980, he softly passed away from the world of possibilities into eternal.

My spiritual life was a life of service, and I tirelessly and generously helped many. I shared my life, my wealth and my family with pure intent and devotion. And I am grateful for being able to serve on this beautiful path of spiritual understanding.

After the physical passing of Hazrat Shah Maghsoud my life took a turn. The beauty of love and kindness, the wonderful memories of the past were put into the fire of ambition and greed. Masks were taken off and unfriendly yet true faces appeared. Alas, such a sad experience, history was being repeated.

Yet, I did not lose hope and reliance in God and my daughters Nahid and Tannaz and their compassion and kindness gave me a new energy for life. Nahid built me a cottage in her garden, and I have moved in and been living with her and her family since 1985.

Each one of us is born into destiny. Our days pass swiftly as each piece of the puzzle is added to the great mosaic of life. Born into a wealthy, aristocratic family, I lived the majority of my years with my husband, Hazrat Shah Maghsoud, in a rich and spiritual universe, truly my share of existence was richness. Many things can be told about having lived such a diverse way of life. I am grateful that Allah gave me the chance to be among His servants.

May He grant us a life of honor and service and may our road of destiny remain smooth and protected. *Amin*

*Excerpts from and basd on her original autobiography in *Sufi Women: The Journey Towards The Beloved: Collected Essays*, pp. 20-26, Copyright 1998, International Association of Sufism, Publisher.

Mary Ann D. Fadae, Ph. D.

Dr. Fadae received her Ph.D. in Arabic and Islamic studies from Indiana University and has taught courses on Arabic, Islam and Sufism, and the history of Western Civilization. A convert to Islam, Dr. Fadae is a member of the Jerrahi Order of Turkey whose main U.S. branch is in Chestnut Ridge, NY. She has given numerous talks to academic, church and civic groups regarding the beliefs and practices of Islam and Sufism and is involved in interfaith work. Her primary focus and concern is to create an understanding of the teachings of Islam and to eliminate fear and stereotyping.

Dr. Fadae has published articles, reviews, and a book entitled *The Key to Salvation: A Sufi Manual of Invocation*, 1996 (under the name of Danner) that is a translation of a 13th-Century Shadhili work on *dhikr*. Currently she is translating *Allah: al-Qasd al-Mujarrad fi Ma`rifat al-Ism al-Mufrad (God: The Pure Goal Concerning Knowledge of the Unique Name)* also by Shadhili Shaykh Ahmad Ibn `Ata' Allah al-Iskandari that will be published by Fons Vitae. She has been a member of the International Association of Sufism since 2003 and in 2012-2013 served as president of the Association of International Women. Dr. Fadae can be reached at mdfadae@iupui.edu.

Sheikha Azima Lila Forest

Sheikha Azima Lila Forest is a Sheikha in the Sufi Ruhaniat International and a Unitarian Universalist minister. In the Ruhaniat, she holds the posts of *siraj* (senior minister), healing conductor, SoulWork practitioner, retreat guide, and farmer in the Ziraat concentration. Her present areas of concentration are dreamwork, Reiki healing, SoulWork, shamanism, and spiritual retreat guidance. She is an activist and volunteer in organizations promoting locally and sustainably grown and raised foods. Azima has been a frequent speaker at the annual Sufism Symposium. She is also involved in education regarding soul healing needed by combat veterans with PTSD (Post-Traumatic Soul Disorder). A native of San Francisco, Azima was also a resident of Auroville in South India from 1993 to 1997; she now lives in Silver City in the mountains of southwestern New Mexico.

John Fox

"Poetry is a natural medicine that extends solace and relief,
gives cathartic voice to suffering, reveals insight and shows us what it means to be human."
John Fox

John Fox is a poet and certified poetry therapist. He is author of *Poetic Medicine: The Healing Art of Poem-Making* and *Finding What You Didn't Lose: Expressing Your Truth and Creativity Through Poem-Making* and numerous essays in a range of books on subjects of spirituality, education, writing, medicine, psychology and healing. His work is featured in the PBS documentary, *Healing Words: Poetry and Medicine.* A book of his poems, *the only gift to bring*, will be published by Seasonings Press in the Spring of 2015.

John contributed two chapters (one is co-authored) to *Whole Person Health Care*, a 3 volume published by Praeger/ Greenwood. He contributed *Poetry Therapy, Mindfulness and Creativity* to the newly published *Mindfulness and the Art Therapies: Theory and Practice*, published by Jessica Kingsley. His chapter *Poetry's Call: An Exploration of the Words Let and Letting* appears in *Letting the Beauty We Love Be What We Do: Stories of Living Divided No More*, published by Prose Press.

Since 2000 he has been adjunct associate professor at the California

Institute of Integral Studies in San Francisco, California. He has taught courses in poetry therapy since 1997 at Sofia University (formerly ITP) in Palo Alto, CA. Since 2005 he has taught at the Sophia Center for Culture & Spirituality at Holy Names University in Oakland, CA. From 1993 – 2012 John taught at John F. Kennedy University in the Graduate School of Professional Psychology and then the Arts & Consciousness Department in Berkeley, CA. Beginning in June of 2012, The Institute for Poetic Medicine offers training in the practice of poetry therapy.

John has brought poetry as healer to pastoral care departments medical schools and hospitals through the United States including Stanford, Harvard, University of Florida at Gainesville, University Hospital in Cleveland, Ohio, Seoul National University Hospital in Korea, St. John of God Hospice in Ireland, The Fred Hutchinson Cancer Center in Seattle, Washington, Children's Hospital at Legacy in Dallas, Texas and many others places. He works throughout the United States in all kinds of settings. He has taught internationally in Ireland, England, Israel, Kuwait, Germany, United Arab Emirates, South Korea and Canada.

For twelve years John led week-long retreats to Canyon de Chelly working in friendship and collaboration with Diné guides, Jon and Lupita McClanahan. He wanted to show people the indigenous roots of poetry-as-healer on the North American continent.

Spirituality inspires the core of this poetic medicine calling John has followed since the age of thirteen. While walking this path, Sufism has exerted a profound influence and blessing. John's poem *Home Equity* was included in *Essential Sufism* by James Fadiman and Robert Frager. He has presented three times at the International Association for Sufism conferences.

John is past president of the National Association for Poetry Therapy 2003 – 2005. He is President of The Institute for Poetic Medicine, a nonprofit he founded in 2005. John lives in Mountain View, California. You can write to him at john@poeticmedicine.org and find out more about his work and the training provided by the Institute at www.poeticmedicine.org

Robert Frager, Ph.D.
Robert Frager, Ph.D. (Harvard University) has taught Psychology at Harvard, University of California, Berkeley, and University of California, Santa Cruz. In 1975, he founded Sofia University (formerly the Institute of Transpersonal Psychology).

Professor Frager has been an Aikido instructor for over 45 years and is the president of the Western Aikido Association. He has received a 7th degree black belt in Aikido, making him one of only a handful of Westerners to have been awarded this rank.

Professor Frager is a sheikh in the Halveti-Jerrahi Sufi Order, whose center is in Istanbul. He is president of the Jerrahi Order of California located in Redwood City, California. He has been a Sufi sheikh since 1985 and he lectures on Sufism and Sufi psychology in the United States and in Europe.

Sheikh Frager has written four books on Sufism: *Essential Sufism* (HarperSanFrancisco, 1997); *Heart, Self, and Soul: The Sufi Psychology of Growth, Balance, and Harmony* (Quest Books, 1999); *Love is the Wine: Teachings of a Sufi Master in America* (Hohm Press, 2009); and *Sufi Talks* (Quest, 2012). He is the editor of *Sharing Sacred Stories: Current Approaches to Spiritual Direction and Guidance* (Crossroad, 2007) and co-author of the classic personality psychology text *Personality and Personal Growth* (7th edition, Pearson, 2013).

Rev. Canon Charles P. Gibbs

A lover of the Mystery, Reverend Canon Charles Gibbs has sought to be of service all his life. An Episcopal priest, a visionary and a poet, Charles is blessed by his friends and colleagues of diverse faiths with whom he shares a commitment to serve the world through spiritual transformation and cooperative engagement for the good of all life on this sacred Earth. As son, brother, husband, father, father-in-law and grandfather, he cherishes and is inspired by his family. Mindful of the abundant blessings that come even through life's biggest challenges, he seeks to live each moment in gratitude.

For seventeen years, until his retirement in 2013, Rev. Gibbs served as the founding Executive Director of the United Religions Initiative (http://www.uri.org), a global movement whose purpose is to promote enduring, daily interfaith cooperation, to end religiously motivated violence, and to create cultures of peace, justice and healing for the Earth and all living beings.

During his tenure, he led a global chartering process that involved thousands of people, and included the planning and production of five global summits and eight regional conferences. The URI signed its global Charter in June 2000 and as of July 2013 had nearly 600 member Cooperation Circles active in 84 countries around the world. Their work includes peacebuilding, interfaith education, advocacy for the rights of women and children, environmental awareness, economic development and building social cohesion; and touches the lives of over 2.5 million people  each year across the globe. URI is a Non-Governmental Organization with consultative status at the United Nations. It was honored by the UN's Alliance of Civilizations for its innovative peacebuilding work.

In his work for the URI, Rev. Gibbs traveled extensively, working with religious, spiritual and other leaders in Africa, Asia, Europe, the Middle East, the Americas and Southeast Asia and the Pacific. He was a featured speaker at many international gatherings including: the World Congress of Muslim Philanthropists (Doha, Qatar); the Parliament of the World's Religions (Barcelona, Spain; Capetown, South Africa; and Melbourne, Australia); the Annual Symposia of the International Association of Sufism (San Rafael, California); the United Nations; and the United Nations Alliance of Civilizations in Rio de Janeiro, Brazil.

With colleague Sally Mahé, Reverend Gibbs co-authored *Birth of a Global Community*, an account of the birth of URI. He contributed a chapter to *Interfaith Dialogue and Peacebuilding*, published by the United States Institute of Peace. He also co-authored, with Barbara Hartford, a chapter in *Positive Approaches to Peacebuilding*. His essay, "Opening the Dream: Beyond the Limits of Otherness," appears in the anthology, *Deepening the American Dream*. In addition, he has published many articles on interfaith work, including several blogs on the *Huffington Post*.

Before becoming the URI's Executive Director, Rev. Gibbs served for six years as Rector of the Episcopal Church of the Incarnation, San Francisco, California. For six years prior, he served as the Executive Director of the San Rafael Canal Ministry, an interfaith ministry of service and outreach that served a community of immigrants and refugees in Marin County, California.

Before being ordained, Charles taught writing at the University of Minnesota and also worked in the theater. His wife, Debbie, is a career educator, currently serving as Head of the Lowell School in Washington, D.C. Their daughter, Naomi, is an editorial assistant at Houghton Mifflin Harcourt in New York City. Their son Ben and daughter-in-law Megan are career educators working in inner city schools in Houston, Texas; and the parents of young twins – Henry and Abigail.

For personal enjoyment, Charles loves daily walks, Qigong, being near the water, meditating, writing, reading and listening to music, visiting museums with his wife, and, when his children are around, playing games and the occasional line of bowling.

Rev. Canon Charles P. Gibbs has a B.A., in Theater Arts, Pomona College, Claremont, California, 1974; M.A., Writing, University of Minnesota, Minneapolis, Minnesota, 1982; M. Div., Church Divinity School of the Pacific, Berkeley, California, 1987.

Rev, Canon Gibbs is a member of the Evolutionary Leaders Group, 2007 – present http://www.evolutionaryleaders.net.

He has received many honors including: Honored for Work for World Peace by the International Association of Sufism, San Rafael, CA, 2010; Honored as one of Fifty Interfaith Visionaries by the Temple of Understanding, New York, NY, 2010; Honored at the Lanao Month of Peace Celebration, Iligan City, Philippines, 2009; United Religions Initiative Pakistan Peace Award, Lahore, Pakistan, 2008; D.D., *honoris causa*, Church Divinity School of the Pacific, Berkeley, California, 2003; Inaugural Distinguished Alumnus Award, Holland Hall School, Tulsa, Oklahoma, 2003; Award for Fellowship and Service, Rotary Club, Lahore, Pakistan, 2001.

Sonia Leon Gilbert

For forty-two years, Sonia Leon Gilbert has been a president of the Bawa Muhaiyaddeen Fellowship and Mosque that has fourteen branches in the United States, Canada, England and Sri Lanka. During that time, the study of the Sufi Way, as exemplified by her exalted teacher, M. R. Bawa Muhaiyaddeen (ral.) has been her focus and her work. Wisdom she has gained is included in her many speeches and is her guide to continued enthusiastic engagement in numerous Interfaith Dialogues. She is a regular speaker at the International Association of Sufism Symposia and is an ardent supporter of Interfaith Endeavors. Author of articles and speeches, she recently contributed a chapter to the book *The Revelation of the Breath.* Her essay, "The Divine Vibration in the Breath - A Song of Life" was included in this book for its salient observations on consciousness.

In earlier years, Sonia Leon was a voice graduate of the revered Curtis Institute of Music in Philadelphia, Pennsylvania. Her operatic career spanned the concert stage, radio, and television, and she performed with some of the greatest singers of the latter 20th century. From 1986 to 1998, she was the owner of two gem magazines, notably the international publication *Lapidary Journal.* In addition to these two mineral and jewelry arts magazines, she co-founded a third gem news magazine, *Colored Stone,* in 1987. Concerns for the spiritual, socio-political and physical environment also initiated her partnership in One Light Pictures LLC, a company involved in documentary film productions. One of the documentaries, interviews with great artists and photographers in Cuba during the time of revolution, was seen throughout the United States on Independent Lens.

Currently, much time is given to careful guidance to those in the Bawa Muhaiyaddeen Fellowship. Most important is the recognition and love for the children and grandchildren who are carrying on with dedication and wisdom the Beauty of the teachings of Bawa Muhaiyaddeen.

Murshida Khadija (Chishti) Goforth

Murshida Khadija (Chishti) Goforth first encountered the Ruhaniat-Inayati-Chishti Sufi lineage in her early 20's via the film "Sunseed" at Beverly Hills, California's Doheny Plaza Theatre. Shortly after, she happened upon the 1970's *What's My Line?* television program whose Mevlevi Sufi sheikh mystery guest's occupation was "whirling dervish." Her lifelong inner call intensified, as what she had been seeking in life seemed to be seeking her. After a two-year search for a Sufi guide, she embarked upon years of rigorous spiritual practice, study, *khilvat/*retreat, and service balanced with teaching five subjects to as many as 130 public junior high school students daily.

Decades later, Murshida Khadija continues to explore the comprehensive four-school *(Chishti, Qadiri, Surawardhi, Naqshbandi)* Universal Sufi legacy brought West from Hyderabad, India in 1910 by Pir-o-Murshid Hazrat Inayat Khan (1882-1927), the embodied, experiential teachings of his American student Sufi Ahmed Murad Chishti/Murshid Samuel Lewis (1896-1971) including Dances of Universal Peace, Spiritual Walk and Whirling Meditations; the spiritual transmission of Shams-i Tabriz and Mevlana Jelaluddin Rumi; group process; spiritual psychology and teachings of the world's sacred traditions.

Since the 1970's, Murshida Khadija has helped catalyze experiences which open hearts, facilitate embodied wisdom, and support development of the God-ideal at festivals, colleges, universities, churches, spiritual centers, and women's programs including the Becoming Program for women in transition from the prison system (1988-91) and renewal retreats for Roman Catholic religious orders.

In 1976, she brought Sufi teachings and Dances of Universal Peace to Spokane, Washington's Vedanta (Sivananda) Yoga Center and in 1977 co-founded Garden of Noor, an early American *khankah*/Sufi center where visiting teachers offered workshops and, in the spirit of Murshid SAM's peace vision, gathered circles of various spiritual traditions to "Eat, Dance, & Pray together" in seasonal celebrations. Murshida Khadija was among the original certified Dances of Universal Peace teachers (1978), demonstrating Dance leadership and proficiency in Murshid SAM's centering, elemental, astrological yoga and *tassawuri* walks, all still central to her learning.

Family became her primary spiritual concentration during the mid-1980's when Murshida Khadija married and gave birth to her daughter. During this time she also co-founded *Abaja!* African-American Music & Dance Company with Nigerian teacher Tokumbo Shomotun and a circle of other mostly-new mothers, studying and performing authentic, traditional West African *Yoruba, Hausa, and Igbo* tribal dances locally and at Seattle's International Folklife Festival. In 1990 she brought Dances of Universal Peace to the Sisters of Loretto worldwide conference in St. Louis, Missouri, invited by Sister Mary Luke Tobin (1908-2006), the order's superior, a longtime friend of Thomas Merton, one of fifteen women delegates invited to the historic Vatican II, and a DUP devotee. She and Murshida Khadija had met through friends the previous year; thrilled to find a "Murshid SAM Sufi," "Luke" (as she was called) rushed everyone through dinner so there would be time to Dance. During this time Murshida Khadija was also invited to offer Sufi teachings at Usui Reiki Master international trainings by Grand Master Phyllis Furumoto. Murshida Khadija represented Mevlana Jelaluddin Rumi's spiritual transmission during the early 1990's, serving as Seattle, Washington's *ateshbaz* (Mevlana's cook: "one who plays with fire") and local *postneshin;* with her husband Sheikh Mansur Kreps and others, co-founding *Zaviya Niyaz,* a major early American Mevlevi center. In this role, she led zikr, taught classes and organized caravans,  *semas* and events, helping establish that *tariqat* in America. A profound moment was serving as *semazenbashi*/dance master (1994), told that she was the first woman to do so in centuries, at the Konya, Turkey *dergah* of Mevlana Jelaluddin Rumi in a history-making *sema* including both men and women *semazens*. Murshida Khadija also Turned as a *semazen* at Istanbul's historic Galata Mevlevihane, one of Turkey's first *semahanes* with her husband and ten-year-old daughter Jamiell, also a *semazen*.

Soon after, Murshida Khadija completed Mevlevi organizational responsibilities, responding to a call from her teacher Pir Murshid Moineddin Jablonski (1942-2001), spiritual successor to Murshid Samuel Lewis, to work closely with him serving Ruhaniat development. He confirmed her as a *sheikha* in San Francisco, CA (1989), asking Murshid SAM's friend and Ruhaniat Godparent Joe Miller (1904-1992) to bestow the *sheikha's* robe, and in 1993 gave her the spiritual surname "Chishti." Murshid Moineddin served as Khadija's living teacher for over 25 years; their learning continues.

Murshida Khadija was introduced to "Three Selves Work" spiritual psychology by San Francisco, CA amanuensis Rev. Frida Waterhouse (1907-87), continuing with Pir Moineddin in a form he further developed as "Soulwork." He eventually referred *mureeds* to Murshida Khadija for individual sessions. She completed a M.S. degree in Applied Psychology (1991), studying counseling, embodied psychotherapies, and group process under the direction of Dr. Walt Powers at Eastern Washington University, Cheney, Washington.

A major contribution was guiding the Ruhaniat ethics agreement through years of group reflection involving both *mureeds* and teachers.

Formalized over 15 years ago, this document continues with only slight modification to unite the *tariqat* in mutual respect and compassionate action when challenges in roles and power differential arise. Murshida Khadija helped initiate the movement of Ruhaniat *jamiats* (*tariqat* meetings) around the United States beyond the San Francisco gatherings of the school's early years, providing cohesion within the growing *mureed* community. She also spearheaded fundraising for Pir Moineddin's first computer, a pioneering internet link from his rural Maui, Hawaii home with *mureeds* worldwide.

For years, Murshida Khadija served as a Ruhaniat trustee and co-founder, board member and sometimes-spiritual director of Sufi circles and events including Northwest Sufi Camps *Sacred Ground* (1988); *Wholeheartedly Human* (1991) and *HEART: Heaven & Earth* (2010) and Inland NW Sufi Camp. In 1993, she was first recognized as a *murshida*/senior Sufi teacher by Sufi Order International Murshida Arifa Jean Miller (1917-1997) and Sufi Ruhaniat International Murshid Saadi Shakur Chishti, an initiation formally confirmed by Ruhaniat Pir Moineddin in his lineage, also acknowledged by Sufi Movement International Pir Hidayat Inayat Khan (1917). Murshida Khadija was delighted to join Sufis of *tariqats* from throughout the world as she presented Dances of Universal Peace and walking meditations of Murshid Samuel Lewis at early annual International Association of Sufism symposia (1995-96).

Since 2004, with American *dervishes,* Murshida Khadija has organized annual New York City gatherings celebrating Mevlana Jelaluddin Rumi's spiritual legacy. In 2005 she emceed *Mysticism of Sound,* a Sufi sacred music concert at St. Peter's Church in New York City. In 2007, with *dervish* friends she presented teachings at Fordham University's New York Interfaith *Conference on the Abrahamic Prophets.* Also in 2007, honoring the International Year of Rumi *RUMI: Poet of Peace* at Sacred Heart University, Bridgeport, CT, she offered Turning and meditation with *dervish* colleagues for several hundred university and community participants.

Ordained by Sufi Order International Pir Vilayat Inayat Khan as a *cherag* (minister) in 1976 and by Pir Moineddin as a *siraj* (senior minister) in 1987, Murshida Khadija celebrated 31 years of ministry by organizing a Universal Worship Service uniting Ruhaniat, Sufi Order, and Sufi Movement ministers in 2007 on Pir-o-Murshid Hazrat Inayat Khan's 80th URS at his New Delhi, India *dargah.* Based upon his 1910 worship service, it included scriptures and music from the world's sacred traditions. This URS, hosted by the Sufi Ruhaniat International, demonstrated growing cohesion among branches of the Chishti/Inayati *tariqat* "tree" he planted in the West upon arriving from India a century before. In 2014 she returned to India to again organize an URS Universal Worship Service at the request of Ruhaniat Pir Shabda Kahn.

Murshida Khadija represented Sufis at Long Island's *Voices of Faith for Peace* sacred music celebrations (2008-09). In 2008 she served as *semazenbashi/* dance master for Boston's Huntington Theatre's *Cry of the Reed* world premiere, introducing the acting company to Sufi esotericism, historical perspectives, ceremonial elements, and Turning. At New York's Brooklyn Museum's 2009 *Light of the Sufis: Mystical Arts of Islam, dervish* colleagues from several *tariqats* from throughout the United States joined her in whirling and music in the museum's Beaux Arts Hall. In 2011 Khadija served as *semazenbashi* for Boston Center for the Arts Company One's production of *1001,* facilitating actor workshops emphasizing whirling, meditation, and Sufi perspectives. In 2011, she represented the Sufi tradition with other New York City clergy in an interfaith service commemorating 9/11, and in 2012, she served as an interfaith leader of the inaugural New York Peace Walk.

With other Sufi Ruhaniat International *murshids,* Murshida Khadija seeks guidance and serves organizational cohesion in a diverse, rapidly growing, international spiritual community. She currently serves Seattle, Washington and New York City Ruhaniat circles and Western Washington's Unity Zikr, uniting (Chishti) Inayati/Ruhaniat/Sufi Order, Mevlevi, Halveti-Jerrahi, and Rifa'i-Marufi *tariqats* in practice, community meals, and charitable endeavors. In addition, she offers a three-year training program (2011-13) for prospective Service of Universal Peace *cherags* (ministers). Grateful for the learning arising in each new day, other interests include feminine perspectives, group process, ministry, and shamanic parallels with Sufi practice. In the Sufi Ruhaniat International lineage, Murshida Khadija now serves as a *murshida/* senior esoteric school teacher, Dances of Universal Peace senior mentor teacher, Service of Universal Peace *siraj/*senior minister, and Dervish Healing Order conductor and initiator. A mother and grandmother, her life includes travel, community, graphic design, astrology, photography, and HEART. She has welcomed many friends to the Sufi path whose spiritual journeys find them also "going forth" in a similar, often-pioneering spirit of service.

William C. Gough

William Gough graduated from Princeton University with Bachelor and Master degrees in electrical engineering and is a registered professional engineer (nuclear). At Harvard University's Kennedy School of Government, he researched and studied the Interaction between Science and Public Policy. Gough was a manager at the US Atomic Energy Commission's controlled fusion research program, where in 1968, he co-invented with Dr. B. J. Eastlund the Fusion Torch concept that would produce sustainability for the material world. He has written two papers with Dr. George Miley (University of Illinois) on the application of the Fusion Torch concept to close the materials cycle from use to reuse, and for the production of hydrogen from water. These papers were presented at meetings of the American Nuclear Society in 2008. See the references in the recent paper, *A Route to Ecological Sustainability* at http://www.fmbr.org/papers/ecological_sustainability.pdf

He was the manager of the fusion power program for the electric utility industry at the Electric Power Research Institute (EPRI), and then the US DOE site manager for high-energy physics and synchrotron radiation at the Stanford Linear Accelerator Center (SLAC). His published works appear in *Scientific American*, the *Environmental Engineers Handbook*, and other publications. In 1980, he co-founded a nonprofit organization, The Foundation for Mind-Being Research (http://www.fmbr.org), which in 2014 is expanding into an Institute for the Advancement of Science and Consciousness (i-asc.org). Since 1988 he has pursued his study of the science of consciousness, full time, and has assisted in the evolution of consciousness studies in an effort to bring this field into wider recognition as a bona fide science.

Jonathan Granoff

Jonathan Granoff, President of the Global Security Institute, Adjunct Professor of International Law at Widener University School of Law, is also Co-Chair of the Task Force on Nuclear Nonproliferation of the

58

International Law Section of the American Bar Association. He serves on numerous governing and advisory boards including the Global Dialogue Institute, Middle Powers Initiative, Jane Goodall Institute, Nuclear Age Peace Foundation, Lawyers Committee on Nuclear Policy, Tikkun, the Bipartisan Security Group, and the Bawa Muhaiyaddeen Fellowship. Mr. Granoff is both a Member of the World Wisdom Council and a Fellow of the World Academy of Arts and Sciences,

and has represented the International Peace Bureau at the Nobel Peace Laureate Summits. He lectures worldwide emphasizing the legal, ethical and spiritual dimensions of human development and inner and outer peace and security, with a specific focus on the threats posed by nuclear weapons and environmental responsibility, including formal expert testimony before the Secretary General's General's Disarmament Advisory Board as well as the U.S. Congress. He was honored to serve as Master of Ceremonies at the United Nations for a Celebration of Love to commemorate the 800th anniversary of the passing of Khwaja Moinuddin Chisti. He is an award-winning screenwriter (*The Constitution*), a regular Blogger on the *Huffington Post*, and featured in more than 75 publications. He is engaged in numerous international affairs, including matters involving the Millennium Development Goals, having produced a documentary on the MDGs (Point of Peace). He has studied with the Sufi Master Bawa Muhaiyaddeen since his youth and is honored by receiving his namesake, Ahamed Muhaiyaddeen. His studies continue. For more information, see http://www.gsinstitute.org and http://www.bmf.org.

Shaikha Camille Adams Helminski

Shaikha Camille Adams Helminski is the Co-Director of The Threshold Society (http://www.sufism.org) which is dedicated to facilitating the direct personal experience of the Divine. She has been working within the Mevlevi tradition of Sufism for over thirty-five years and has helped to increase awareness of the integral contribution of women to the spiritual path of Islam with her book, *Women of Sufism*. She was the co-founder and

co-director of Threshold Books that made many classics of the Sufi tradition available in English. She has co-translated many volumes of Sufi literature, including *Jewels of Remembrance* (excerpts of the *Mathnawi* of Jalaluddin Rumi), and is the first woman to translate a substantial portion of the Qur'an into English in the book, *The Light of Dawn,* selections from the Qur'an for daily contemplation. She has authored two anthologies for the Book Foundation (http://www.thebook.org), *The Book of Character* and *The Book of Nature, A Sourcebook of Spiritual Perspectives on Nature and the Environment.* She also translated, with Refik Algan, *Rumi's Sun, The Teachings of Shams of Tabriz.* Her most recent publication is *Rumi and His Friends, Stories of the Lovers of God.*

Camille has also been designated as one of the spiritual leaders of WISE (Women's Islamic Initiative in Spirituality and Equality, http://www.wisemuslimwomen.org) and is a member of the WISE Shura Council. As core faculty members of the Spiritual Paths Institute (http://www.interspiritualwisdom.org), Camille and her husband Kabir have also taught programs in Interspirituality rooted in contemplative practice and through close association with Sufi teachers around the world are working to integrate the classical methods of Sufi education with modern needs.

Shaikh Kabir Helminski

Shaikh Kabir Helminski is the Co-Director of the Threshold Society (http://www.sufism.org), a non-profit educational foundation that has developed programs that provide a structure for practice and study within Sufism. He is also an American representative of the Mevlevi Order that is based in Turkey. In 2009, Kabir was named as one of the "500 Most Influential Muslims in The World." He has translated many volumes of Sufi literature, including many works of Rumi, the most recent with his wife Camille, *The Rumi Daybook.* He is the author of two books on Sufism: *Living Presence* and *The Knowing Heart,* as well as two texts for the study of Islam, *The Book of Language* and *The Book of Revelation.*

Kabir began the study of Sufism with Suleyman Dede of Konya and was officially recognized as a Shaikh of the Mevlevi Order in 1990 by the late Celalettin Celebi, Head of the Mevlevi Order. From 1980 until 1999 he was the Co-Director of Threshold Books, one of the foremost publishers of Sufi literature. Between 1994 and 2000 he toured with the whirling dervishes of Turkey, bringing the spiritual culture of the Mevlevis to more than 100,000 people.

He has an M.A. in transpersonal studies and an honorary Ph.D. in literature from Selçuk University of Konya, Turkey. In recent years, Kabir and Camille began the Baraka Institute (http://www.barakainstitute.org) bringing scholars and spiritual teachers together to explore the possibilities of "Transformation Through Spiritual Experience." Kabir and Camille live in Louisville, Kentucky and focus on Sufi music, writing, and teaching and developing new forms of spiritual education together with an international team of scholars and Sufis.

Judith Hill

Judith Hill is a lifetime astrologer, researcher and an award-winning author of many acclaimed books. She has performed approximately 9000 personal readings. Judith is the founder and owner of Stellium Press, dedicated to fine astrological, spiritual and whimsical titles (accepts no manuscripts). She is also the founder of The Lost Secrets of Renaissance Medicine Conference.

For ten years, Judith pioneered the scientific, statistical research of Astro-seismology and Astro-genetics. She internationally published papers with breakthrough research in both fields and received a personal research grant from the renowned physicist Arthur Young and his Institute for the Study of Consciousness in Berkeley, California. Ms. Hill has served as the Educational Director for the San Francisco National Council for Geocosmic Research (NCGR).

She founded *Redheads Research* - an international ten-year research project of astrology and genetics that resulted in an international publication. She also successfully matched five charts to five biographies in an NCGR sponsored skeptics' challenge in 1989. Ms. Hill's breakthrough astro-genetics research was featured on TV's *Strange Universe*.

Hill wrote for four years for the journal, *Sufism: An Inquiry*. Her articles likely represented the first time articles on astrology appeared in a scholastic quarterly outside of the astrological press. She also has over thirty articles published in numerous journals including: *Borderlands; NCGR Journal; Correlations; The Mountain Astrologer; Dell Horoscope; Above and Below; Sufism: An Inquiry;* and *Linguace Astrale.* Her radio appearances have included KCBS, KPFA, KBOO and The Laura Lee Show. Hill served as the Educational Director for The National Council of Geocosmic Research. She has served on the Faculty of The Institute for Stellar Influence Studies.

Hill's speaking engagements have included: The International Association of Sufism; The Theosophical Society; Sacred Places Conference; Oregon and Washington Astrological Associations; The National Council for Geocosmic Research; The Institute for the Study of Consciousness; and The American Federation of Astrologers, Inc.; *The Laura Lee Show*; *The Mitch Rabin Show*; and the *Job 1 Show* based in New York City.

Hill's first paid astrological reading was at the age of fourteen, following a four-year intensive training with a skilled relative. She has been reading charts for every possible type of person ever since! Judith is also a Chartered Herbalist with the Dominion College of Herbal Sciences and is widely versed in Vedic Astrology, History, Theology, Art, Music, Metaphysics, Feng Shui, Phrenology, Psychology, Anthropology, and Handwriting Analysis.

Syed Ahmadul Huq

Syed Ahmadul Huq is one of those very few personalities who has ably disproved the notion or the proverb that knowledge, learning and wealth do not usually go hand in hand and that one keeps a safe distance from the other. Syed Ahmadul Huq, while removing this distance, is known in Chittagong as a man of profound knowledge and learning with an enviable research-oriented background of our history, culture and traditions. He is the founding chairman of one of the leading industrial projects of the country.

A widely traveled man, Ahmadul Huq visited countries like Saudi

Arabia, America, Jordan, Syria, Iran, Dubai, Burma, India, Pakistan, Thailand, Malaysia, Singapore, Indonesia, Hong Kong, Japan, Kenya, Tanzania, England, France, Germany, Italy, Belgium and others. Syed Ahmadul Huq has to his credit a number of publications, such as A *Short History of Chittagong, Export Prospects of Ginger in the U.K., Export Guide to India,* and *Tour report of the Businessmen's Trade Delegation to Central and East African Countries.* His essays on Maulana Jalluddin Rumi, Hafiz, and the influence of Persian literature on Bengali earned him a widely recognized reputation. His latest book is the Bengali version of *Diwan-e-Shams Tabrezi* by Maulana Jalaluddin Rumi. This book is under print. He is the founder of the Allama Rumi Society in Bangladesh and was selected as a speaker on the Unification of Muslim Sects in the World Muslim Conference held in Mecca in 1991 under the auspices of the Government of Iran. He participated in the conference as a State Guest of the Islamic Republic of Iran.

He belongs to Maizbhandari Order, founded by Maulana Syed Ahmadullah and Maulana Syed Golam Rahman of Maizbhandari, Chittagong.

Ibrahim Jaffe, M.D.

Dr. Ibrahim Jaffe is a licensed medical doctor, who, for the last 25 years, has pioneered advanced energetic and spiritual healing in the West. This approach using the integration of Sufi spiritual healing, the invocation of the 99 Divine Names and *Quranic Dua* in combination with allopathic and prophetic medicine, has led to over 35,000 healings including cancer and other serious and life-threatening diseases.

Ibrahim is known for his depth of wisdom, love, mercy, and compassion. He has dedicated his life to creating world peace through helping people to heal themselves and find the love within. His teachings reach across all faiths and beliefs. Most recently, he was awarded the "Man of Peace" award at an Interfaith International Peace Conference.

After studying many different spiritual paths, Dr. Jaffe found Sufism. Sufis are known for their deep and ecstatic love. Sufism had a profound and powerful transformation of his own spirit as well as completing his understanding of healing.

Currently, Dr. Jaffe is the President of the University of Spiritual Healing and Sufism in Napa Valley, California. He is also the *Murshid Murrabai Ruhi* (spiritual director and caregiver of the spirit) within the Shadhiliyya Sufi Order, under the guidance of Shaykh Muhammad Al-Jamal.

He resides in Northern California where he teaches, lectures and practices spiritual medicine.

Bawa Jain

Bawa Jain has more than 25 years of progressively increasing responsibilities, working in diversified fields under challenging and compelling circumstances across cultures, ethnicities and geographical locations with the world's religious, political, business and civic leaders at the highest level. He is a strategic planner with exceptional speaking abilities, he is very versatile, conversant with complex religious and political protocols, a specialist in international mediation in very sensitive circumstances, and widely traveled, possessing vast experience in international organizing across the world. He has successfully built initiatives from conceptualization to completion. Bawa Jain was invited to serve as Secretary General of the Millennium World Peace Summit, which, for the first time in history, brought together over 1200 of the world's pre-eminent religious leaders from over 120 countries at the United Nations. He established The World Council of Religious Leaders (WCORL) and currently serves as its Founding Secretary General. Bawa Jain founded the Gandhi-King Award that honors those who exemplify the life and legacy of Mahatma Gandhi and Martin Luther King, Jr. Past recipients include former United Nations Secretary General Kofi Annan, President Nelson Mandela, Dame Jane Goodal, Mata Amritanandamayi and President Mwai Kibaki.

Bawa Jain was invited to develop and jointly launch the Religious Initiative of The World Economic Forum in Davos, Switzerland. He is the founding chairman of The World Youth Peace Summit – an initiative that has brought together young leaders from over 100 countries in an effort to harness and explore new and innovative youth-driven initiatives to address Global challenges. He was also elected Chairman of the United Nations Annual Conference for non-governmental organizations commemorating the 50th anniversary of The United Nations. Bawa Jain launched WCORL's "Religion

One on One" initiative which brought together two of the world's oldest religions, Judaism and Hinduism, which resulted in a signed "Declaration of Mutual Understanding and Cooperation" and the creation of "A Standing Committee" for Hindu-Jewish relations for ongoing bilateral relations. Additionally, he is the founder, chairman and CEO of a multi-million dollar corporation of diversified construction and development firm with countrywide operations headquartered in Delhi, India. Bawa Jain wrote a special publication in

cooperation with the Office of the United Nations High Commissioner for Human Rights entitled: *Sacred Rights: Faith Leaders on Tolerance and Respect*, to commemorate the World Conference on Racism, Racial Discrimination, Xenophobia, and Related Intolerance, Durban, South Africa. He also contributed a chapter for a book entitled *Toward a Global Civilization? The Contribution of Religions*, published by Peter Lang, New York. Bawa Jain also compiled, edited and published two commemorative publications in honor of his Spiritual Father - Guru, His Holiness Acharya Sushil Kumar ji Maharaj in 1993 and 1994. He contributed a chapter for a book on *Inter-Group Leadership* – Religious Diplomacy for the Kennedy School of Government and also compiled, edited and published The 1ˢᵗ Hindu Jewish Leadership Summit Report 2008. Bawa Jain has a Bachelor of Commerce (with honors) in Business Administration from The University of Delhi, India, and a postgraduate diploma in Industrial Marketing and Sales Management from the Institute of Marketing Management, Delhi, India. He attended the oldest private institution in Asia, Bishop Cotton School in Shimla, India**.**

Shaykh Muhammad Hisham Kabbani

Listed as one of the World's 500 most Influential Muslims by Georgetown University, Shaykh Muhammad Hisham Kabbani is a world renowned scholar of Islam and the spiritual science of Sufism. Hailing from one of the most prominent Sunni families of Beirut, Shaykh Kabbani's maternal uncle Shaykh Mukhtar Alayli was the head of Dar al-Fatwa (Office of Islamic Rulings) in Lebanon and another maternal uncle, Shaykh Abd Allah Alayli, Head of the Association of Muslim Scholars of Lebanon, was a leading intellectual figure in the Arab world, renowned for his ability to address difficult issues within Islamic law.

Shaykh Kabbani took his undergraduate degree in Chemistry at the American University of Beirut and then studied medicine at the University of Louvain, Belgium. After completing his medical studies, he traveled to Damascus to study Islamic Shariah under Shaykh Salih Farfur. In addition to learning religious knowledge from such great scholars as Sayyid Muhammad Arabi al-'Azzuzi, Shaykh Salih Farfur, Shaykh Abu al-Khayr al-Maydani, and Sayyid Makki al-Kattani, he continued his ongoing study under Shaykh Abdullah Faiz al-Daghestani and Shaykh Muhammad Nazim al-Haqqani.

He traveled with both shaykhs to many parts of the world over the years, including England, France Germany, Holland, Italy, former Yugoslavia, Turkey, Saudi Arabia, Egypt, Malaysia, Singapore, Pakistan and Sri Lanka and finally America where he currently resides. Under the guidance of his Sufi masters, he entered intense seclusion many times in order to develop his spiritual capacity and mastership of power over the self. Shaykh Kabbani also participated in many spiritual pilgrimages and visitations (*ziyarat*), including doing several Hajj trips with his master and many on his own.

In August 1991, Shaykh Kabbani arrived in the United States where he began a new chapter in his life, establishing himself first in New Jersey and then moving to California. Seeing the lack of traditional Islamic teachings, and in particular the deprecation of Sufism and the overwhelming influence of extremist interpretations of Islam, Shaykh Kabbani set out to correct an obvious void in the Islamic milieu in America. First he began establishing numerous centers throughout North America, where the classical normative Islam is taught and practiced. At that same time, taking advantage of budding internet technology, Shaykh Kabbani established a strong presence on the web from which to teach classical Islam and the Sufi Path. Besides the official Naqshbandi website, which presents the teachings of the Naqshbandi-Haqqani Sufi Path, Shaykh Kabbani has established the Sufilive.com website, which provides ongoing live and taped broadcasts by Shaykh Kabbani's spiritual master Shaykh Nazim Adil, as well as broadcasts of Shaykh Kabbani's almost daily teaching. He also established the As-Sunnah Foundation website [www. sunnah.org], that provides extensive detailed information on the beliefs of classical Islam. Additionally, he created the Haqqani Fellowship website, a social networking site for Sufis and people with spiritual inclinations and eShaykh.com, an extremely popular site providing Islamic religious rulings, advice, dream interpretation and prayer requests.

His spiritual centers attract people from all walks of life who yearn for reality, as well as those who seek his counsel, including politicians, social scientists, media outlets, academia, faith leaders, community activists and common folk. Daily prayers are observed and in weekly congregational gatherings, attendees practice group Dhikr (chanting of Divine Names and other liturgies), observe special holidays and celebrations, and perform Sufi Sama, Hadrah and whirling. These centers are dynamic hubs of activity for the surrounding communities, and often are deeply involved in charity work, community outreach and interfaith relations.

Shaykh Kabbani was an active participant in the Sufi Symposium conference, first established in 1993 by Dr. Nahid Angha and Dr. Ali Kianfari under the auspices of the International Association of Sufism. This conference has continued annually up to the present day, attracting ever-increasing number of participants, both from the presenting Sufi shaykhs as well as attendees.

Committed to interfaith outreach and the establishment of world peace, Shaykh Kabbani serves as chairman and founder of the Washington D.C. based Islamic Supreme Council of America, a religious non-profit focused on academic program development.

Shaykh Kabbani chaired two highly successful International Islamic Unity Conferences, the first taking place in Los Angeles in 1996, with over 7000 attendees and hosting over 150 presenters. The second International Islamic Unity Conference took place in Washington, D.C. in August of 1998, which Shaykh Kabbani used as a media platform even to condemn terrorism and Islamic extremists on international broadcast TV. Both conferences brought together an unprecedented array of religious scholars and international leaders from all over the Muslim world who adhere to and promote classical Islam, as taught by Prophet Muhammad (s). Moreover, these were some of the first conferences to introduce the traditional practices of *dhikr* and Mawlid an-Nabi (the celebration of the birth of Prophet

Muhammad) to an American audience.

Observing the lack of entertaining, thought-provoking media for Muslims, Shaykh Kabbani founded and directed an award-winning production team to produce a 100 page full-color quarterly national journal distributed by Barnes and Noble. The Muslim Magazine became a flagship for a new breed of Islamic journals which soon followed in its footsteps, such as Islamica and others.

Shaykh Kabbani is often called upon by world leaders and statesmen, particularly to address issues of Islamic extremism and its cure. He has met with former United States presidents Bill Clinton and George Bush Jr., former vice president Dick Cheney, as well as many other national leaders, including Prime Minister of Turkey Recep Tayyib Erdogan, Afghan President Hamid Karzai, the Malaysian Prime Minister Abdullah Badawi, the Indonesian President Susilo Bambang Yudiyono, Vice President Yusuf Kalla (to strengthen joint projects on "Jihadi rehabilation" for Indonesian youth) and former Foreign Secretary of the United Kingdom Jack Straw-- in addition to many others. He is often a guest speaker at universities and conferences, including Harvard, Yale, McGill, Georgetown, USC, UC Berkeley, University of Chicago, and the world's largest university, the University of Indonesia, and many others.

Shaykh Kabbani has expanded his work internationally, establishing teaching centers in Southeast Asia, India, Africa, the Caribbean, and South America. Up to the present day, Shaykh Kabbani spends much of his time visiting his hundreds of thousands of students around the world.

In the United Kingdom, Shaykh Kabbani is the Founder of the registered charity focused on social cohesion amongst local faith communities, *The Center for Spirituality and Cultural Advancement [CSCA]*. The CSCA was inagurated with an event to honor HRH the Prince of Wales, Prince Charles of England and to demonstrate British Muslim diversity of culture and artistic expression. Shaykh Kabbani has also made several trips around Africa, meeting with political figures, scholars, diplomats and common people from every walk of life. Shaykh Kabbani was hosted by the Grand Mufti of Ivory Coast, where he met with Ivory Coast's president Laurent Gbagbo. In Kenya, he met Prime Minister Raila Odinga, a close friend of President Obama and in Morocco he met with representatives of King Mohamed VI.

A prolific author, Shaykh Kabbani's 30-plus published works include: the *Encyclopedia of Islamic Doctrine and Beliefs* – this 7-volume, 1500-page set describes the beliefs of Islam according to the classical approach of major schools of jurisprudence and doctrine. *Classical Islam and The Naqshbandi Sufi Way* – detailed biographies of the 40 masters of the Naqshbandi Sufi *silsilah*, or chain of transmission; *Exegesis of The Chapter of Sincerity, Surat al-Ikhlas; Encyclopedia of Muhammad's Women Companions; Angels Unveiled; Pearls & Coral,* Volumes I and II – classical Islamic teachings in an informal style*; Symphony of Remembrance* – this book presents the spiritual background behind the practice of Divine Remembrance in the Sufi Way; *The Ninefold Ascent,* a course towards spiritual realization; and *At the Feet of My Master,* spiritual talks delivered at the request of Mawlana Shaykh Nazim for his visitors in Cyprus.

Shaykh Kabbani is a powerful, moderate voice for mainstream Islam. He has consistently called for an end to violence in the name of religion and urges Muslims to unite against all forms of radical ideology, be it religious, ethnic, or political.

Pir Shabda Kahn

Shabda Kahn has been a student of Sufism since 1969. He is a direct disciple of the American Sufi mystic Murshid Samuel Lewis (Sufi Ahmed Murad Chisti), and he worked closely with the American mystic Joe Miller. Shabda is currently the *Pir* (spiritual director) of the Sufi Ruhaniat International (http://www.ruhaniat.org), a Sufi lineage tracing from time immemorial and brought to the West in 1910 by the great Indian Sufi master, Pir-o-Murshid Hazrat Inayat Khan.

As Pir of the Sufi Ruhaniat, Shabda is responsible for guiding the lineage stream and directs its Board of Trustees. He also directs the Ruhaniat's Jamiat Khas (the leader's circle) and is the spiritual guide for the Dances of Universal Peace worldwide (http://www. dancesofuniversalpeace.org). Shabda is also the director of the Chisti Sabri School of Music. He is co-author of *Physicians of the Heart: A Sufi View of the Ninety-Nine Names of Allah* (http://www.physiciansoftheheart.com).

Shabda and his wife, Tamam, live in Marin County, California. They had two adult children, Ammon, still living and Solomon ~ deceased, and they have two granddaughters and many godchildren.

Shabda holds a regular *Zikr (Dhikr/ Dikr)* class in Marin (http://www.marinsufis.com/) and travels much of the year, offering the flower of Sufism with which he was entrusted. Sharing the mysticism of the heart, he has taught throughout North America, Europe, Estonia, Poland, Czech Republic, Russia, Morocco, Turkey, Syria, Brazil, Colombia, Ecuador, New Zealand, Australia and India. He brings warmth, humor and clarity in his efforts to help seekers on their path to awakening. Shabda has been instrumental in guiding over a decade of Sufi youth retreats.

Background and History: Pir Shabda attended McGill University in Canada and City College of New York. In 1968 he heard "Baba" Ram Das, who was just back from India, give a talk on the radio in New York City. Pir Shabda was moved by his words to give away everything, drop out, and become a "seeker." He heard the Sufi Order International's Pir Vilayat Inayat Khan speak in New York the same year, and then set out to attend the 1969 summer Sufi Camp in Colorado taught by Pir Vilayat. It was there that he met several of Murshid Sam Lewis's students including (now) Murshid Wali Ali Meyer.

Murshid Samuel Lewis and the Sufi Ruhaniat International: Inspired by the perfume of connections through Murshid Samuel Lewis' students, Pir Shabda moved to California to meet Murshid Sam and was initiated by him on February 16, 1970. In the fall of 1970, Shabda traveled with him for five weeks on the East Coast as his personal assistant. Murshid Sam Lewis left his body in San Francisco on January 15, 1971.

After Murshid Sam's death, Shabda became an assistant to the next leader of the *Ruhaniat*, Pir Moineddin Jablonski. At his recommendation, Shabda was initiated as a Sufi sheikh by Pir Vilayat Khan at the tomb of Hazrat Inayat Khan on the occasion of the 50th anniversary of his passing, on Feb 5, 1977, in New Delhi, India. In October 1995, Pir-o-Murshid Hidayat Inayat Khan, second son of Hazrat Inayat Khan and head of the International Sufi Movement, initiated Shabda as a Murshid. In February 2001, just before he died, Pir Moineddin appointed Shabda as the next Pir of the *Ruhaniat*.

The Dances of Universal Peace: One of the legacies of Murshid Samuel Lewis are the Dances of Universal Peace, a body-centered spiritual practice using movement, sacred chant and music. Conceived in 1968, today the dances are enjoyed in over 50 counties with more than 200 circles in the

United States. Pir Shabda Kahn first received the Dances of Universal Peace directly from Murshid Samuel Lewis and began leading dances in the summer of 1970 when Murshid Sam was still living. He has been leading, playing music for, and teaching the Dances of Universal Peace ever since. As Pir of the Sufi Ruhaniat, Shabda is the Spiritual Guide for the Dances of Universal Peace worldwide.

Pandit Pran Nath: Indian Classical Music Lineage: Pir Shabda met his next great teacher, Pandit Pran Nath, in 1972 and began the daily practice of North Indian classical music in the Kirana style. Pandit Pran Nath (November 3, 1918 – June 13, 1996), Master North Indian Classical Vocalist, was a Sufi mystic and called himself "*fakir*." Through Pir Shabda and a handful of other students, Pandit Pran Nath planted the 800-year-old oral tradition of Chisti Sufi Indian Classical vocal music in the Western world. He requested that Shabda carry on the lineage under the name of Chisti Sabri School of Music, after the great 13th century Sufi mystic Hazrat Allaudin Sabir; this has become an umbrella for Pir Shabda's music teaching and performing.

Pir Shabda has appeared in concerts ranging from "Visions for a Perfect World" at New York's St. John the Divine Cathedral for His Holiness the Dalai Lama, "New Music America" in Chicago at the Delhi University Music School and "Shivaratri Festival" in New Delhi. Shabda has guided more than a dozen music journeys to Mother India setting up impromptu vocal schools for Western students.

12th Tai Situpa Rinpoche: Tibetan Buddhist Lineage: In 1984 Shabda became a disciple of the illustrious 12th Tai Situpa Rinpoche, a venerated Tibetan Buddhist incarnate lama of the Kagyu Lineage. In the late 1980s, at Rinpoche's request and under Rinpoche's guidance, Shabda set up and directed a series of large events in the Bay Area and Mt. Shasta featuring His Holiness the Dalai Lama, just after he was awarded the Nobel Peace Prize.

Pir Shabda has used the teaching of this Buddhist lineage and the Buddhist lineage of Murshid Sam's Zen Roshi, Nyogen Sensaki, to continue the work of universal mysticism that Murshid Sam embodied. As part of this effort, Pir Shabda began a form of retreat practices called "Sufi Sesshin"—sitting meditation alternating with Dances of Universal Peace or other meditative movement practices. Since 2002, he has taught this form worldwide and leads a yearly 10-day "Sufi Sesshin" in Petaluma, California.

Tamam Kahn

Tamam Kahn is a senior teacher in The Sufi Ruhaniat International. She has spoken about Sufism, conducted poetry workshops and presented her own poetry at conferences and Sufi gatherings for two decades. In 2009 she was invited to recite her poetry at an international Sufi conference, The Sidi Chiker World Meetings of Tassawuf Affiliates, in Marrakech, Morocco. Her poems have been translated into German and Spanish for Sufi presentations in Germany in 2009 and Ecuador in 2011 and 2013.

She is author of the book, *Untold, A History of the Wives of Prophet Muhammad* (Monkfish Books, 2010). This book combines ten years of research with 70 poems and narrative celebrating the lives of Prophet Muhammad's wives. It is translated and published in Indonesia. *Untold* won an International Book Award in 2011.

Tamam was the editor-in-chief of *The Sound Journal, A Sufi Newsletter for the West* for over twenty years. It is being considered for online publication under a new name. Tamam received her M.A. from San Francisco State University in Eastern Art History, her B.A. from Sarah Lawrence College and attended Stanford University Graduate School. She and her husband Pir Shabda Kahn, head of the Sufi Ruhaniat International, have taken many groups to India and the Middle East. Here is a biographical excerpt from the preface of her book, *Untold*:

"In the late sixties I was a college sophomore at Sarah Lawrence. My advisor was the brilliant Adda Bozeman. In her World Politics and Culture class, I uncovered the modern Middle East; I devoured the few books on Islam available in English. I went to the new mosque in Washington; I spoke to an imam; I wrote a paper titled "Arabic Literature in Translation," but Islam remained a mystery to me. Eight years later in California, I heard The Sufi Choir, the musical expression of American Chishti Sufis. Through them I came to know my future husband, the musician Shabda Kahn. He grew up in New York, the son of German Jewish immigrants and had become part of the universal Sufi lineage of the Indian mystic, Hazrat Inayat Khan, whose message was one of "love, harmony, and beauty..."

72

Shabda and I married and moved into a house near San Francisco called, "The Garden of Allah" with students of his deceased American teacher, Samuel L. Lewis. I began to study and found the American Chishti path inclusive. I learned traditional Sufism in most of the world is the path of mysticism within Islam. We began to meet other Sufis, a teacher (murshid) from Jordan, the Mevlevi whirling practitioners (dervishes), and a Moroccan spiritual guide (muqaddam). We became teachers and group leaders; we traveled to the Middle East and I was finally able to see minarets, a keyhole door, working camels. (*Untold*, pp. 4-5.) Tamam and Shabda had two adult sons (the youngest, Solomon, is recently deceased). Both have been recognized by their peers as talented DJs, combining a variety of music and rhythms. Tamam realized that her poetry about the wives of Muhammad seemed to reach an "older audience," so she worked with her sons to come up with the rhythm and cadence associated with a poetry genre called "spoken word." This is a gentler, more poetic form than "rap." Sometimes there is music with the piece, but often it is recited alone with strong rhymes. Here is a section of a spoken word piece. Prophet Muhammad's widow, Umm Salama (who was close to Fatima and 'Ali) talks about the responsibility—the weight—of holding early history as it changed with Muhammad's death:

Angel of Death: Umm Salama's last words
The Angel of Death, he just went past
came slow —left fast. Here's the word at last.
Seems my library card's come up date due.
My age is 88 —less two.

He said the gate to paradise is left ajar,
told me it's not so far, but before I go
that angel wants to know,
who's gonna take the weight?

Now as for that, it's been my prayer
to check my life in. I'm prepared.
Haven't seen Rasoul in 50 years –
about death, I'm clear. No fear.

I drink the Word-of-God, call Allah and wait.
I commiserate with everyone because 'Ali is,
Hasan is, Husayn is —dead. People dumb down
all the GOOD things Muhammad said.

I'm the wife who's left and I tell hadith straight;
while the angel asks,
who's gonna take the weight?

Seems like dying is a reality bender with pinpricks
of unruly splendor. Here's the blessing descend-er,
O, Allah! I surrender.

Slack the pass-it-on rule, I'm gonna leave earth-school.
I'd be fool to stay. You've got Qur-Ran
and a compassionate plan —
Last words? Now listen up: I want a violence ban.
You hear me? No cruelty against your neighbors;
put down that spear, take a look in the mirror -
Follow the Prophet's real words:
he wanted you all to feel SAFE.

It's never too late to throw down the weight.
Here I go on over to the garden gate —
just watch me ease-on-over to the garden gate,
Allah HU.   Allah HU.   Allah HU.

Tamam writes: "I'm including this in my biography because when I offer information and poems and about the early days of Islam, the spoken word pieces seem to wake people up, and are received enthusiastically. In April, 2011, I was invited to be a featured guest at *Poetry Night at The Black Box Theater* at Lincoln High School in San Jose. It was organized by student poets. They heard me recite my poetry at the Willow Glen Library in that city. They invited me to share my spoken word pieces with the student poets and others. In this way, good stories of early Islam are reaching young people."

Tamam is working on a second book with poetry exploring "formal" rhythmic patterns so as to be closer to the poetry heard in the 7th century. This book will also focus on the family of Prophet Muhammad. Information, interviews, videos, and articles are available on her blog: http://www. completeword.com. In 2013 she won an award in the Soul-Making Keats Literary competition for her sonnet, "Fatima Tells of Muhammad's Death."

Dr. David Katz

Dr. David Katz was born in Madison, Wisconsin and lived with his family in Milwaukee during his first 18 years. He attended Stanford University, where he earned an A.B. with Honors in Philosophy and met his wife and fellow seeker, Anne. He studied medicine at the University of Rochester School of Medicine, obtaining his M.D. in 1975. He completed a Family Medicine residency in Rochester, New York in 1978.

In 1976 Dr. Katz and his wife began their lifelong studies with Sheikh M.R. Bawa Muhaiyaddeen *(rad.)*. Soon afterward Dr. Katz began to integrate his experiences with Bawa Muhaiyaddeen into his medical practices. He states, Bawa taught that God is the active principle in healing, and that all healing is actuated by God's Qualities. Only God is the Healer. We, through God's Qualities, can become the "scalpel in the hand of God." A person becomes truly human through acting with of God's Qualities: Love, Compassion, Truthfulness, Patience, Tolerance, Equality, Justice, etc. By acting with this intention, one is an instrument of the healing Qualities of God. God's Wisdom becomes the guiding wisdom of the healing instrument.

Dr. Katz currently practices family medicine in West Sacramento, California. He is an Associate Professor of Family Practice at the University of California Davis School of Medicine and teaches medical students and residents in his clinical practice. He is also a retired Medical Director of CommuniCare Health Centers in Davis, California. Last year he was elected to the Board of Directors of Western Clinicians Network, an association of clinical leaders of community clinics in the Western United States.

Dr. Katz is the President of the California Branch of the Bawa

Muhaiyaddeen Fellowship. He and his wife Anne live in Sacramento, California.

Sean Kelly, Ph. D.

 Sean Kelly received his PhD (1988) in Religious Studies from the University of Ottawa and has taught in the departments of Religious Studies at the University of Windsor, the University of Ottawa, and Carleton University (all in Canada). Since 1997 he has been professor in the Philosophy, Cosmology, and Consciousness program at the California Institute of Integral Studies in San Francisco. He has published articles on Jung, Hegel, transpersonal theory, and the new science and is the author of *Coming Home: The Birth and Transformation of the Planetary Era* (2010) and *Individuation and the Absolute: Hegel, Jung, and the Path toward Wholeness* (Paulist Press, 1993). Sean is also coeditor, with Donald Rothberg, of *Ken Wilber in Dialogue: Conversations with Leading Transpersonal Thinkers* and co-translator, with Roger Lapointe, of French thinker Edgar Morin's book *Homeland Earth: A Manifesto for the New Millennium*. Along with his academic work, Sean has trained intensively in the Chinese internal arts (taiji, bagua, xingyi, and yiquan) and has been teaching taiji since 1990. His current interests focus on the intersection of consciousness and ecology in the Planetary Era.

Hazrat Inayat Khan

Hazrat Inayat Khan, founder of the Sufi Order and Movement, came to the West as a representative of the musical and spiritual traditions of his native India, bringing with him a message of Love, Harmony, and Beauty that was both the quintessence of Sufi thought and a groundbreaking contribution to the harmonizing of East and West in the realm of applied spirituality. As a vocalist, musicologist, and player of the vina, Inayat Khan dedicated his early life to mastering the intricacies of classical Indian music, and won the title of *Tansen* from the *Nizam* of Hyderabad. While in Hyderabad he was initiated and trained by Qutb al-Aqtab Sayyid Abu Hashim Madani. Madani was a teacher in the Chishti lineage of Sufism who additionally maintained and transmitted the traditions of the Suhrawardi, Qadiri, and Naqshbandi orders. At the end of Inayat Khan's apprenticeship, Madani enjoined him to travel to the West on a mission of spiritual harmony.

On September 13, 1910, Hazrat Inayat Khan began an odyssey which would encompass three continents and transform the lives of thousands. He eventually settled in Suresnes, a suburb of Paris. During his sixteen years in the West, he created a school of spiritual training based on traditional Sufism and infused with a vital vision of the unity of religious ideals and the awakening of humanity to the divinity within.

Pir Vilayat Inayat Khan

Pir Vilayat Inayat Khan was the eldest son of Hazrat Pir-o-Murshid Inayat Khan, and the *Pir* of the Sufi Order International. Pir Vilayat was a teacher of meditation and of the traditions of the East Indian Chishti Order of Sufism. His teaching derived from the mystical tradition of the East brought to the West by his father, combined with his knowledge of the esoteric heritage and scholarship of western culture. He taught in the tradition of Universal Sufism, which views all religions as rays of light from the same sun. Pir Vilayat initiated and participated in many international and interfaith conferences promoting understanding and world peace. In 1975 he founded the Abode of the Message, which continues to serve as the central residential community of the Sufi Order International, a conference and retreat center, and a center of esoteric study. Pir Zia Inayat Khan is Pir Vilayat's son and successor as Pir of the Sufi Order International.

Pir Zia Inayat-Khan, Ph. D.

Pir Zia Inayat-Khan, Ph.D., is a scholar and teacher of Sufism in the tradition of his grandfather, Hazrat Inayat Khan. He received his B.A. in Persian Literature from the London School of Oriental and African Studies, and his M.A. and Ph.D. in Religion from Duke University. He received his spiritual training from his father, Pir Vilayat Inayat Khan, whom he succeeded in 2004 as worldwide president of the Sufi Order International (http://www.

sufiorder.org). In the same year he founded Suluk Academy (http://sulukacademy.org), a school of contemplative studies with branches in the U.S. and Europe. Four years later he founded Seven Pillars House of Wisdom (http://www.sevenpillarshouse.org) as a forum for interfaith and interdisciplinary collaboration.

Pir Zia is editor of *A Pearl in Wine: Essays in the Life, Music and Sufism of Hazrat Inayat Khan* (2001) and *Caravan of Souls: An Introduction to the Sufi Path of Hazrat Inayat Khan* (forthcoming) and author of *Saracen Chivalry: Counsels on Valor, Generosity, and the Mystical Quest* (2012). He is a Fellow of the Lindisfarne Association, Advisor to the Contemplative Alliance, and recipient of the U Thant Peace Award. With Shaikh al-Mashaik Mahmood Khan he jointly leads the Knighthood of Purity of the Hazrati Order (http://www.knighthoodofpurity.org). He lives with his wife and two children in rural upstate New York. More information on Pir Zia's work can be found at http://www.pirizia.org.

Seyed Mehdi Khorasani

Dr. Seyed Mehdi Khorasani was born in the holy city of Karbala, Iraq. He comes from a distinguished line of Persian spiritual leaders and teachers. His father, Ayatollah Mirzah Hadi Khorasani, was a leader in the Shia' community comprised of 250 million followers worldwide. Ayatollah Mirzah Hadi Khorasani was the author of 143 books on various subjects. Seyed Khorasani's great-grandfather, Mir Kalan (Great Emir), was a revered spiritual and political leader of his tribe in Khorasan.

An author of 18 books in Persian and English, he has written: *Thoughts on Islam, Islam: The Rational Religion,* and *Words of Wisdom and Songs of Love.* Seyed Khorasani established the Islamic Society in London in 1960 and then emigrated to the United States in 1974. In the U.S. Mehdi Khorasani established the Islamic Society of California and the Islamic Society of Northern California Redwood Mosque located in Fairfax. One significant interfaith event Mehdi organized and held was his inviting the Dalai Lama to San Francisco for a historic gathering of Buddhist and Muslim leaders at the Mark Hopkins Hotel in April 2006.

Shah Nazar Seyyed Ali Kianfar, Ph.D.

In the universe, in the history of the journey from eternity to eternity, the destiny and the mystery of each being is wrapped within Being itself. During this eternal journey one is alone, unique as its own self, with no one else identical. "No one can carry the burden of the other one," reads the Qur'an.

The birth of the human, his presence, and his journey is indeed a mystery, a mystery that we want to unveil so we can have assurance about our destiny, where we are heading, and how the hand of destiny will lead our lives. However, there are signs in that journey that help us to unveil the journey ahead. These signs come along at the right time and have been guiding and directing our lives towards a predesigned destiny beyond our choices.

The first sign for me came when I was very young: it is a memory that remains strong in my mind. It was one summer night in Teheran, the capital city of Iran, during the month of Ramadan, the month of fasting. Usually, from the very first day of Ramadan, the city turns to a new lifestyle. People get up very early in the morning, prepare food at dawn, stand for praying, and recite the Qur'an. After dawn, some people go to bed, and others begin to meditate and reflect. Movement throughout the city is more peaceful and calm, and there is an atmosphere of kindness and generosity in the air.

In my family fasting was mandatory, my mother prepared her children well, and everyone in my house prepared ahead of time for the month of fasting. My mother taught us how to pray and how to read the Qur'an. She herself had memorized the Qur'an in its entirety. She also carefully watched my father so that he did not stop his fasting for any excuse.

Teheran becomes very hot in the summer, when some families sleep in their garden or backyard or on their balcony. My first memory is from one of those summer-time Ramadan nights when we were all sleeping in the backyard, under the bright sky. My mother always urged me to pray and repeat the salutation to the Prophet and His family before I went to sleep.

On that special night, my mother, who was from the generation of the Prophet (Seyedeh), asked me to look at the sky and search for my star. Everyone, she said, has a star in the sky. I remember being so moved and excited to learn that I had a star in the sky and I eagerly began looking to find it. After a little searching I told my mother, "I found it," and she replied that every night I should look at that star. I don't remember if I looked for that star again or not. But what I do remember is how that moment of finding made such a strong impression on me, for it planted a deep quest and longing in my heart.

Seventeen years later I graduated from a police university and was working in one of the police stations in Teheran. One day, in the early afternoon, I was very surprised to receive a visit from one of my old friends, a relative of mine whom I hadn't seen since we graduated from high school. I asked him where he had been and what brought him here to see me. He said, "I will let you know whenever you get ready to leave your office." I told him I could leave in a couple of hours and he said he would wait for me.

We got ready to leave and when we were in the car I asked him again, "Now do you want to tell me?" He said, "I have been sent by my teacher to bring you to him. You know, I am a Sufi, and my teacher is a Sufi master." I knew a little about Sufis, but had never studied Sufism. Sufism, in general, is very well known in Iran, for Iran has been the land of Sufism and historically has many famous Sufis like Mansur Hallaj, Hafiz, Saadi, Rumi, and many others who travelled to different countries and established many different Sufi schools. So when he said he had become a Sufi I was not surprised, but I wondered how his teacher knew me. He said, "You can ask him when you come to visit him." I accepted his invitation with no resistance.

When we arrived, my friend guided me into the room where about twenty people sat around in a circle. The Master was at the head of the room. Even though he was dressed in ordinary clothing it was so clear he was the Master. He greeted me with a very warm and deep voice and, as he allowed me to sit, he said, "We know you and have been waiting for you." That moment was the beginning of my introduction to Sufism beyond my choice or will. After I passed several *cheleh* (40 days of purification and meditation under the supervision of the Master), I found a star in my heart through his guidance and his supervision and was appointed to teach and lead the newcomers to our Tariqat (school). During a special gathering, I was honored to receive from the Master the title of his spiritual son and was given the Sufi name, Shah Nazar, Sight of the King. King in Sufi terminology relates to the Vilayat (Amir al Momenin Ali.)

I later went to the University of Tehran and earned my doctorate studying philosophy and erfan, under the encouragement of my Master Moulana Shah Maghsoud Sadegh Angha. Then, in 1978, we moved to the USA and I began my Sufi teaching first in California and then in different states and meanwhile, with the help of a few Iranian scholars as well as Dr. Nahid Angha, my love, my friend and my partner in life, I established and chaired a department of Philosophy and Islamic Sufism in a private university in Los Angeles.

Not long after, by the will of God and His guidance, Dr. Angha and I created a new movement introducing the great treasure of the East to members of our human family in the West. This was the conception of our idea to establish the International Association of Sufism (IAS) in order to bring together Sufis from around the world for sharing, networking, becoming a community, and with appreciation, keeping the door of communication open. The IAS is a non-profit, humanitarian organization and a United Nations NGO/DPI that we founded in California in 1983 to create and provide a global forum for a continuing dialogue amongst Sufis, scholars, interfaith leaders, poets and artists from diverse cultures, nations and schools; to bring together Sufi principles and scientific understanding; and to promote equality and human rights. To my knowledge, the IAS is the first organization in history to bring together Sufis from different schools and around the world, with the goal of friendship, companionship, dialogue, harmony and peace.

Since its inception, we have developed many departments, including: the Sufism Symposium, Songs of the Soul Festival, the Sufi Women Organization, the Institute for Sufi Studies, Voices for Justice, Sufism Psychology Forum, Taneen Sufi Music Ensemble, and IAS Publications, including the periodical Sufism: an Inquiry, the world's longest running journal on Sufism. Since that time, Sufism: An Inquiry has been a living reflection of the dynamic energy and growing global community of people living from the heart. The journal aims to foster the study and advancement of the idea of religion, the interrelation between the principles of religion and the principles of science, and the role of inner practices that foster equanimity and the expression of love and wisdom.

I have given lectures and taught classes nationally as well as internationally. This includes speaking engagements at UNESCO, the University of California-Berkeley, the California Institute of Integral Studies, Dominican University, the Parliament of the World's Religions and more. I tour and lecture giving talks on Sufism, Islam, spirituality and the relationship between Science and Spirituality at conferences held in Australia, Egypt, Scotland, Spain, the United States, and Uzbekistan. I have met numerous religious and spiritual leaders of the world.

My approach in explaining the subtle, mystical world of Sufism to western audiences relies as much on contemporary science and psychology as it does on traditional Sufi philosophy and a contemporary applicability and understanding of the deep esoteric meaning of the Qur'an. My teachings spring from philosophical and rational principles confirmed by my spiritual and inner experience. I am one of a few individuals who holds the essence and lineage of Uwaiysi Sufism and have dedicated my life to this service.

We continued our Uwaiysi tarighat (school) and taught from that framework. We also established the Institute for Sufi Studies for students to learn and practice Sufism. The pursuit of knowledge and the quest for the Divine are essentially identical in Sufism. The vital link between knowledge and practice is to be found within, in the attainment of the inner knowledge of the heart. Through the perfection of such an understanding, the individual comes to know not only one's self, but also the Divine. In the Institute for Sufi Studies, I teach classes on the Qur'an, Hadith and the Bible in order to introduce the meaning of the verses that need to be revealed to the human heart by practice.

The Uwaiysi tarighat is based entirely upon inner experience. The history of the Uwaiysi Path goes back to the legendary figure, Uwaiys-i-Gharan, who lived during the time of the Prophet Mohammed (swa), in the seventh century. As the one who initiated this tarighat, Uwaiys-i-Gharan's teaching extends beyond the limitations of time and space. His way of understanding and achieving reality, by receiving inspiration and teaching from a physically absent teacher, remains a model for all inner travelers. He exemplifies the need to remain ever watchful over your heart. As he said, "Your heart will return to you."

I decided to extend this model and idea of teaching and practice into the realm of psychology and thus established the 40 Days: Alchemy of Tranquility program, a Sufi-Psychology system that brings western psychology, psychological principles, and Sufi teachings together. This is based on the ancient practice of "chelleh," a forty-day technique of fasting and practice to purify the self from what is not self. As the Prophet Mohammad says, "Whoever knows one's self, knows one's Lord."

Throughout the ages, Sufism has been open to all and has been truly multi-national, especially for the past millennium. Truth is universal and belongs to no one nation or culture, but to all humanity. In the present time, Sufism spreads from the borders of Australia to West Africa, from India to the shores of America. Recognizing the value of polishing the heart and substance of faith prior to its division into different religious expressions, we helped and partnered with the world interfaith movement. We appreciate the gift of unity and togetherness we have created. We have participated in many interfaith events, dialogues and conferences throughout the United States and around the world in an effort to promote peace and to increase understanding among faith traditions. Through this journey, we have developed bonds of deep friendship and mutual appreciation with countless faith leaders, philanthropic organizations and educators, all of whom wish to promote peace and increase understanding among faith traditions.

As an extension of this interfaith work, we are building the Garden of Light Praying Room in Napa, California to serve as a landmark of unity. We consider this a public service to the community as a house for praying. This building sits on sacred space with a direction oriented towards qibla, and serves as a serene and suitable area for visitors of all faiths and spiritual traditions to pray and reflect.

All that we have accomplished is through the will of God and the blessing of my beloved Master, Moulana Shah Maghsoud Sadegh Angha, and the faithful and devoted group around us.

Hamaseh Kianfar, Ed. D.

I was born in Teheran, and am Moulana Shah Maghsoud's first grandchild. We moved to England then to California where I grew up. My grandfather named me after his book *Hamaseh-i-hayyat, The Epic of Life*. Being born into a Sufi family gave me the opportunity not only to learn the beauty of

this spiritual path, but also to engage from an early age with a great number of outstanding individuals.

I have learned that this path of spiritual learning is based on understanding reality, reality that cannot be understood through speaking words, but rather through the heart's intuition and illumination. Such knowledge requires becoming united with the real, and the real is unchanging. A human being is capable of discovering the center of that knowledge within his/her own heart, through purifying oneself of limitations and of anything other than the identity of the "I" that is fixed and unchanging. I have found my heart through the teachings of this path.

As a member of the International Association of Sufism, the Sufi Women Organization, and Sufi Youth International, together with my sister Sahar and several of my spiritual sisters and brothers, we established and contributed towards many projects over the years, including: Domestic Violence Prevention; Cross Cultural Studies; Youth Program; and United Nations Campaigns. I have travelled extensively and presented at many roundtable discussions, and lectured on behalf of SWO and the IAS.

Together with a few Sufi youth, I established Voices for Justice, a youth department of the IAS and an Ambassador of UNICEF. Voices for Justice was established to advocate for the rights of children by providing a forum for public awareness through education and community service programs, so that every child and every young adult might have the opportunity to fulfill his or her highest potential. Together we have created a few important programs and service projects. Voices for Justice was nominated for the Heart of Marin Award.

In my professional life, I received a doctoral degree in education, and have served as a director and clinical director of several non-profit organizations in Northern California; I have also worked as a medical case manager for HIV positive women and children. My passion for the study of HIV/AIDS led me to complete a doctoral dissertation focused on the role of forgiveness and imagination in allowing HIV positive women to move forward in their lives in a meaningful way. I have co-authored and published several research papers on that subject.

I have written many articles on Sufism and biographies of Sufi Masers, and with my sister Sahar co-authored *Sufi Stories*, and many articles for *Sufism: An Inquiry*.

Sufism has taught me that to become knowledgeable, one must break the limitations of finitude. As long as the bubble is bound to its limited form, it is not the ocean. To become the ocean it must break its limitation and dissolve in the ocean. What richness!

Sahar Kianfar, JD

I was born in Teheran, and moved to Brighton and then to California, and grew up in Marin County. I am the third grandchild of Moulana Shah Maghsoud and he named me after one of his books: *Sahar*.

Being born into a Sufi family provided me with a rich environment of teachings and learning, meeting multicultural groups of Sufi masters, interfaith leaders, scientists, poets, and human rights advocates. Throughout the years since the founding of the International Association of Sufism and the launch of the first Sufism Symposium, I engaged with many Sufi masters and students from *tariqat(s)* around the globe, making my own connections and friendships along the way.

As members of the International Association of Sufism, and the Sufi Women Organization, my sister Hamaseh and I, together with several of our spiritual sisters and brothers, launched Sufi Youth International. It was in 1999 that, as a group of youth from both the Sufi and Interfaith communities, we sponsored the Encouraging Wisdom: Youth and Leadership forum. We led several panel discussions at the Sufism Symposia. We have also developed several other projects over the years, including: Domestic Violence Prevention; Cross Cultural Studies; Youth Program; United Nations Campaigns. I have travelled extensively and presented at many roundtable discussions, and lectured on behalf of the SWO and the IAS.

I have learned that as human beings, we rely on our senses and regard them as the doorway to knowledge, and it is not always an easy task to take a different step to build the foundation of our understanding. But to learn to distinguish between the real and the mirage, and to understand the real as reality is, we are to practice discipline and educate ourselves to learn to live harmoniously with the reality of being. It is here that we need a teacher who guides us on our path. I am grateful for being born into such an outstanding family and for having such great teachers.

My professional life is also rich. I have received a masters degree in Islamic Studies (with an emphasis in Islamic law) from the University of Cambridge and a juris doctorate from the University of Michigan, Ann Arbor. I am licensed in California and New York, and am a senior attorney with an international practice. I have given lectures on numerous subjects, including Islamic law and Sufism, at universities, international corporations, and cross border organizations in North America, Asia, Europe, Africa and the Middle East. I co-authored *Sufi Stories*, and many articles for *Sufism: An Inquiry*.

I am grateful for such a rich life, a spiritual upbringing, a life of service and dedication. I currently reside in London with my husband and son, Kian, Moulana Shah Maghsoud's first great grandson.

Patrick Marius Koga, MD, MPH, FRSPH

A Fellow of the Royal Society for Public Health, London, with an academic career in psychiatry, psychology, and public health spanning three decades, Dr. Koga received his training at the University of Medicine and Pharmacy, Timisoara, Romania, and Tulane University, New Orleans, USA. His work focuses on mental health services and policies for traumatized refugees and immigrants. His current appointments include Director, Refugee Health Research at University of California, Davis, Dept. of Public Health Sciences in the School of Medicine; Core faculty, UC Global Health Institute, Center of Expertise on Migration and Health; and Researcher, UCD Center for Healthcare Policy & Research. Past appointments include Professor of Psychology, Institute of Transpersonal Psychology (ITP); Dean of International Medicine & Professor of Psychiatry, Cambridge Overseas Medical Training Programme, UK; Clinical Associate Professor of Psychiatry, Tulane School of Medicine; Medical Director,

Samaritan Counseling Center; and Consultant, UNHCR.

Dr. Koga's Research interests include cultural, religious, and spiritual modulators of resilience in PTSD in refugees; moral disengagement of religious leaders and toxic faith of perpetrators of mass atrocities and genocide; subclinical PTSD in police brutality; fractal geometry modeling of psychiatric diagnosis; and integration of mental health interventions in virtual reality environments. For the past twenty years he has given over 100 invited lectures, keynotes, and workshops on PTSD in the USA and internationally in Bosnia, Serbia, Slovenia, Czech Republic, Romania, United Kingdom, Morocco, Spain, South Africa, Turkey, and Kyrgyzstan. Since 2012 Dr. Koga has been providing psychiatric evaluations at Sacramento County Refugee Health Clinic to refugees from Afghanistan, Iraq, Iran, and other countries.

A member of the World Psychiatric Association, Section on Religion, Spirituality and Psychiatry, and a former political refugee from Romania, Dr. Koga is the Founder of Veteran, Immigrant, and Refugee Trauma Institute of Sacramento (VIRTIS), a translational research institute with a philosophy rooted in transpersonal psychology. Dr. Koga is a lifelong student of world religions and an Advaita Vedanta initiated disciple of the late Swami Shraddhananda of Ramakrishna Order of India. Email: pmkoga@ucdavis.edu

Chafik Kotry

I was born in 1948 in Egypt and migrated to Canada in 1971. My experience in Canada was essentially split into having two careers: a) a professional musician; and later on, b) a Personal Fitness Trainer/Consultant and a motivational speaker.

The inclinations of my Soul-search were evident from early in my youth, beginning when I was captured by the music of Ray Charles. It was like his exuberance, joy, aches and pains spoke to me personally. I was 12 years old at that time. It was only upon maturity that I understood that the connection with him transcended the music and became a Soul to Soul bonding.

This development in me took place hand in hand with another ongoing one, which was a burning desire to transform my underweight and skinny physical condition to a muscular athletic type. I succeeded greatly in doing so by age 20. This physical accomplishment pales next to what really happened in the inner restructuring of my spiritual and mental state that manifested itself

in my life and continues to do so to this very day.

But this is not to say that the physical development was for naught. In fact, the highly euphoric energy developed and experienced within my workouts literally elevated my Soul to higher spiritual realms. Some of the most profound contemplations I have had came directly after the workouts and lasted for a few days after. My Mind simply threw off the shackles of limiting thought; my Insight and Vision became very keen. I have learned that my workouts infuse me with euphoria, thus, liberating my Soul and bringing it to the forefront of my being. At such a point, I feel that I am in Soul Existence. At this point, the world takes on a very different meaning, veils drop, love and compassion reign, understanding deepens, insight sharpens and the essence of life reveals itself effortlessly.

All these factors transformed my whole being into an actualization of Oneness, where the Spirit/Mind/Body Energies all blend and interchange FREELY. It was through the discipline, sacrifice, hard work, and dedication that I achieved such a physical standard which became my most essential tool, and I was a living example in showing others how to build themselves physically. It also gave me the opportunity to teach the interconnection between Mind and Spirit. A very important feature that results from this union is the honing of one's intuitive powers. It is the building of this triad within the Human Being that I teach.

My own Inner Transformation became evident in my work with clients as a Personal Trainer, where I would work on "The Whole Person" to establish genuine Health by IGNITING the Mind-Body-Spirit Connection, therefore paving the road to a thriving interchange of energies within the person that they could use to create their own inner experience.

As for my reading interests, they remain constant and widely varied. Alongside my Sufi studies, they include the subjects of Taoism, Buddhism, Judaism, Christianity, Ancient Egypt, North American Indians, Stoic Philosophers, mysticism and the spirituality of all faiths and cultures as well as motivational and Self-Help books.

I believe that the Human Being has still to discover his or her true potential; we are functioning while severely handicapped by looking outside for answers and by being totally distracted from our inner path. We have a treasure in our own individual makeup that is waiting to be CLAIMED. Can we really afford to let the opportunity slip by?

I returned to Egypt in 2002 to look after my aging mother who passed away in March 2008. I got married to my wife Racha in 2003, and we have been blessed with two beautiful children: Adam (almost five years now) and Maya (three years and seven months). I am presently living in Alexandria, Egypt. I still give Spiritual/ Motivational Talks and Music Concerts. I am also compiling thoughts for the birth of a book in the very near future, with the intention of helping people liberate themselves from binding and limiting thoughts, while freeing their Soul to do its uninterrupted and intended work in a highly energized body.

Rodney Mansur Kreps, Ph. D.

At age 40, Mansur Rodney Kreps was introduced to the Chisti lineage of Abu Hashim Madani, Inayat Khan, Samuel Lewis and Vasheest Davenport. He has served as a sheikh in the Sufi Ruhaniat International and has worked closely with the Mevlevi Order of America. He and his wife Khadija served as *semazen-bashis* in 1994 at Rumi's tomb in Konya, Turkey. Mansur believes that the growth of group process and endeavoring to see everyone as equal in God are necessary and holy works in spiritual and other areas. His most significant application of this belief was creating and maintaining a highly productive workplace for seventeen years where people loved to be. He holds a Ph.D. in Theoretical Physics from Princeton University and is a Fellow of the Casualty Actuarial Society. He is now 75 and working towards simplification and completion.

Stanley Krippner, Ph. D.

Stanley Krippner, Ph.D., is a professor of psychology at Saybrook University in San Francisco, USA. Professor Krippner is a pioneer in the study of consciousness, having conducted research in the areas of dreams, hypnosis, shamanism and dissociation, often from a cross-cultural perspective, and

with an emphasis on anomalous phenomena that seem to question mainstream paradigms. He is the co-author of *Extraordinary Dreams and How to Work With Them* (SUNY Press, 2002), *Perchance to Dream* (Nova Science, 2009), *Mysterious Minds* (Praeger, 2010), *Debating Psychic Experience* (Praeger, 2010), *Demystifying Shamans and Their World* (Imprint Academic, 2011), *The Voice of Rolling Thunder* (Inner Traditions, 2012) and is the co-editor of *Varieties of Anomalous Experience: Examining the Scientific Evidence* (APA, 2000) as well as dozens of other books. He also has over 1000 published, scholarly articles, chapters and papers.

Makam Postneshin Jelaleddin Loras and The Mevlevi Order of America

"If you are quiet and in a state of prayer when you Turn, offering everything of yourself to God, then, when your body is spinning, there is a completely still point in the center.....We do not turn for ourselves.....We turn for God and for the world and it is the most beautiful thing you can imagine."
Murshid Suleyman Hayati Dede

The mission of the Mevlevi Order of America is to be a living embodiment of the Mevlevi Way, through sharing the teachings of the great 13th century poet and mystic, Mevlana Jelaleddin Rumi. This order offers cultural programs, open workshops, and public presentations in the spirit of inclusion, equality and love. Members of the Mevlevi Order of America serve under the inspiration of Murshid Suleyman Hayati Dede and the guidance of his son and successor, Makam Postneshin Jelaleddin Loras.

The transmission of the Order comes in an unbroken chain from Rumi. His students and followers have maintained his teachings and practices from his time to the present day. The Mevlevi Order of America is part of that living tradition. It was founded by Jelaleddin Loras under the guidance of his father, Suleyman Dede, the Sheikh of Konya, appointed by Celaleddin Bakir Celebi, head of the Mevlevi Order, and the 21st descendant of Rumi. Dede visited Europe and America many times, planting the seeds of Mevlana wherever he went. He brought inspiration, compassion and love to those who met him.

In 1978 Dede sent Jelaleddin to America to share the Mevlevi tradition. From early childhood, Jelaleddin was raised and trained by the Mevlevi community of Konya. Under his father's instruction he came to America with the task of creating centers and training Western men and women. Known as Efendi – "Friend" to his students, he has spent more than thirty-five years in this service, exploring and refining how to present the Mevlevi path to the western heart.

Today there are Mevlevi Order of America centers across the United States and in Europe. Under Efendi's spiritual guidance, his students pursue the journey of sincere seekers on a perennially modern, and centuries old path into the Divine Mystery.

Olga Louchakova-Schwartz, M.D., Ph.D.

I was born in Leningrad, Russia, on Sept 23, 1957. My ancestry on my mother's side comes from two 12th century Hungarian brothers by the name of Baturin (Batorii). A falconer and a cup-bearer, they settled in the city of Ryazan near Moscow. Later, this branch of the family intermarried with a family of a Tatar prince named Dolgov. The male side of the family comes from Jewish intelligencia of southern Ukraine named Kirtchik, and a Belorussian Jewish artist named Nirman. Love of learning, art, and social service ran in my family; we had a home library of more than 3000 volumes. Several generations of women in my family received a university education and had professional careers, and were very empowered. My grandmother's last message to me, before her death in 1977, was "learn, learn, always keep on learning." I spent my childhood between Leningrad, Estonia and the Crimea. When I was about seven years old, I discovered that one can observe and control one's mind. While in high school, I was interested in art history, foreign languages, and nuclear physics. The memories of one of the major events of the Second World War, the siege of Leningrad, were very fresh in my family. Influenced by it, I founded, and for several years directed, the school's museum of the local history of the Second World War. In 1974, I completed

my high school education with honors, and decided to continue my family tradition of medical service by entering the Leningrad Pediatrical Medical University. Early on, I was involved in research in immunology and biochemistry. Upon graduating as an MD I was hired as a researcher at the Institute of the Study of Children's Infections at the Soviet Ministry of Health. I married in 1978, and a year later my daughter Alexandra was born.

Within the first year of my work in science, a remarkable encounter directed my interest towards the study of consciousness. I witnessed a folk healing of a boy with deathly viral meningitis. Even though the child's encephalogram showed that he had been "brain dead," the healing brought back his speech and capacity to interact with other people. Impressed by the potential of alternative healing, I turned to autogenic training, a self-regulation system available in Europe in the 1980s, which I studied on my own. This training rapidly opened my channeling and clairvoyance capacities. When in 1983 I was offered a position as a neuroscientist at the Pavlov Institute of the Soviet Academy of Sciences. I gladly accepted this appointment because of my interest in the brain and consciousness. I researched neuron-glia interactions and the autoimmune diseases of the nervous system. With grants from the Shemyakin Institute of Bioorganic Chemistry and the Chasov Institute of Cardiology, I registered three biotechnological patents, completed my second doctorate degree in neuroscience in 1989, and began the biotechnological production of my new diagnostic kit for multiple sclerosis.

At Pavlov I had access to the special repository of the Library of the Academy of Sciences, where I could read the letters of Pavlov and Freud, Byzantine legends, and translations of mystical and philosophical Arabic, Persian and Indian texts, including those treated by the Buddhologist Shcherbatsoi. I started feeling more and more dissatisfied with science, partly because of the cruelty of scientific experiments on animals and partly because of the limitations of the natural scientific approach to knowledge. By that time I had observed many remarkable healings and paranormal phenomena for which science had no explanation. I decided to learn psychology and took a psychotherapy training at the Bechterev Neurological Institute; however, my questions remained unanswered. I divorced, re-married, and witnessed my daughter reaching her adolescence. A lucky chain of circumstances led me to the Russian spiritual underground school, which was formed by scientists interested in spiritual practice and transformative education. There I studied various transformative approaches, including Gurdijeff's system and Kundalini and Vajrayana Tantra with Yoga Tummo (the yoga of "inner heat"), meditative running, mountain expeditions and silent retreats in dark subterranean caves. Soon I was mandated as a teacher in this school, and, together with the rest of our faculty, taught many courses in spiritual transformation and researched remote geographical locations for traces of esoteric teachings. Teaching meditative practices of concentrated attention and energy turned out to be my special gift. I also continued as a scientist, working at Pavlov and collaborating in psychedelic research conducted by the Ministry of Health. During Perestroika I taught transformative practices in hospitals, at the army, at schools and other places where these practices could help people cope with societal transition. In 1992, I was invited to teach in the United States. My hosts were the Albert Hoffmann Foundation, the Kundalini Research Network, the Institute of Noetic Sciences, and the Esalen Institute. After several people asked me to start a spiritual school, I founded the Hridayam® School, which grew rapidly, with departments in San Francisco, Los Angeles and Fresno. I continued my own spiritual studies with traditional Advaita-Vedanta teachers, and kept part-time academic appointments at the California Institute of Integral Studies, the Graduate Theological Union, and other schools. After ten years of teaching, I felt that my duties as a full-time spiritual teacher were about to be completed. I felt that I learned a lot about consciousness; now I needed to understand the human person and the Spiritual Heart. What I thought to be spirituality was changing into gnosis, i.e. self-knowledge. In addition, I discovered phenomenological philosophy and a practice of phenomenological research, and that changed both the character of my research and my own consciousness. I limited my activities with the Hridayam® School, and returned to full-time academic research and teaching. While I received many spiritual teachings of Bektashi, Malamatia, and Jerrahi Sufi masters in Turkey, I felt that the roots of the teachings of the Heart are more in Iran and Central Asia and perhaps in early Christianity. I needed to travel, and continue research. I am finding remarkable treasures of wisdom in Islamic philosophy, and keep studying languages in order to read teachers like Suhrawardi or Ibn Arabi in their own language.

Having previously thought that the best way to pass knowledge on is through personal teaching, I gradually came to believe that writing is a better way, and that what I have learned about the Spiritual Heart and intuition has to be recorded and be described in scientific terms.

In 2001, I joined the core faculty at the Institute of Transpersonal Psychology. At ITP, I founded the Neurophenomenology Center, to use dense-array encephalography in the study of "the meditating brain." I continue my affiliation with the Graduate Theological Union, and find nourishment in friendships with people all over the world who, like myself, love phenomenology, true gnosis, and transformation. At present, my chief activity is writing and lecturing. I am married to Martin Schwartz, Professor of Iranian Studies at UC Berkeley whom I met in 2008. I hope to continue my life journey in his company.

Gausul Wara Hazrat Shah Sufi Maulana Syed Mainuddin Ahmed Al-Hasani Wal Hossaini Maizbhandari

Honorable descendant of holy Prophet Muhammad (SM), Gausul Wara Hazrat Shah Sufi Maulana Syed Mainuddin Ahmed Al-Hasani Wal Hossaini Maizbhandari (K) born on February 10, 1938 and departed on August 17, 2011 was indeed a friend who answered for the needs of thousands of his devotees belonging to different castes, creeds and religions and of his admirers that have come into his contact. He was lovingly called "Baba Mainuddin" by his devotees. With the height of his spiritual semblance and services to humanity, it was made clear to everybody that he worked with the inspiration to know the truth of life. Syed Mainuddin Ahmed led an illustrious campaign to spread Islam, peace and interfaith harmony in the past several decades as the incumbent leading light of Maizbhandar Darbar Sharif based at Fatikchari, Chittagong, Bangladesh.

A most convenient cultural belt of south-eastern Asia, Bangladesh is evidently rich in cultural heritage. From time immemorial travelers, adventurers, fortune hunters and some great Sufi saints of Islam came to Bangladesh to spread the religion of Islam whose shrines lay scattered all over the country. Tariqah-E-Maizbhandaria or the Maizbhandari order sprang up from that locality through Gausul Azam Hazrat Maulana Syed

Ahmadullah Maizbhandari (R) in the middle of the 19th century A.D. He was one of the renowned *Ulemas* and saints of the Sub-Continent. Tariqah-E-Maizbhandaria was widely spread and consolidated by his nephew and his successor Gausul Azam Hazrat Maulana Syed Gulamur Rahman Baba Bhandari (R). Baba Bhandari was one of the greatest saints of the Sub-Continent. Innumerable miraculous events took place in his life. At the time of holy departure to eternal life, Baba Bhandari® left four sons and two daughters

behind. Syed Abul Bashor®, the second son of Baba Bhandari, was one of the renowned *Ulema*, a fierce orator for which he was called the Gaus-E-Zaman of the age. Syed Abul Bashor was called by the *Ulemas* the "Store-House of *Tasauf* and *Towhid* (*Tauheed*). He was also called "Sultanul Mashaikh." On April 5, 1962 Syed Abul Bashor (R) at the instruction of Baba Bhandari (R) declared his third son, Syed Mainuddin Ahmed Maizbhandari, his successor.

Baba Mainuddin worked as the source of consolation for the spirit in distress and fountain of wisdom for the spirit in thirst of knowledge. Although he started a worldly career in the materialistic field of accounting for a bank, he was suddenly drawn to the spiritual realm by his father and *Murshid* (Spiritual Guide) to assume the figure of a strong and loving spiritual father for millions of devotees in the last five decades. The special *"bayet-e-khas"* from Murshid Hazrat Gaus-e-Zaman Syed Abul Bashar Maizbhandari(R) empowered Baba Mainuddin with *belayeti* strength, a divine power that works within a devotee to take him or her to the highest level of spirituality to immerse in the existence of the Creator Himself.

Hazrat Shah Sufi Maulana Syed Baba Mainuddin Ahmed started his long journey of preaching the principles of Sufism both at home and abroad in 1962. He was a well-known figure in the world and has taught in the sphere of Sufism throughout the world. Millions of Sufi students as well as Sufi teachers are his keen disciples. He is the honorable president of Ahley Sunnat Wal Zamat, Bangladesh. Millions of Sunni *Ulemas* and *Pir Mashaikhs* flocked together under his banner. He was the honorable Adviser of the International Association of Sufism since 1996. He has hoisted the flag of the Maizbhandari order all over the world. It is through his effort that *Jasn-*

E-Julus-E Eid-E-Miladunnabi (SM) rally had been observed in Dhaka, the capital of Bangladesh, every year on the 12th of *Rabiul Awal* from 1987 to 2011. Every year he spent at least two months preaching Sufism in Asia, Europe, Africa and America working to spread the light of the Maizbhandari order. Renowned Sufi scholars of the world love and appreciate him with great enthusiasm.

Baba Mainuddin is one of the greatest lovers of mankind in the world. He loves everybody irrespective of caste and creed. The people of other religions also respect him highly and come to receive theological teachings. He believes in love and affection. Baba Mainuddin taught his disciples to become submissive. He says, "submission leads to the way of success and audacity leads to the way of destruction." A perfect Muslim never shows audacity and pride. Satan or *Iblis* was expelled from the *Darbar* of Almighty Allah for audacity and pride. A perfect Sufi is always a gentleman. A brute never becomes a Sufi.

Baba Mainuddin, at home and abroad, preached to embrace of the essence of divine love; his unique way of preaching Islam to the people evoked love and affection for Allah as well as all His creations. His life and works, in fact, depict his unflinching determination to create love among the entire human community. To him "Islam" means peace, Total Peace. It is a religion of love -- Love for the creator and his creation. Baba Mainuddin's approach towards religion with love has been well acclaimed in the international arena. The acclamation had been well exposed by the laurels that are being conferred upon him. He was a regular attending member in the Sufism Symposia held by the International Association of Sufism (IAS). He was given the title of 'Shaikhul Islam' in 1997 by the aforementioned association.

Syed Mainuddin Ahmed attended the Millennium World Summit of religious and spiritual leaders in 2000, where he had called upon the world community to follow the 'Medina Charter' to establish Global Peace. He traveled widely in Europe. On September 17, 2000 he went to Uzbekistan to attend the "International Workshop on Sufism and Religious Dialogue." During his visit to Eastern Europe, Tashkent Islamic University gave him a grand reception. All of his activities in the International arena did not go unnoticed by the world as was proven when the National Council of Ghana and U.S.-based Universal Islamic Centre honored him with the "Worthy Grand Ambassador for Islam, Universal Peace, Reconciliation, Spiritual

Uplift of Humanity International Award" of the decade in the year 2005.

Syed Mainuddin Ahmed Maizbhandari (K) was the name of a saint who contributed immensely to human welfare and spiritual uplift. His name is globally endorsed and acclaimed. Moreover, the present Prime Minister of Bangladesh Sheikh Hasina decorated Baba Mainuddin with the title, "Sufi Padak" in 2004 as recognition for his relentless work in the cause of humanity and peace in the garb of Islam. Numerous other organizations throughout the world have awarded Syed Mainuddin Ahmed for his outstanding striving to strengthen the Sufi movement worldwide.

Syed Mainuddin Ahmed always advocates on behalf of peace and tranquility and opposes hatred, cruelty, and brutality. He says, "Humanity means religion." Humanity and religion go hand in hand. He is dead against racial, tribal and religious discrimination. All these bad elements must be eradicated to established peace, security, happiness and tranquility all over the world.

Baba Mainuddin was a patron of education. He established 25 Islamic institutions, including orphanages, Madrasas, Mosques, and free clinics in his *Darbar Sharif*, inside and outside the country. We should extend our hands of co-operation to these religious and humanitarian institutions. He has at least four thousand *Khankas* in Bangladesh, India and many other countries of the world where people are receiving primary education of Islam and practicing Islamic rituals.

Tarika-E-Maizbhandaria is a popular *tarika* (*tariqah*) now inside and outside of the country. For the integrity and solidarity of Sufism and Tarika-E-Maizbhandaria he has dedicated his whole life. Baba Mainuddin's whole life is full of *Karamats* (miraculous events). Thousands of people were benefited by his noble blessing and pleasant sights and are still benefiting. Baba Mainuddin is now a symbol of heavenly love. His heavenly presence and guidance are still giving uncounted people the direction towards the enlightened path. His work is the inspiration for the people who love to see the light of the truth in this life and hereafter.

Baba Mainuddin had bestowed his son, Shahzada Syed Saifuddin Ahmed Maizbhandari, with the spiritual blessing to carry on the responsibilities of running the *Darbar* and to continue spreading the Maizbhandari Order to the world, and his daughters Syeda Saima Ahmed and Syeda Shaheda Ahmed are supporting this divine work to be accomplished.

Shaikhul Islam Gausul Wara Syed Mainuddin Ahmed Al-Hasani Wal

Hossaini Maizbhandari (K) was a successful Sufi spiritual leader whose name and fame prevail all over the world. He left us on August 17, 2011. May Allah bless him.

Shahjada-E Gausul Azam Maizbhandari Syed Saifuddin Ahmed Al-Hasani Wal Husaini Maizbhandari

Awlad-E Rasul (*Sallallahu Alaihi Wa Sallam*) Shahjada-E Gausul Azam Maizbhandari Syed Saifuddin Ahmed Al-Hasani Wal Husaini Maizbhandari (*Madda Jillihul Ali*) has been nominated as legitimate successor by great Ambassador of Peace and Islam, Shaikhul Islam Hazrat Shah Sufi Maulana Syed Mainuddin Ahmed Al-Hasani Wal Husaini Maizbhandari (Kaddasa Sirruhul Aziz) or Baba Mainuddin (1938-2011). After the holy departure of our holy prophet (*Sallallahu Alaihi Wa Sallam*), the world witnessed numerous "*Wail Aulias*" and Sufi saints rushing to the various parts of the world to preach and spread the religion of Islam. Bangladesh is a famous country in the world where innumerable Sufi saints came and preached the religion of Islam with their utmost efforts, while the existence of a great member of *tariqahs* (*tarika*) in this region as its testimony. Among them Tariqah-E-Maizbhandaria has much eminence.

Tariqah-E-Maizbhandaria was established by Gausul Azam Hazrat Maulana Syed Ahmadullah Maizbhandari (R) in the mid-19ᵗʰ century. This *tariqah* (*tarika)* was furnished and consolidated by his nephew and successor, Gausul Azam Hazrat Shah Sufi Maulana Syed Gulamur Rahaman Al Hasani Wal Hossaini (Baba Bhandari) (R). Baba Bhandari's second son was Syed Maulana Abul Bashor (R). Sultanul Mashaykh Syed Abul Bashor Maizbhandari (R) made his third son Shaikhul Islam Hazrat Maulana Syed Baba Mainuddin Ahmed Al-Hasani Wal-Husaini Maizbhandari (Kaddasa Sirruhul Aziz) his successor during his lifetime in 1962.

Since 1962, great Ambassador of Peace and Islam, Shaikhul Islam Baba Syed Mainuddin Ahmed Maizbhandari (Kaddasa Sirruhul Aziz) preached the religion of Islam and enhancing the Tariqah-E- Maizbhandaria with utmost efforts both at home and abroad. And of late this eminent Sufi, Baba Syed Mainuddin Ahmed Maizbhandari, announced Shahjada Syed Saifuddin Ahmed Al-Hasani wal Husaini Maizbhandari (*Madda Jillihul Ali*) to be his successor or torchbearer.

Shahjada Hazrat Shah Sufi Syed Saifuddin Ahmed Al Hasani Wal

Hossaini Maizbhandari was born on February 24, 1967. From the very beginning of his boyhood, he led a very gentle and pious life and was also a whole hearted devotee of Almighty Allah. After his graduation, his *Murshid Qiblah*, Baba Mainuddin, endowed him with the responsibility of running the Darbar-E Gausul Azam Maizbhandaria *Sharif.* He was entrusted with *Khilafat.* Syed Saifuddin has thousands of disciples both at home and abroad.

He is the honorable President of "Anjuman-E-Rahamania Mainia Maizbhandaria", which was established to uplift the economic condition of the poor and underprivileged section of society. He is also the Vice President of the "Sunni Supreme Council" as well as "Ahley Sunnat Wal Zamat Bangladesh." To keep up the sanctity and interest of Ahley Sunnat Wal Zamat, he has arranged many meetings, seminars and spiritual discussions involving religious scholars, academics and peace activists. He always keeps communications with great scholars, Islamic thinkers and Sufi saints. He is the honorable Chairman of the national "Eid-E-Miladunnabi Celebration Committee," and the Secretary General of "Gausul Azam Baba Bhandari Parishad".

Since 2007 he has been the honorable President of Sufi Unity For International Solidarity (SUFIS) which is working to strengthen unity and harmony between the followers of different faiths in the spirit of humanism to resist all anti-religious activities. He always advocates on behalf of peace and tranquility and opposes hatred, cruelty and brutality. He believes that, "Humanity means religion." Humanity and religion go hand in hand. Through his extended works, he is trying his best to establish global peace. He moves all over the world. For the sake of Peace, Islam and Sufism, he has visited the United States of America, Canada, England, Denmark, France, Holland, Thailand, Indonesia, Malaysia, Germany, Ghana, Nigeria, Singapore, India, Russia, Uzbekistan, Qatar, South Africa, Kuwait, Saudi Arabia, Pakistan, United Arab Emirates, Egypt and many other countries of the world. Several times he has participated in the dialogues and workshops arranged by International Association of Sufism and other organizations of the world. Through his movement, he has established numerous Sufism practice centers (*Khanka*) in many places in the world.

He has established a number of educational, religious and social institutes, such as *madrasas*, mosques, schools, religious research centers, charitable clinics, an Arsenic Free Water Treatment Program, vocational training centers, Imam Training Projects, and *Tasauf* Practicing Centres in Bangladesh and other countries. There are 4000 *Khankas* (Religion Practicing Centres) run under his supervision. He is the honorable Managing President of all of these *Khankas*. Apart from his engagement in preaching Islam, Syed Saifuddin Ahmed Maizbhandari also puts efforts to instilling into the young children a sense of peace and harmony under the banner of a children's forum, "Mainia Shishu Kishor Mela." With an aim to infuse among the children the spirit of Islam, the forum regularly organizes different programs like cultural, painting, and calligraphy competitions.

Syed Saifuddin Ahmed Al-Hasani Wal Husaini Maizbhandari (*Madda Jillihul Ali*) founded the "Syed Mainuddin Ahmed Maizbhandari Trust," a non-political, socio-religious organization. He is the honorable Trustee of the Trust. The Trust has many programs. About 100 orphanages across Bangladesh are under this Trust from which the orphans receive their education, food, and living facilities free of cost. For the efficiency of the *Khalifas* of *Darbar, sharif* training programs are underway. Muslim scholars and Sufi teachers attend the workshop to enhance the knowledge of *Khalifas* on Sufism. The Sufi students and teachers have the opportunity of meditation there. "Meditation paves the way of rectification of the soul," Every year the trust holds a large number of seminars, symposia, meetings, workshops, *Waj* and *Milad-Mahfil* both within the country and abroad under his leadership.

Some socio-economic programs are also run by this Trust. The Trust distributed large numbers of rickshaws to rickshaw pullers. The Trust lends money to the poor, widows, orphans and indigents without any interest. The Trust extends its hands at the time of any natural calamities in any part of the country. It always rushes to the affected areas with alms and food. The Trust is always busy with humanitarian programs. Every year the government of Bangladesh observes a nation-wide Plantation Week while the Trust also runs a yearlong plantation campaign in various parts of the country for the sake of a better environment.

Valuable books have been published under his strict supervision that are very helpful for Sufi students and disciples. These include the *Noor-E-*

Rahman, a popular monthly magazine written on various subjects of *Tasauf*, *Tariqahs (tarikas)* and *Ahley Sunnat Wal Zamat*. The other publications of "Anjuman-E-Rahamania Mainia maizbhandaria" and "Syed Mainuddin Ahmed Maizbhandari Trust" include *Haqikats Semah*, *Sajrah-E-Quadiria Gausia Maizbhandaria*, *Jharna*, *Dalilul Muhebbin*, *Pir Muridir Itiktha*, *Kolir Robi*, *Drop of Truth*, *Way of Salvation*, *Life History of Baba Bhandarir®*, and the Quarterly *Sufi Voice* English Journal.

Syed Saifuddin Ahmed Maizbhandari has three sons: Syed Mehboob-E-Mainuddin, Syed Mashuk-E-Mainuddin and Syed Hasnain-E-Mainuddin. This spiritual leader traveled and is still traveling throughout the world to preach the religion of Islam like his great father and spiritual teacher, eminent Sufi Gausul Wara Syed Mainuddin Ahmed Al Hasani Wal Hossaini Maizbhandari (Kaddasa Sirruhul Aziz) did before him. May Allah Bless him and prolong his life.

Sharon G. Mijares, Ph.D.

Imagine walking into a large hotel in San Francisco and joining with people from Africa, the Middle East, India, Turkey, Europe, Canada, America and various nations around the world — all gathering with the shared intention of contributing to the art of peace-making, joining to share knowledge, art, music and hearts. In my mind's eye I can still see the rooms filled with booths selling perfumed oils, gorgeous scarves and Middle Eastern and African clothing. I remember passing these booths, listening to recordings of Sufi music, smelling perfumed incense, and taking time to read (and often buy) intriguing and meaningful books — each one a reminder of the divine presence and the purpose of the symposia. This was just on the breaks. The Zikrs, workshops and panels expanded and lifted our hearts.

This gathering of the peaceful has a history that began with the efforts of the International Association of Sufism (IAS). I cannot remember if my first symposium was in 1994 or 1995, but I do know that each one has carved an indelible mark upon my heart. It has been part of an ongoing journey that continues to expand my global connections—a continuation of the Messenger calling me to the Sufi path in 1989.

At that time I had made an inner affirmation that the "unity of religious ideals" was my path in life (see: Hazrat Inayat Khan. The Unity of Religious Ideals. Volume 9, The Sufi Message of Hazrat Inayat Khan. NY: Omega Publishing). It was no coincidence that a publication from Omega publishing advertising books arrived in my mail. Of particular significance were books written by the late Hazrat Inayat Khan (1882-1927). Although I did not order any books, I cut out a photo of Inayat Khan, calling it a "very striking face," and put in on the front of my refrigerator. Within two months I quit my job and moved to Northern California following the unexpected decision to enroll in Matthew Fox's Institute for Culture and Creation Spirituality. One of the courses was a class on the Dances of Universal Peace and the faculty for the class was Saadi Shakur Chiste (Neil Douglas-Klotz) — a member of one of the Inayati lineages of HIK, the Sufi Ruhaniat International. Within a few years this religious ideal expanded to include the IAS.

I first met one of the IAS Co-founders, Dr. Ali Kianfar, in 1994 when we were both members of Saadi Shakur Chiste's (Neil Douglas-Klotz) doctoral committee. Within a month or two, following a doctoral gathering regarding the results of Saadi's research on Middle Eastern wisdom, poetry and movement, I received a phone call from Dr. Kianfar inviting me to speak on the IAS Sufism and Psychology panel discussing the "Alchemy of Transformation."

As a presenter I had an even greater opportunity to meet with other presenters and to get to know the members of the IAS. It was truly a gathering of heart-centered Sufis. As a person who has always cherished the ideal of meeting with people of various spiritual traditions, I was overjoyed to make friendships with Sufis from various Sufi orders that had both similarities and differences from my own Sufi group, the Sufi Ruhaniat International. I have always been very grateful for the opportunities to express my own beliefs at these symposia, joining with members of many other Sufi orders also focused on global peace and spiritual unity.

In the beginning years, I primarily expressed my beliefs related to the importance of balancing feminine and masculine expressions as part of life's alchemical journey. Soon I began to note its importance in the outer world as well. In fact, gender balance became an important focus, both inwardly and outwardly, in much of my own life — guiding my dreams, revelations and other spiritual experiences. I have always recognized its importance.

Not long after I started attending the Sufism Symposia, IAS co-founder, Dr. Nahid Angha, created the Sufi Women's Organization (SWO) and Dr. Angha invited me to join with herself, Sonia Gilbert, Rabia Ana Perez, Azima Lila Forrest, Muzeyyen Ansari, and many other women creating the SWO.

Later Dr. Aliaa Rafea and her sister Aisha Rafia from Cairo, Egypt joined us as this circle expanded.

Dr. Angha has shown tireless dedication to gathering women, recognizing the importance of the female voice and presence in helping to heal the many imbalances in this world. In fact, the IAS itself is an example of gender balance in that Dr. Kianfar and Dr. Angha co-jointly began the organization and have co-led all of its numerous efforts. The Sufi Women's Organization became a very large part of my life. It led to my being invited to join Dr. Angha and daughter Seyedeh Dr. Hamaseh Kianfar, Dr. Arife Ellen Hammerle, Dr. Leili First and beloved Sonia Gilbert in New York City to represent SWO at a United Nations' NGO gathering. Having come from a very difficult early life I never would have imagined I would have had such an experience! Being able to attend both the NGO gathering and the United Nations' Millennium Peace Summit for Religious and Spiritual Leaders was one of the highlights of my life. It was also a memorable experience to go with Dr. Angha and her daughter, Seyedeh Hamaseh Kianfar, via the New York subway, to eat Italian food in Greenwich Village and afterwards walk to visit the famed Empire State Building. For many years after this experience, they joked about this journey — and their safety on the streets of New York because of my black belt in Aikido. These adventures may seem small — given the seriousness of our current world conditions — but love and friendship add joy where joy is needed. Also, I have always appreciated learning more about other cultures and their religious beliefs.

My journey with the IAS and SWO is a connectedness of the heart. It has led us to meet regularly on the West coast (San Francisco, Marin County, Seattle and San Jose) and the East coast (NYC and Philadelphia as guests of the Bawa Muhayaddeen Fellowship) of the United States. After 9/11, the various IAS presenters expanded as Christian ministers, Jewish Rabbis and Buddhist monks added their presence and voices to the discussions taking place. Many close friendships were sealed. These were the people who cared beyond their own affiliations — joining in a larger vision of peace and brother/sisterhood. These same groups made an effort to travel to symposia year after year — all joining in the spirit of love. Many of us also traveled to Barcelona, Spain, joining others with like-hearted intent at the 2004 Parliament of World Religions.

It also led to a joint symposium with our Egyptian friends and the Egyptian Society for Spiritual and Cultural Research (ESSCR). This particular symposium emphasized the theme of "Sufi Perspective on World Peace and Responsibility." It greatly expanded my own friendships. This was not long after I had co-authored a book on the need for global gender-balance with Dr. Aliaa Rafea and an Israeli woman. Entering the Hilton conference room in new Cairo on the second day of the symposium I said, "I want to come spend three months here." Within two years I was landing in the Cairo airport being escorted to Dr. Aliaa's new home for that three-month stay — an opportunity to expand this circle of Sufi women.

Following the Egyptian IAS gathering, Dr. Rafea and I had begun a second book as co-editors titled, *A Force Such As the World Has Never Known: Women Creating Change*. Soon thereafter, Dr. Angha joined us and together we gathered approximately 25 women from a variety of countries throughout the world to join in our project. These women relate how they contributed to environmental, nutritional, political, educational and religious transformation. There are also chapters from women working with dance, Quranic recitation, health, psychology, along with women's reproductive rights and birthing practices. Muslim, Christian, Jewish, Buddhist, Hindu, Shinto, Native American and even non-religious women have joined in this shared tribute of caring for the human family. Those three months in Egypt allowed time to begin the work on this book, to deepen my relationship with Aliaa and her family and also meet more peace workers. Life keeps expanding.

Next, IAS traveled to Edinburgh, Scotland in 2011, where once again we shared Zikr, various Sufi practices, prayers and friendships. Of course, these gatherings always includes meeting and making new friends, sharing good food while expanding heart fields.

These words are but a small example of the many ways my life has been impacted by this fellowship of the heart — this community initiated by the International Association of Sufism.

Murshida Kamae A. Miller (Edinburgh, Scotland, 1944-2011)
Kamae was a writer, artist, held an M.A. in Creativity and Spirituality, and was a teacher of sacred movement in the Sufi tradition. She facilitated workshops on

women's spirituality, dance, walking meditation, and creativity in the U.S., Canada, Europe, Russia, and Australia. Deeply devoted to harmony in the human family and for this planet, she was engaged since her teenage years in being an active voice and body for Peace.

Kamae moved to San Francisco in the 1970's and began her formal Sufi training. She immersed herself in the joys and rigors of daily life with the community at Khanqah SAM and with her guide Murshid Wali Ali Meyer. Kamae was one of the first trailblazers to bring the Dances of Universal Peace around the world and to seed the Walks of Murshid SAM internationally. She took Murshid SAM's directive to heart and from the early 1980's was engaged in sharing this lineage treasure outside the boundaries of the United States. Kamae developed an approach to the Walks based on self-discovery rather than "doing them right."

Kamae was editor of the book, *Wisdom Comes Dancing, Selected Writings of Ruth St. Denis on Dance, Spirituality and the Body*. While there are numerous biographies of Ruth St. Denis, *Wisdom Comes Dancing* is unique in its focus on the mystical aspects of the life of this 20th century icon. The book is a treasure for those who want to know more about the relationship of Miss Ruth and Murshid Samuel Lewis.

Kamae was a cherished teacher within the Sufi Ruhaniat International community. She was a courageous leader and friend to her *mureeds* and students. Her words on idealism speak to her nature: "I am fortunate in requiring my heroes to have human qualities, thereby removing their need to be perfect...no one person being the star … the only measure of success being the opening of hearts to beauty and the sacredness of all." Kamae passed on March 30, 2011 in Edinburgh, Scotland.

Daniel Abdal-Hayy Moore

Born in 1940 in Oakland, California, Daniel Abdal-Hayy Moore's first book of poems, *Dawn Visions*, was published by Lawrence Ferlinghetti of City Lights Books, San Francisco in 1964. The second book, *Burnt Heart/Ode to the War Dead*, was published in 1972. He created and directed The Floating Lotus Magic Opera Company in Berkeley, California in the late 1960's and

 presented two major productions, *The Walls Are Running Blood* and *Bliss Apocalypse*. He became a Sufi Muslim in 1970 affiliated with the Darqawi-Habibiyya Tariqat of Shaykh Muhammad ibn al-Habib of Fes, Morocco. He performed the Hajj in 1972 and has lived and traveled throughout Morocco, Spain, Algeria and Nigeria, landing in California and publishing *The Desert is the Only Way Out* and *Chronicles of Akhira* in the early 1980's (Zilzal Press).

Residing in Philadelphia since 1990 and a member of the Bawa Muhaiyuddeen Fellowship, in 1996 he published *The Ramadan Sonnets* (Jusoor/City Lights) and in 2002, *The Blind Beekeeper* (Jusoor/Syracuse University Press). He has been the major editor for a number of works, including *The Burdah of Shaykh Busiri*, translated by Shaykh Hamza Yusuf, and the poetry of Palestinian poet Mahmoud Darwish, translated by Munir Akash. He is also widely published on the worldwide web, including on the sites The American Muslim, DeenPort, and his own website and poetry blog:

(http://www.danielmoorepoetry.com, and http://www.ecstaticxchange.wordpress.com).

He has been poetry editor for *Seasons Journal, Islamica Magazine*, a 2010 translation by Munir Akash of *State of Siege* by Mahmoud Darwish (Syracuse University Press) and *The Prayer of the Oppressed* by Imam Muhammad Nasir al-Dar'i, translated by Hamza Yusuf. He has read his poetry in Egypt, Morocco, England and America and has had a major study of his work in Arabic published by University of Fez scholar Aziz el Kobaiti Idrissi. In 2011 and 2012 he was a winner of the Nazim Hikmet Prize for Poetry, in 2013 he won an American Book Award for his book, Blood Songs, and was listed among the 500 Most Influential Muslims for his poetry. The Ecstatic Exchange Series is bringing out the extensive body of his works of poetry of which there are forty-one titles as of February 2014.

SONG OF OUR SOULS
If we could string out the songs of our souls
the way clotheslines are strung from building to building

or light years strung out from star to star
seismic rumbles and something opening its
eyes for the first time
streaks of otherworldly blue turning
gray in cold sunlight
to flow to where ears who hear them are rubbed into the
forward thrust of their streams
straight shots to the heart in this godly earth God's given us
earth to earth and galaxy to galaxy
one sung note in our breaths from our souls enough
to ignite in all of us His Light throughout…

YOU'LL SING A SONG
You'll sing a song from somewhere out of your depths
and light will hit it and it'll be
a diamond brooch worn at the back of
Layla's head in a sunny glade

It'll be a drop of water hanging at the
tip of a leaf in a dark rainforest radiating diamond light

A deep chasm with a train trestle above it and an
old fashioned train chugging along
oblivious to all danger over a giant arc filled with blue smoke

When you open your heart to sing
the whole room becomes a single ear
or even no ear at all but more like a
sharp point say of a needle about to
enter a cloth to sew
a saintly sleeve to the main body of the divine garment

The exact tip of the needle the sound-receiver
for the entire universe made drunk in the
sudden echoing orbit of your song

Musa Muhaiyaddeen (E. L. Levin)

Musa Muhaiyaddeen (E. L. Levin) has a rare gift for making the teachings of Sufism accessible to Westerners. He teaches in a very grounded way, distilling esoteric concepts into practical, useable every-day guidance. Musa Muhaiyaddeen is the author of *The Road to Infinity* and the newly released book, *The Elixir of Truth, Journey on the Sufi Path* (available on Amazon.com).

For the last two decades, Musa has been a regular speaker at the International Association of Sufism Symposium, a major gathering of Sufis in the United States. It was at his recommendation that the Symposium met at the Philadelphia Convention Center in 2006, in honor of Muhammad Raheem Bawa Muhaiyaddeen, a Sufi Master from Sri Lanka who came to live and teach Sufism in the West. Muhammad Raheem Bawa Muhaiyaddeen resided in Philadelphia until his passing in 1986.

Musa has spoken on Sufism in Asia, Africa and Europe as well as in the United States and Canada. When he is not traveling, he gives weekly talks to a committed group of truth seekers in Philadelphia. He began these spontaneous talks over ten years ago. The talks are wide ranging on various aspects of Sufism and contain such titles as, "Handling Illusion," "Karma," "Letting Go" and "Diseases of the Heart." These powerful talks carry a resonance whether you listen to them or read them in one of his books.

Musa's journey began while he was in graduate school, he found himself confronted with profound questions which permeated his consciousness. Questions like: *Why am I here? Where did I come from? How was I created? Who is my Creator?* His desire for answers led him to spiritual books that he read extensively. He quickly realized, however, that enlightenment was not to be found in a book. He needed a teacher.

Through a marvelous series of events in 1972 Musa and his wife, Asiya, found themselves on Easter Sunday sitting at the feet of Bawa Muhaiyaddeen who had come to live and teach in a small row home in West Philadelphia. During that encounter, Bawa, who spoke no English, pointed to a manuscript sitting on the shelf to his left. He asked someone to read from it. Musa was astonished to find that it contained answers to questions he had hoped to ask but had not yet put into words. Asiya had her own remarkable encounter with Bawa Muhaiyaddeen, one that left her with no doubt that this man from Sir Lanka was a perfected being. From that day on, Musa and his wife became Bawa's faithful disciples. They committed to

108

spending as much time in his presence as they could, commuting to Philadelphia several times a week. After some time Musa and his family moved to the Philadelphia area so they could be closer to Bawa and the community of students.

Under Bawa's tutelage, Musa began the self-work that is at the heart of Sufism. From 1972 until 1986, Bawa Muhaiyaddeen worked to establish a community in Philadelphia now called the Bawa Muhaiyaddeen Fellowship. Bawa brought Musa close to him and instructed Musa to share what he had learned with the world community. Musa is Co-President of the Bawa Muhaiyaddeen Fellowship. Every year from 1991 to 2001 Musa led pilgrimages to Mecca and Medina, taking hundreds of people in total.

In the years that followed, some of Musa's friends established The Witness Within website (http://www.thewitnesswithin.com) to make the weekly talks Musa is giving in Philadelphia available to a wider audience. Those weekly talks continue to this day. There are over 120 of these talks already posted and more are added regularly.

Musa explains that there is only *one* important story and that is God's story. What we need to understand is that story. To quote Musa, "There is this mystery of man's relationship to God, and every man has this relationship to God. We need to explore this relationship and make that exploration something that is a life-long priority. We identify with our bodies, but we are *not* our bodies. Similarly, we identify with our culture, language and religion; but we are not any of those things either. Our true story is the story of our real identity. We need to find *what* and *who* that is. Just as we have duties to our family, and within the work sphere, at the same time we *also* have to do what is necessary to understand what reality is and who we are in that reality. That, in fact, is our primary duty. Man's destiny is directly related to his state of consciousness. As man moves from the egocentric self towards the exalted levels of wisdom, he transcends his illusory worldly circumstances and moves towards his true destiny in reality.

"Man's real work in this world is this transformation of his consciousness from animal qualities to the light filled wisdom that is free of elemental influences and resides within the grace filled qualities of God."

Sheikh Aly N'Daw

Sheikh Aly N'Daw was born in Senegal in 1950. He was a student when he met his Spiritual Master, Sheikh Abdoulaye Dieye, who initiated him to hidden sciences, metaphysics and Sufism. He gave up his profession as a Mathematics lecturer to exile himself on Reunion Island by the orders of his Master. He propagated the Bambian philosophy of "Peace and Service to Mankind" in the Islands of the Indian Ocean before traveling to different parts of the world to teach people to become liberated human beings in order to accomplish their mission on earth.

Like his predecessors in the Initiatory Chain of Khidmatul Khaim, he has devoted his life to serving man according to the Prophetic model. He has consolidated the Khidmatul Khadim International Sufi School which has a mission of serving men without distinction as to race, color or creed. The Master has spared no effort in the edification of Peace Builders around the world, teaching by his example the importance of the choice of any human being "TO BE" in order "TO HAVE" and then "TO DO" for the welfare of all. A firm believer in the principle of Peace, he has laid the foundation for a sound economy to benefit the less fortunate of our society. He urges his disciples to promote interfaith dialogue and to make non-violence their creed.

To humanity, he has offered a token of love – liberation therapy and the initiatory way to peace – the steps of which lead any man who makes the choice to incarnate peace and sow the seeds of peace on this terrestrial journey. His message is "Be Peace to build Peace and serve the whole of humanity."

Yogacharya Ellen Grace O'Brian

Yogacharya Ellen Grace O'Brian is the Founding Minister and Spiritual Director of the *Center for Spiritual Enlightenment* (CSE) with headquarters in San Jose, California, now in its 33rd year of service. CSE is a ministry in the spiritual tradition of Kriya Yoga that serves people from all faith backgrounds who are seeking Self- and God-realization. Yogacharya O'Brian was ordained to teach in 1982 by Roy Eugene Davis, a direct disciple of Paramahansa

Yogananda who brought the teachings of Kriya Yoga to the West.

She is the author of several books on meditation and spiritual practice including *Living the Eternal Way: Spiritual Meaning and Practice in Daily Life*, as well as CD lessons on the classic spiritual works: *The Gospel of Thomas*, *The Bhagavad Gita* and *The Upanishads*. A frequent speaker at conferences and retreats both nationally and internationally, she offers a message on the value of meditation for seekers of spiritual truth and the importance of ethical and spiritual awakening to contribute to world peace. Devotional music and poetry are important to her as a way to express and experience love for God. She has lead the devotional chanting kirtan group, Gitanjali, for more than a decade and has published two books of devotional poems. She is the editor and publisher of the quarterly magazine, *Enlightenment Journal*, which offers inspiration for spiritually conscious living. Her articles also regularly appear in *Truth Journal* magazine published by CSA Press.

Yogacharya O'Brian is the Founder and President of Meru Seminary, training leaders in the Kriya Yoga tradition, as well as Founder and Chair of the community nonprofit educational organization, Carry the Vision, which provides educational programs in nonviolence. She received the 2008 Human Relations Award from the Santa Clara County Office of Human Relations recognizing her contribution to positive human relations and peace in Santa Clara County. She is Vice-Chair Emeritus of the Board of Trustees of the Council for a Parliament of the World's Religions.

Abdullahi El-Okene, Ph. D.

Abdullahi El-Okene was born in Okene, Nigeria on Thursday June 6, 1957 (8th, Zhul-Qa'da 1376AH). With regards to western education, he obtained a Bachelor's degree in Engineering from Ahmadu Bello University in Nigeria in 1979, his M.S. in 1984 and his Ph.D. in 1995. He is currently a Professor of Engineering and was at one time Head of Agricultural Engineering of Ahmadu Bello University, and later a Programme Leader heading the Agricultural Mechanization Research Programme of the Institute for Agricultural Research in Samaru, Zaria.

On the Islamic Platform, Abdullahi is a student of Shaikh Ahmad Tijani and Shaikh Ibrahim Nyass is his role model. Abdullahi studied and travelled widely with Shaikh Tahir Bauchi of Nigeria and Imam Hassan Cisse of Senegal and had the blessing of brief studies with Shaikh AbulFathi, Shaikh Shereef Ibrahim Saleh al-Hussainy, Shaikh Ismaila Sufi, Shaikh Aliyu Harazim al-Hausawi, Mallam Habu Danbami, Khalifa Ghali of Shaikh Yahuza-Zaria, Ustaz Ismaila. He studied the Qur'an with Mall Aliyu Ogaminana where he graduated in 1968. Abdullahi follows the schools of thought of Imam Malik with regards to Sharia (Shariah); al-Ash'ari with regards to *Tauheed (Towhid)* and Divine Attributes; *Warsh* with regards to recitation of the Qur'an; and al-Tijani with regards to methods of *Zikr* (*Dhikr*) (*Dikr*).

Abdullahi believes in all six compulsory articles of Islamic Faith, the Consensus of Ulama, with respect to Qur'an and Prophetic Traditions and is totally against blind criticism of what is not clearly forbidden by the Qur'an and *Sunnah*. Abdullahi is currently the Chairman and Coordinator of the International Organization of Tijaniyyah Brotherhood based in Nigeria.

Sr. Elizabeth Padilla

Sr. Elizabeth Padilla is currently the Program Manager for the Anubhuti Mediation & Retreat Center administered by the Brahma Kumaris World Spiritual Organization (BKWSO). She has been a spiritual student and educator since 1985. Her professional experience has been in Administration, Human Resources and Program Management since 1990. Previously, she was a working actor in San Francisco for 12 years in such productions as Beach Blanket Babylon in the leading role of Snow White and with American Conservatory Theater.

Sister Elizabeth has been trained as a facilitator in Appreciative Inquiry method and Self Managing Leadership. She now designs and facilitates retreats, seminars and workshops on such topics as stress management, healing relationships, self-empowerment and forgiveness. She has been involved with the BK Environmental Initiative since 2010 and has been facilitating and promoting *Awakening the Dreamer Workshop* in India and internationally with the BKWSO. Sister Elizabeth is a very talented singer and a theater artist. She is now fulfilling her life's dream by reaching the heart and spirit though her songs and work.

Murshid Nawab Pasnak

Murshid Nawab Pasnak is a senior member of the International Sufi Movement, and travels extensively to give lectures, retreats and seminars based on the Sufi teachings of Hazrat Inayat Khan. He is also an editor and author, with a number of books to his credit. Originally from Canada, he is presently living in Norway.

Murshida Rabia Ana Perez-Chisti, Ph.D.

Murshida Rabia Ana Perez-Chisti is an ordained minister, senior teacher and National Representative of the Sufi Movement International of the USA, representing Universal Sufism in the West. See http://www.sufimovement.net.

Dr. Perez-Chisti also acts as the *Moin-ul-Maham* for the USA (head of the Religious activity) and serves as part of a collaborative leadership on the Pir-O-Murshid council and the executive committee of the Sufi Movement International (SMI). She has directed a training program that ordains *cherags* (ministers of the Universal Worship founded by Hazrat Inayat Khan in the United States) that educates students in the study of the religious scriptures of the world. This SMI study program has continued for three decades preparing hundreds of students in interfaith studies, spiritual ethics and counseling procedures that permit them to move into chaplaincy, prison reform, and social programs that help humanity.

She holds degrees in psychology, philosophy and religion. In terms of academic responsibilities, she is presently a faculty member in the clinical psychology program at the California Institute of Integral Studies in San Francisco. She has functioned as vice president and academic dean at the University of Creation Spirituality in Oakland, California and academic chair of the Ph.D. Global Program at the Institute of Transpersonal Psychology (now called Sofia University) in Palo Alto, California. She served as a faculty member at Naropa University for 11 years, and

is a lecturer at the University of California-Berkeley, Stanford University, San Diego State University, John F. Kennedy University and Sonoma State University. She specializes in subjects such as Comparative World Religions, the Abrahamic Mystical Traditions, Buddhist Abidhamma using original translations from the Pali language, Ethics, Eastern and Western Philosophy, Women Saints and Prophets: East and West, Jungian Psychology, Psycho-spiritual Synthesis and Culture and Consciousness Studies.

Dr. Perez-Chisti has worked as the director of the Prison Library Project that networked with wardens of the local prisons to bring greater contemplative and educational literature into the prison libraries and also provided spiritual counsel to inmates and their families. She served as a start-up member of the San Francisco AIDS Hospice program. In the Mission of Charities in San Francisco and in Calcutta, she worked with Mother Teresa to support the homeless and marginalized communities in both areas. She was the coordinating director of the Emergency Relief Fund International that helped coordinate food and medicine dispersal to areas of Somalia and Ethiopia during periods of severe famine. She is presently supporting LGBT communities dealing with end-of-life care.

Some of her journal articles include: "A Feminist Approach to Three Holy Women's Intuitive Processes: Exploring Aspects of Transcendental Phenomenology and Hermeneutics through a Correlation of the Researcher's Experience, "*ReVision Magazine: A Journal of Consciousness and Transformation,* Spring Edition (San Francisco, California, 2010); "Originally Blessed: Love of the Mother of the World," Creation Spirituality Community (Golden, Colorado, 2008); "Women's Prophetic Contributions to Sufism," *Italian International Sufi Journal* (Verona, Italy, 2003); *Causation Correlation and Liberation in the Abhidhamma* (Washington, D.C.: UFI Publications, 1998); *Sufi Women: Journey to the Beloved* (contributor). (San Rafael, California: International Association of Sufism, 1998); "The Cosmic World: How We Participate in Thee and Thou and Us" (2001); *A Journal of Consciousness and Transformation Quarterly: ReVision,* Vol. 23; *Transformation Quarterly,* Number 3 (Washington, D.C.: Heldref Publication); *Commentary on Meister Eckhart's Notion of Emptiness* (1999); *Toward the One Magazine* (Edmonton, Canada).

[1]Dr. Perez-Chisti is a phenomenological and hermeneutic researcher. Her interests extend to the study of many languages, yoga, dance and the martial arts as she holds a black belt in Shorin-Ryu Karate, a degree in herbal medicine from Dominican College in Vancouver, Canada and enjoys maintaining an organic vegetable and herb garden.

To access more information regarding the Sufi Movement International (Universal Sufism of the West) activities in the Bay Area and abroad, see www.sufimovement.net.

Swami Prabuddhananda

Swami Prabuddhananda is minister-in-charge of the Vedanta Society of Northern California in San Francisco, California, a post that he has held since 1970. He is a monk of the Ramakrishna Order of India and was in charge of the order's *ashrama* in Bangalore, South India, prior to coming to the United States.

Hazrat Wahid Baksh Rabbani

One of the first members of the International Association of Sufism, Captain Wahid Baksh Rabbani (Pakistan) was a devoted Sufi master. *Hazrat* Wahid Baksh Rabbani, who departed from this world on April 20, 1995, was an eminent Sufi saint of this century in the Chistia spiritual order. His life and work, spanning 85 years, present a perfect example of the great Sufi masters of the past, to whom Islam owes the most of its present day vitality. *Hazrat* Wahid has written many books and his book, *Islamic Sufism,* was well received by the Sufi communities.

Captain Wahid became a student of *Hazrat* Syed Muhammad Zauqi Shah, a great Sufi teacher. In 1970, the *Caliphate* of Hazrat Wahid was announced. Eventually the number of his students grew and as Divine wisdom would have it, he had a very large following from Malaysia which he later visited a few times at the request of his followers. He was a prolific writer about Islamic Sufism and the Sufi path throughout his life.

Hazrat Wahid, in the best of the Sufi traditions of being *Insanul Kamil* (Perfect Man), lived a life that will inspire and provide guidance to thousands for centuries to come. His followers surely have a daunting task ahead. Captain Wahid is buried in Allahbad, LiaqatPur District, Pakistan.

Aisha Rafea

Assayyedah Aisha Rafea is a devoted writer, researcher, and trainer who specializes in personal growth, focusing on galvanizing people's souls, mindsets and behavior. She uses her "The Genuine Me" approach to help people solve their problems by stripping away their emotional clutter and untrue beliefs to be able to move peacefully and softly ahead in their lives. She uses cognitive behavioral techniques and meditations to have people gain consciousness of their deeper selves and let them transform their lives to be more meaningful and fulfilling.

Assayyedah Rafea is a co-leader of the women's group in the Egyptian Society for Spiritual and Cultural Research (http://www.esscr.org). Her spiritual teacher, *Assayyed* Ali Rafea (who is also her brother) has been creating a wonderful environment in which each member of the spiritual family is encouraged to express themselves genuinely and freely. Regarding the fruits of such a liberating and inspiring environment, *Assayyedah* Rafea writes: "One of the most precious things that our Teacher has taught us is how to prepare ourselves for the birth of "the teacher within" to guide our steps along the earthly journey…The more humans are trained to dig into their deepest potentials and express them in genuine works of love and service, the more they gain harmony within and without. Harmony leads to human fulfillment; a journey in which humans' consciousness expands enough to see their oneness with all aspects of creation and also their special mission according to their distinct faculties, and capabilities. This is a basic human right."[1]

Since her childhood, Assayyedah Rafea started to learn and acquire knowledge about human nature from her father, a prominent Egyptian Spiritual Teacher, Master Rafea Muhammad Rafea (1903-1970). She wrote the following about what she has learned from her father: "My father had always taught us, his disciples and children, to open our hearts and minds to listen to any word of truth coming from any source, first and foremost, from our own souls. He used to teach that the core message of all revelations in their diverse expressions is to support human beings in search of their real identities as Divine creation, and in that sense, religion is the science of the human soul in search for her relation with her Creator within and in all creation. He says: 'The loftiest of all sciences is the one related to humans' knowledge of their own Selves. And the most cherished of all gains for a human being is to realize being really *human.*' I have learnt from my father that Islam, as revealed to the Prophet Muhammad, is a revelation that invited people to discern their deeper oneness and their belonging to each other beyond any differentiation of color, culture, race, or religious affiliations."

In four books and diverse articles written in Arabic, *Assayyedah* Rafea expresses her vision that without spirituality, people tend to turn the most precious teachings of revelations into dogma and stagnant tradition. She is also a co-author with Ali and Aliaa of the book, *Beyond Diversities: Reflections on Revelation,* and *Islam From Adam to Muhammad and Beyond* (also published under *The Book Of Essential Islam,* by The Book Foundation, Watsonville, California; Bath England, 2004).[2]

"The True 'Me': Focused, Free, Fulfilled" is a self-development program that *Assayyedah* Rafea designed with teamwork. It is based on the vision that each and every one of us is a unique treasure to be discovered, not raw material to be molded. The highest purpose of the program is to support children, as well as adults, to be spiritually, psychologically, mentally and morally fulfilled. The bottom line of the journey is to awaken the consciousness of participants to the Divine essence with its unbounded capabilities. Children are trained to be participants in creating an environment in which each person gives freely and lovingly to their own fulfillment and in service to all creation impartially.

"Be Yourself…Be Happy," is a Self-growth program that aims to liberate humans from limiting beliefs and attitudes that restrict their chances for being happy, fulfilled and psychologically balanced. The program supports participants to connect with their innermost nature (their true Self) that can turn all limiting beliefs and attitudes into chances for growth. This program has three levels, including some adaptation: 1. general self-development; 2. training the trainer, for care-givers of children; 3. parenting. Under that same title, "Be Yourself…Be Happy" *(Kun Nafsak…Takun Sa'ida)*, Assayyedah Rafea writes regularly for the Egyptian weekly magazine *October*, and presents principles of spiritual psychology and how they can empower us to transform the challenges of life into chances for personal growth.

In several papers and articles presented at international Sufi and interfaith conferences, *Assayyedah* Rafea expressed her vision of Islam. These works include: "The Soul's Longing," [3] "A Spiritual Approach to Women Would Change the World Positively,"[4] "Peace Among Religions,"[5] "The Human Civilization In Search of Wholeness,"[6] "Listening to the Inner Voice,"[7] "Islamic Spirituality: Enhancing Women's Leadership,"[8] "Sufi Way to Peace, Peace in World Religions,"[9] and "The Language of the Qur'an."[10]

Professor Dr. Sayyeda Aliaa Rafea

Professor Dr. Sayyeda Aliaa Rafea grew up in a Sufi environment where her father was a Sufi master and from the lineage of the Prophet Muhammad. From an early age, she was conscious that she should play a role in conveying the Sufi message of love. She sensed that Sufism is not merely a personal matter, but a whole way of life and a worldview that would enhance the quality of life for human beings everywhere, which could help change the world to be a better place to live. She studied philosophy and psychology at Cairo University with the idea that understanding the intellectual heritage of humanity is necessary to build cultural dialogue among nations. Later on, doors were opened for her to acquire knowledge from different fields. Upon her graduation, she got married and traveled to the UK where she pursued free studies in philosophy and psychology. She was particularly interested in Spinoza, and presented a seminar on his philosophy in relation to the Muslim Sufi Ibn Arabi at the University of Wales. She was also introduced to C.J. Jung's school of analytical psychology, and read his collective works. In her pursuing of the impact of Jung on intellectual thoughts, she came across the work of Eric Fromm, and was impressed by his analysis of American society. She realized that a result of a consuming capitalist society made people become more indulgent in day-to-day demands, race for material gains, and suffer a spiritual void. Sayyeda Aliaa realized that spirituality is part of our social reality; that is, without a social environment that values spiritual principles and practices, it may be difficult to draw people's attention to the importance of the spiritual aspects in their lives. However, a Sufi should struggle in creating a social environment that is convenient for spreading a Sufi worldview and at the same time use his or her worldview to support people in their day-to-day life.

In 1979, she started a Master's degree program at the American University in Cairo (AUC) and became a teaching and research assistant at the university. She changed her major from Philosophy and Psychology to Sociology and Anthropology. Her interests in relating between religiosity and social environments directed her to study the then upcoming phenomenon of veiling amongst students. Her analysis showed how the religious aspects of the phenomenon intertwined with politics and social reform in Egyptian society. Veiling was then a symbol that conveyed a message of the necessity to adhere to Islamic discipline in order for our society to base

its plan for development on Islamic ethics. She was concerned about reducing Islam to a set of forms that highlight dogmatic ways of thinking.

Once she finished her Master's degree, Sayyeda Aliaa planned to pursue a Ph.D. program, but the AUC did not offer a Ph.D. degree in Social Sciences, so she made contacts with Egyptian universities. Her plan was interrupted by travelling to the United States to accompany her husband as a visiting professor at San Diego State University. She saw this as an opportunity to study at a U.S. university, but was unlucky, as the only university nearby (University of California, San Diego) offered a program that included an M.A. and a Ph.D. together with many courses, and required two years of residency in the U.S., which was not convenient for her.

When she returned to Egypt, she had another chance to study abroad, as the British Council offered her a grant to study at the University of London. She turned this offer down, however, due to her family demands. She highlights human relations over career ambitions, and believes in the Divine's mercy and help. Despite what seemed to be lost chances, she has never regretted her choices. She had a clear vision about what she wanted to do with her life: that is, to live in peace with herself and her surroundings and to manifest peace around her. She would never be consistent with her inner self if she overlooked her family's needs.

Sayyeda Aliaa is now a full-time professor, writer and spiritual activist. She worked as a visiting professor at Randolph-Macon Women's College in 2002, where she taught a course on Islam and the World and another on the Universal Message of the Egyptian Civilization. She has authored and co-authored many books, including: *Egyptian Identity: An Anthropological Study of The School of Art and Life; Islam From Adam to Muhammad and Beyond* with Master Ali and Aisha Rafea, co-authored with Dr. Sharon Mijares et al.; *The Root of All Evil: An Exposition to Prejudice, Fundamentalism and Gender Imbalance*

Sayyeda Aliaa was involved in many social activities in Egypt. For example, she coordinated a conference on the "Right of Thoughts and Beliefs," sponsored by the Egyptian Organization for Human Rights. She was formerly Secretary General of Zeinab Kamel Hassan Foundation for Holistic Development. She is also a member of the Egyptian Society for Women's Writers. She is a co-founder of women's gatherings within the Egyptian Society. Sayyeda Aliaa Rafea joined the Global Peace Initiative of Women in 2011, and traveled with them to Kenya in 2012 where she delivered a speech in the UN headquarter, and she travelled with them again to Japan in the same year.

In 2011, She established and is a now a chair of the Human Foundation (HF). She considers the establishment of The Human Foundation as a first step toward advancing the pace of moving towards human development on the basis of humane ethics, embracing love and compassion. Within the HF, she holds regular weekly forum under the title Islam is a Religion of Peace and Love, she also gives a course in the analytical psychology, relating between psychology and Sufism. Professionally, Sayyeda Aliaa is a member at the American Anthropological and Sociological Societies.

Assayyed Ali Rafea

Assayyed Ali Rafea[11] is the son of *Assayyed* Rafea M. Rafea (1903-1970), a Muslim spiritual Teacher whose earthly life was a living expression of love to all humanity. Despite the physical absence of his father, his father's spiritual presence is deeply felt, continuously inspiring his disciples and children while they carry on his mission. It is a mission that is based on the conviction that when human beings are conscious of their spiritual essence, their approach to life becomes deeper, richer and more fruitful on all levels. Fulfilling the meaning of being human is a never-ending process. Religion, he taught, came to support human beings to be awakened to that sublime goal and to give them the means and tools for fulfilling it. As a devotee to service, *Assayyed* Ali Rafea is continuing the mission of his father. He is the spiritual guide of the Egyptian Society for Spiritual and Cultural Research (ESSCR), (http://www.

esscr.org). ESSCR set its goal as the dissemination of knowledge about the oneness of humanity, the oneness of the revelations, prophetic and natural, and conducting research in that area.

To explore and shed light on the oneness of the path to human fulfillment as expressed in all revelations, *Assayyed* Ali Rafea, with his sisters Aliaa and Aisha, wrote the book *Beyond Diversities: Reflections on Revelations,*[12] which is based on research on the major revelations of history: ancient Egyptian beliefs, Taoism, Hinduism, Buddhism, Judaism, Christianity and Islam. The book elucidates the basic concepts that all revelations demonstrate:

All revelations invite humans to discern their connection to the Supreme, the Originator of the Divine Order to gain real life. Revelations guide humans to spiritual growth and supply them with means and tools that are multiple in form and one in essence They all call on humans to handle all aspects of life from the perspective of the higher Self with its high moral traits. To clarify the fact that Islam, as revealed to the Prophet Muhammad, guides humanity to a methodology to live in harmony with the Divine Order, they wrote *Islam from Adam to Muhammad and Beyond,*[13] which is also published under the title, *The Book of Essential Islam.* The book demonstrates that: Islam, as revealed to the Prophet Muhammad, confirmed and clarified the very basic concepts of previous revelations, and presented them in a comprehensive system that can be inspiring to humanity. The Prophet Muhammad built an interfaith dialogue based upon al *Kalimah Assawa* (the basic common principles). "The Islamic Call targeted the whole world while respecting diversity and freedom of choice, and that its universal nature does not seek to abolish variations or impose uniformity."

Islam: Living In Harmony with the Laws of Life, is an anthology of some of *Assayyed* Ali Rafea's speeches compiled and translated by some of his disciples. In this book, religion is approached as "a path that is embedded in our very pure nature (*fitra*)." He says, "Heavenly revelations came to help humans to listen to the voice of the truth within, to discern the truth within, and to attain insight into the truth within.... Any approach to Religion should start from our realization of who we truly are, what is the true essence of our life, and how we can gain our lives."[14]

Even though the speeches included in the anthology depend mainly on the teachings of Islam, as revealed to the Prophet Muhammad, the approach presented can be very inspiring to members of any faith, since it unfolds many universal attributes in human psychology that often influence our interaction with religious guidance.

By the beginnings of 2014, a new anthology of Assayed Ali Rafea is published under the name: *Islam: A Book and A Human*. In this anthology, the Speeches focus on the deep relationship between the spirit of divine Sharia concerning society regulations, and what humans have discovered by themselves as accepted norms such as justice, freedom and human rights. He says that religious teachings can never be contradictory with the human experience in its search for building societies on basis of inborn human values and aspirations. The issues handled in *Islam: A Book and A Human* creatively solve the existing conflict that some Islamists create between religiosity and secularity.

In his biography published in Karen Sawyer's *Soul Companions,*[15] Assayyed Ali Rafea presents his approach to the *Sheikh*-disciple relationship. He says: "I do not accept myself as a traditional Sufi guide. I am an ordinary person who is trying to think freely and go deeper in understanding the wisdom we have on earth coming from different sources. I feel, however, that one should not be completely dependent on outside sources and that knowledge should come from within; from one's own experience. I tell the members of the circle that everything I am saying is not absolute and can be discussed – that they are only hearing wisdom from me because of their love, confidence and belief in me. We are all one…if I am the tongue, they are the ears. If I am the mind, they are the heart and body. We complement each other by love, desire for knowing the truth, and a wish to improve our earthly lives and to be exposed to the mercy of God. I accepted the role of 'guide' to the group under this new definition."

With this spirit of striking sincerity, straightforwardness, devotion and simplicity, *Assayyed* Ali Rafea's enlightened soul shines within the clean hearts of the circle's members. His words echo in their hearts, springing from within their souls. He guides their steps all the way through. *Assayyed* Ali Rafea is also a prominent scholar in computer science. He obtained his Ph.D. in France and is now a professor at the American University in Cairo.

Ingo Ahmad Taleb Rashid

Ingo Ahmad Taleb Rashid was born in Munich, Germany on May 2, 1963 to his German-Polish mother, Ruth Taleb Rashid, and his Iraqi father, Ahmad Ghalib Taleb Rashid. The paternal family line of *Ingo* Ahmad Taleb Rashid descends through two lines back to the Prophet Muhammad (pbuh).

Through his father and grandfather, *Septi* Ahmad Taleb Rashid, *Ingo* Ahmad Taleb Rashid was initiated to the *Tariqa* Naqshbandi-Rashidiya, that was founded by one of his ancestors, *Sheikh* Abu Bakr ar Rashid an Naqshband. *Ingo* Ahmad Taleb Rashid became an ordained *Sheikh* (also spelled *Shaykh* or *Shaikh*) of his *tariqa* in 1987 and has been leading the *tariqa* since 1990.

Ingo Ahmad Taleb Rashid was raised partially in Baghdad, Iraq and then also for a longer portion of time in Munich, Germany. He graduated from Ludwig-Maximilian University in Munich in 1986 with an M.A., with majors in Science of Theatre and minors in Politics and Journalism. In addition to his academic and Sufi studies he pursued interdisciplinary studies of dance, martial arts and movement systems from various parts of the world.

Soon after university, *Ingo* Ahmad Taleb Rashid started to form the foundation of Movement Concept®, a system of teaching and learning based on Sufism. It is influenced by long years of studies in the following fields: Bujinkan Budo Tai Jutsu, classical Japanese sword fighting, Judo, Feldenkrais method, Capoeira, acting, classical and modern dance, and stuntman training. He spent a significant amount of time in Japan studying martial arts and the local culture and, since 1993, he regularly worked with Kazuo Ohno (one of the founders of Japanese Butoh) and his son Yoshito Ohno. He also stayed for a longer period in Brazil studying local martial arts and dance forms.

Ingo Ahmad Taleb Rashid is founder and artistic director of El Haddawi, a project-based dance company and a school for spiritually inclined dance theatre and integrated body art. He choreographed, amongst others, the musical *Peace Child*, one of the first theatre productions in Israel in which Jewish and Arabic children worked together. One of his last bigger productions, *Danse Macabre*, is a mystery play about death and dying that was inspired by the death paintings of the Spreuerbrücke in Lucerne, Switzerland. This dance theatre production premiered in Lucerne and was later staged in Graz, Austria and Wasserburg Inn, Germany.

Ingo Ahmad Taleb Rashid regularly directs and choreographs performances and holds seminars and lectures in Europe, Asia and the Americas. He has been producer of the International El Haddawi-Winterschool at Frauenchiemsee (with guest teachers from different spiritual traditions) since 2001, and producer as well as artistic director of the Chiemgau-Dance-Theatre-Festival since 2008. He leads seminar-travels to different regions of the world, including Central Asia, Far East, Middle East and remote regions of Europe.

The *Tariqa* Naqshbandi-Rashidiya is one line of the Naqshbandi *Tariqa*. It shares the same *silsilah,* starting with the Prophet Muhammad (pbuh), with many other lines of the Naqshbandiya, until *Sheikh* Abu Bakr an Naqshband, who immigrated from Bukhara (a part of former Turkestan in Central Asia) to Baghdad around 1850. *Sheikh* Abu Bakr had to flee from war and revolutionary unrest and took refuge in Iraq, which was part of the Ottoman Empire. Soon he became an *oadi* (judge) in Baghdad and later counselor and political advisor of *Sultan* Abdul Hamid II. (1842-1918). One of the most famous students of *Sheikh* Abu Bakr was *Shahab ud Din* al Alusi, who was a renowned Qur'anic scholar and commentator. Later, the line branched out: one part stayed in Baghdad and another part went to Aleppo, in Syria. Ahmad Ghalib, the father of *Ingo* Ahmad Taleb Rashid, left Iraq during the 1950's and began teaching in the West.

Specifically for the *Tariqa* Naqshbandi-Rashidiya, besides the preferred silent practise of *dhikr* (also spelled *zikr*), is its unique bodywork, which probably is strongly influenced by Central Asian roots. Important parts of the practice are the magic steps (*Chutwa al Karam*) and their combination of sacred dances (*Haraka al Muqaddas*). Some of them are related to *surat* of the Holy Qur'an. They became the nucleus of Movement Concept® and the dance theatre work of Ingo Ahmad Taleb Rashid. A characteristic of this bodywork is an integrative approach designed to facilitate the experience of the unity of being *tawhid* (also spelled *tauheed*). Central to this approach is the concept of the three gates of healing: body, energy and spirit, which are connected through breath.

The home page of El Haddawi is: http://www.elhaddawi.de. The web page for the El Haddawi-Dance-Company is: http://www.elhaddawi-dance-company.com.

Shaykh Ahmed Abdur Rashid

Shaykh Ahmed Abdur Rashid is the founder of the Circle Group, World Community, and Legacy International and is an authorized teacher of the Naqshbandiyya, Mujaddadiyya, Qadriyya, Chishtiyya, and Shadiliyya Sufi Orders. His career includes studies in law and religion, work in professional theater and media, and the design of training programs and curricula. He has applied the essence of Islam and *tasawwuf* (also spelled *tasawuf*) by establishing programs in education, leadership development, peace building, and cross-cultural relations. As an educator, lecturer, and writer, he has worked extensively in the areas of leadership training, cross-cultural dialogue, peace building, and Islam and Democracy.

An American by birth, he is also known by his English name, J.E. Rash. *Shaykh* Rashid has spent much time among the peoples of India, Pakistan, North Africa, Turkey, and the Middle East. He received his *ijazat* from the late *Hazrat* Azad Rasool (may Allah's blessings be upon him) of New Delhi in 1984 and serves students in the United States, United Kingdom, India, Turkey, Afghanistan, Kyrgyzstan, Saudi Arabia, Indonesia, Iraq, Israel, Palestine, Tunisia, Saudi Arabia, Kuwait, Oman, Libya and Egypt. Throughout his work and his teaching, he seeks to build bridges of understanding and to develop practical interfaces among people of diverse backgrounds by emphasizing universal spiritual values, social responsibility, mutual respect, and tolerance.

In 1970, *Shaykh* Rashid founded the World Community to provide a supportive environment where individuals could study the ancient methods of spirituality and strive to refine their inner and outer life. The Circle Group (http://www.circlegroup.org) was established shortly thereafter as a publication center and outlet for disseminating teaching materials. As an educator trained in the Montessori Method by the St. Nicholas Training Centre (London), *Shaykh* Rashid has also established a number of Montessori schools, including a small private school, which came to be known as the World Community Education Center (est.1971), serving children from preschool through high school.

In 1979, he founded Legacy International (http://www.legacyintl.

org), a secular, non-profit organization based in Virginia that is dedicated to promoting peace by strengthening civil society and fostering a culture of participation worldwide. For over thirty-five years, Legacy has been instrumental in creating programs that address pressing needs around the world, including civil society development, public health education, women's empowerment, cross-cultural relations and language training, social innovation, and dialogue, peace-making and conflict prevention. Legacy projects have included the Global Viewpoints Forum in Washington, D.C. (including presentations by Middle Eastern religious leaders and policy makers), a Dialogue Workshop for oil companies and environmental activists, the Leadership Development Initiative (designing curriculum and trainings in citizen participation for schools of the Archdiocese of New York City), and the Virginia Growth Management Forum.

Legacy International has administered numerous programs funded by the U.S. Department of State. Among these are the Community Connections (a U.S. State Department initiative providing capacity building for Russian, Ukrainian, Belarusian, and Central Asian professionals), Youth Leadership Programs (bringing together youth and teachers from different religious and ethnic backgrounds from Bosnia & Herzegovina, Indonesia, and Iraq); and TechGirls (a dynamic tech-based empowerment program for young women from 18 countries across the Middle East). Legacy International's recent work in the Middle East includes the Community Health Initiative (addressing women's and children's health issues in Morocco and Egypt), and the Legislative Fellows Program (building capacity and civic leadership in young professionals from Egypt, Kuwait, Libya, Morocco, Oman, and Tunisia).

Legacy International's Global Youth Village, running annually since 1979, has served more than 4,500 participants from over 105 countries, among them Israeli Jews and Palestinians; Northern Irish Catholics and Protestants; Pakistanis and Indians; Lebanese Christians and Muslims; Albanians and Bosnians; Abkhazians and Georgians; Iraqi (Kurds, Sunni and Shia), Indonesians (Muslim, Christian and Hindu youth) and Americans from all ethnic, religious, racial, and economic backgrounds, amongst many others.

In his life's work, *Shaykh* Rashid demonstrates and emphasizes the connections between inner refinement and outer peace building, an approach he calls "Applied Sufism." He has spoken at many national and international forums, including the Asian Conference on Religion for Peace in New Delhi, the Islamic Unity Conference, the University of Colorado's Golda Meir Center for Political Leadership, the International Symposiums on Science and Consciousness in various locations, the United Nations Environment Program, and the World Bank. His lectures can be found on YouTube and the Circle Group Website.

In 1999, *Shaykh* Rashid took part in an historic meeting called, "An Encounter Between Jews and Muslims" in Cordoba, Spain, bringing together Muslim and Jewish religious leaders and scholars. In the fall of 2000, he served as a delegate to the Millennium World Peace Summit of Religious and Spiritual Leaders at the United Nations. He was also a guest of the Templeton Foundation and the Muslim presenter in a forum on "Peacemaking and Reconciliation" at the 2000 State of the World Forum. A member of the Muslim Peace Fellowship, he spoke at the Fellowship's summer 2000 conference on Islamic perspectives on peace building. He has also chaired numerous panels, including one on educating Muslims for skilled leadership at the 2000 convention of the Association of Muslim Social Scientists (AMSS), held at Georgetown University. He is also a former member of the board of advisors of the International Association of Sufism (IAS).

Shaykh Rashid occasionally sits on Master's degree and Ph.D. committees at the Virginia Polytechnic Institute's College of Architecture and Urban Studies, and he periodically addresses multi-faith gatherings, including forums at the University of Virginia, Randolph Macon Woman's College, and Johns Hopkins University. *Shaykh* Rashid's articles and speeches have been translated into Arabic, Turkish, Russian, Urdu and Kazakh. His articles have appeared in both domestic and international publications including *World Affairs, Education and Urban Society, Sufism Journal, The American Muslim*, the Turkish publication *Bugday*, and *Man and Development*.

He has written the following books: *Applied Sufism: Classical Teachings for the Contemporary* (Wingspan Press, 2007), and *Islam and Democracy: A Foundation for Ending Extremism and Preventing Conflict* (Wingspan Press, 2006). He has contributed to the following books: *Democracy and Religion: Free Exercise and Diverse Visions* (Kent State University Press, 2004) (recently recognized as an Outstanding Academic Title); *Choice: Current Reviews for Academic Libraries* (January 2006); *Taking Back Islam: American Muslims Reclaim Their Faith*, edited by Michael Wolfe (Rodale Press, 2002); *Turning*

Toward the Heart: Awakening to the Sufi Way. Hazrat Azad Rasool (Fons Vitae, 2002).

Shaykh Rashid is currently working on two new books, tentatively title*d: Islam: A Systems Approach to Comprehending the Incomprehensible* and *The Inner Circles: Embracing Awakening.* His most recently published series, *The Anbiya: Five Great Messengers* and *Sufism: What, Who, Why, When, and Where,* are challenges to the modern seeker to commit to a life-long sojourn toward, in, and with the Divine.

Michele Ritterman, Ph. D.

Dr. Michelle Ritterman is recognized as the mother of the integration of hypnosis and family therapy, as seen in her classic text: *Using Hypnosis in Family Therapy* (1982). One of Milton Erickson's leading students, she originated the concept of the symptom as a trance state that is actually suggested by various people and social structures. From this basic concept that Erickson himself admired, she framed therapy as the production of "counter-inductions," hypnotic "sequences" that impact the symptom trance. Diagnoses are rarely useful after induced symptoms have been treated. Dr. Ritterman has trained thousands of psychotherapists around the globe in her approach to working with couples and families. Her approach includes shared and separate-track trances in family and couple interactions, and also the development of therapeutic counter-inductions.

Dr. Ritterman also pioneered the concept of the symptom as a gift and therapy as a mutually dignifying process of cooperative exchanges between therapist and client. She calls this a woman's spin on therapy, based on a non-hierarchical approach to every step of a systematic therapeutic sequence.

Dr. Ritterman is a prolific author whose work has been translated into several languages. Also a dedicated activist, she has served as a spokesperson for Amnesty International and other human rights organizations, and her book, *Hope Under Siege* (1986), with a foreword by Isabel Allende, considers the applications of psychotherapeutic principles in the larger context of political and social reality. In Dr. Ritterman's words, "reciprocity is the highest form of love. And love has everything to do with healing." Her latest book *The Tao of a Woman* (2009) is a tool for us to carry with us, to move from the symptom trance to the healing stance. Her book in progress, *From Trance to Stance,* is her latest understanding in therapy of shifts, such as how it occurs in martial arts. Instead of labeling and envisioning individuals as damaged, she sees people as wonderful, unique works in progress, like Michelangelo's Prigioneri series. She emphasizes that we are all works in progress! Dr. Ritterman believes that the goal of psychology is to help create a "human-friendly society" that caters to the bio-rhythms and other real and natural needs of the human organism.

Please visit Dr. Ritterman's home page http://www.micheleritterman.com/ for a video segment from a book party. You may also download, for free, some of her classic papers like "Stopping The Clock," and "Torture: The Counter Therapy by the State," as well as fun-to-read papers on Milton Erickson's principles, and other subjects basic to the symptom as a trance.

Tony Roffers, Ph.D.

Dr. Tony Roffers received his Ph.D. from the University of Minnesota in Counseling Psychology in 1969. He served on the faculty of the University of California, Berkeley, San Francisco State University, and Saint Mary's College of California, where he trained hundreds of therapists on the Masters and Doctoral levels. Dr. Roffers has been trained in many forms of traditional psychotherapy but has more recently focused on the energy therapies. He was one of the first professionals trained in Advanced Integrative Therapy (AIT) in 1999 and served as Dr. Asha Clinton's educational consultant for designing the AIT Training Program. His history of having food and inhalant allergies led him to a study of energy methods for treating allergies and ultimately to the holistic health model he is developing with Dr. Clinton for the physical track in AIT. He currently maintains a private practice in Oakland, California.

David Rosenthal, "David R."

David R. is a composer, producer, engineer, and multi-instrumentalist. He is also the owner of On The Moon Studio in San Francisco, a recording studio where he produced the Taneen recordings . He graduated from the Berklee College of Music in Boston and has produced and performed with a wide variety of musicians from across the globe, including Taneen.

Dr. Rabbi Rami M. Shapiro

Dr. Rabbi Rami M. Shapiro is an award winning author, poet, essayist, and educator whose poems and essays have been anthologized in over a dozen volumes and whose prayers are used in prayer books around the world. Rami received rabbinical ordination from the Hebrew Union College–Jewish Institute of Religion and holds both a Ph.D. and D.Div. degree. A congregational rabbi for 20 years, Rabbi Rami is currently Co-director of One River Wisdom School in Sewanee, TN (www.oneriverwisdomschool.com), Rami writes a regular column for *Spirituality and Health* magazine called "Roadside Assistance for the Spiritual Traveler" and blogs at www.rabbirami.blogspot.com. His most recent book is *Perennial Wisdom for the Spiritual Independent* (Skylight Paths). He can be reached via his website www.rabbirami.com/.

Bahman A. K. Shirazi, Ph.D.

Bahman Shirazi is interested in the processes involved in the transformation of consciousness and wholeness of personality, drawing on several world spiritual traditions such as Buddhism, Sufism and Integral Yoga, as well as Western philosophy and psychology. After studying psychology at the B.S. and M.S. levels, he sought to integrate Eastern sacred psychological wisdom with compatible trends in Western psychology, in search of discovering a whole-person framework. Bahman's doctoral dissertation, titled *Self in Integral Psychology,* was the first of its kind in the nascent field of integral psychology.

130

It concluded that the self can be understood in terms of three distinct spheres of consciousness: egocentric, psychocentric, and cosmocentric, and that a whole-person approach to self-realization necessitates simultaneous mastery of these domains.

Besides teaching, Bahman has held a number of academic administrative positions at the California Institute of Integral Studies (CIIS), most recently as archivist and historian and previously as director of graduate studies. Currently he is on the faculty at Sofia University, Palo Alto, California (formerly the Institute of Transpersonal Psychology). He has previously taught at Dominican University of California and John F. Kennedy University.

His publications include book chapters and articles in the areas of integral psychology and Sufi psychology, including: "Integral Psychology: The Metaphors and Processes of Personal Integration" (in *Consciousness and Its Transformation*; Sri Aurobindo Ashram, 2001), "Integral Psychology: Psychology of the Whole Human Being" (in *Consciousness and Healing: Integral Approaches to Mind-Body Medicine*-Institute of Noetic Sciences, Elsevier Publishing, 2005), "Dimensions of Integral Psychology" (in *Unity in Diversity: Fifty Years of Cultural Integration*; Cultural Integration Fellowship, 2004), and "The Sufi Path of Self-Transformation" (in *Foundations of Indian Psychology*, Vol. 1., New Delhi: Pearson Publications, 2010).

Bahman has published a number of articles and has been special issue editor for the journals *ReVision* and *Integral Review*. He has presented at a number of conferences internationally in the areas of integral psychology and Sufi psychology and has organized a number of conferences and symposia on integral psychology and integral consciousness.

Huston Smith, Ph. D.

Dr. Huston Smith is a Thomas J. Watson Professor of Religion and a Distinguished Adjunct Professor of Psychology, Emeritus, from Syracuse University. Prior to that appointment he taught at Washington University, St. Louis, and was for fifteen years Professor of Philosophy at the Massachusetts Institute of Technology. His most recent teaching was as Visiting Professor of

Religious Studies at the University of California, Berkeley.

Born of missionary parents in Soochow, Dr. Smith lived in China until he was seventeen. His youth there provided an appropriate background for his subsequent interests in comparative philosophies and religions. His interest in education beyond the classroom led Professor Smith to produce three television series for the Public Broadcasting System, "The Religions of Man," "The Search for America," and (with Arthur Compton) "Science and Human Responsibility." His films on Hinduism, Tibetan Buddhism, and Sufism have all won international awards. His phonograph record, "The Music of Tibet," which embodies his discovery of the capacity of certain lamas to sing multiphonically, was acclaimed by *The Journal of Ethnomusicology* as "an important landmark in the study of extra-European music, and in fact of music itself."

Holder of twelve honorary degrees, Professor Smith was one of six professors in 1964 to receive the national E. Harris Harbison Award for Distinguished Teaching in the United States and was featured guest that year on the opening and closing programs of ABS's "Meet the Professor" series. In 1961 he was invited as the first Charles Strong Lecturer on World Religions to the Universities of Australia. Twice he has been appointed Distinguished Visiting Lecturer to the United Chapters of Phi Beta Kappa, and in 1964 he was Annual Lecturer to the John Dewey Society. In 1996 Bill Moyers devoted a 5-part PBS Special, "The Wisdom of Faith with Huston Smith," to his life and work. The series was nominated for an Emmy Award.

Author of over seventy articles in professional and popular journals, his book *The World's Religions* (formerly titled *The Religions of Man*) has been for almost half a century the most widely-used textbook for courses in world religions and has sold over two-and-a-half million copies. His thirteen other books include:

- *Condemned to Meaning*
- *The Soul of Christianity*
- *Islam: a Concise Introduction*
- *A Seat At the Table: Native American Spirituality* (also a film)

-The Huston Smith Reader (essays collected and published by the University of California press)

-The Search for America, Huston Smith, ed. - book that followed the film series

-Tales of Wonder: Adventures Chasing the Divine, an Autobiography with Jeffery Paine

-Forgotten Truth

-Beyond the Post-Modern Mind

-The Purposes of Higher Education

-The Illustrated World's Religions

-One Nation under God: The Triumph of the Native American Church

-Cleansing the Doors of Perception: The Religious Significance of Entheogenic Plants and Chemicals

-Buddhism: A Concise Introduction with Philip Novak

- The Way Things Are with Philip Cousineau

-Why Religion Matters: The Fate of the Human Spirit in an Age of Disbelief (which received the Wilburn Award for the most important book on Religion published in 2001).

Dr. Smith fathered three daughters. His wife, Dr. E. Kendra Smith, is a psychologist. They live in Berkeley, California.

Harlan Stelmach, Ph. D.

Dr. Harlan Stelmach is Professor of Humanities and former Chair of the Humanities Department at Dominican University of California where he teaches undergraduate and graduate courses in the Humanities. His graduate work in the field of ethics began at Harvard University where he received his Master's degree. He completed his doctoral work at the Graduate Theological Union in 1977 in an interdisciplinary program in ethics and social science. As a post-doctoral visiting scholar at the Haas School of Business, UC Berkeley, he specialized in business ethics. Dr. Stelmach has served as the director of the Center for Ethics and Social Policy in Berkeley. He has also served on a number of non-profit boards, including the Graduate Theological Union, Marin Interfaith Council, Interfaith Center at the Presidio, Center for the Common Good and the Pacific Network for Mission Education. He is co-author with Dr. Robert Traer of *Doing Ethics in a Diverse World*.

Harlan Stelmach graduated from Oceanside High School in 1963. He

went on to earn a B.A. from Whittier College in Whittier California, focusing on International Affairs and Latin American Studies. His sophomore year he spent at the University of Copenhagen in Denmark in the Whittier's Study Abroad Program. Upon receiving a Rockefeller Fellowship, he attended Harvard University in Cambridge, Massachusetts where he received an MTS (Master of Theological Studies) degree at the Divinity School. Concurrent with his work at Harvard, he also earned a Certificate of Ecumenical Studies in Geneva, Switzerland in a joint program of the World Council of Churches' Ecumenical Institute and the University of Geneva.

In 1977 he was awarded his Ph.D. from the Graduate Theological Union in Berkeley, California in a cooperative program with the University of California, Berkeley. His course of study was in the interdisciplinary fields of Religious Studies, Social Ethics and Social Theory. His dissertation research focused on the new religious consciousness of the 1960's and 1970's and was partially funded by a grant from the Ford Foundation.

At present, Dr. Stelmach is a tenured Full Professor and Chair of the Humanities Department at Dominican University of California in San Rafael, California. He teaches courses in medical ethics, moral philosophy, Native American thought, religion and public life, religion in Latin America, sociology of religion and a "great books" course for all humanities majors. His other responsibilities have included the administration of eight academic programs from religion and philosophy to art history and music and the supervision of thirty faculty members. He was responsible for initiating four new programs: 1) a university-wide service learning program, 2) a new interdisciplinary major in women and gender studies, 3) a pre-professional BFA program in Dance in cooperation with Alonzo King's LINES Ballet Company and, 4) a new B.A. program in Sustainable Community Studies. He is the former Chair Elect of the Faculty Forum.

He recently co-authored a book with Robert Traer entitled, *Doing Ethics in a Diverse World*, published by Westview Press. This is an introductory textbook helping students to confront the many challenges they face in a pluralistic and interdependent world. He has also published in *The Journal of Teaching Ethics, The Pacific Coast Theological Journal* and *The Ecumenical Review.*

Dr. Stelmach has presented papers at numerous conferences and seminars. Recently he presented a paper at the San Diego Convention Center during the American Academy of Religion's (AAR) Annual Meeting. The paper was entitled "Niebuhr's Immoral Society and Bellah's Good Society: A Conversation about Moral Man." This was the keynote address at the Niebuhr Society Section of AAR.

Other papers he has presented include: "The Future and the Structure and Content of the Cloning Debate" at the Conference on Science and Religion in San Rafael, California and "Civic Engagement and Religious Pluralism, A Liberal Education Challenge," delivered at the annual meeting of the American Association of Colleges and Universities in Washington, D.C. He has presented on various topics worldwide including locations such as: England, Germany, Poland and Costa Rica, and many U.S. states including California, Pennsylvania, Illinois, Minnesota, New York and Connecticut. His list of papers and public lectures is long and impressive.

Prior to coming to Dominican University, Dr. Stelmach was Core and Associate Professor at St. Mary's College in Moraga and the University of San Francisco, in San Francisco, respectively. He has also served as the Associate Dean at the Graduate Theological Union and has been a visiting professor at the University, Berkeley. He is the former Executive Director of the Center for Ethics and Social Policy in Berkeley.

Harlan Stelmach began his education in Oceanside city schools. He attended Ditmar Elementary School, South Oceanside Elementary School, Jefferson Jr. High School and Oceanside High School. He comes from a large family that came to Oceanside in the early 1950's. Four of his siblings went to Oceanside High School and all were involved in student government and athletics; two sisters were Salutatorians of their graduating class.

Harlan lettered in freshman baseball and basketball and was a three-year varsity letterman in both sports. He was captain of the baseball team. He was All-League in baseball his sophomore, junior, and senior years. He lettered in cross-country one year and was Intramural Tennis Champion. He also coached the City of Oceanside's Babe Ruth All Star Team, which included future major league star, Chris Chambliss. He played several years on the Oceanside town baseball team, the Oceanside Buccaneers, founded by his brother and his father. His father managed the team for almost twenty years and eventually founded the North County Baseball League.

Taking after his father, Harlan was the founder of the Albany Berkeley Girls Softball League, now in its 30th year. He served as the Commissioner of the League for eight years. It began at a time when only nine girls were playing organized softball or baseball in Albany and Berkeley combined. Now there are over three hundred girls participating. Some of the founding players are now coaches for their own daughters in the league or as Little League Coaches for their sons. Many girls went on to play fast pitch softball in high school and college, including his daughters. Building on his academic training in ethics, he viewed his work with the League as civic and moral development for youth and the adult role models, helping them to understand healthy competition.

At Oceanside High School, Harlan held student government offices including ASB president, ASB Athletic Commissioner, and Freshman and Sophomore Boy's League Representative. He was Boy's State Representative and was honored with the Bank of America Outstanding Student Award.

Dr. Stelmach's family is very important to him and is part of his success story. His wife is a Physical Therapist and both daughters are in the field of education. One is an Assistant High School Principal and the other was an Art and English teacher at Richmond High School and now is a Teacher Mentor. Academics have always been a central part of their lives. His parents also valued education. They both became college graduates during the depression. They instilled the love of learning in all six of their children, all of whom are college graduates. Among their thirteen grandchildren, two have their Doctorates, and five have obtained Masters Degrees.

Harlan is a truly involved and focused person in all that he undertakes. He is an outstanding leader, teacher and an excellent role model for those seeking careers in the academic world. His dedication and love of learning made him an outstanding candidate to receive the Oceanside High School Hall of Fame Award for excellence in the field of Academics.

Rev. Heng Sure Ph. D.

Rev. Heng Sure ordained as a Buddhist Bhikshu (monk) at the City of Ten Thousand Buddhas, in Talmage, California, in 1976. A native of Toledo, Ohio, Heng Sure met his teacher in religion, the late Ven. Master Hsüan Hua, while finishing an M.A. in Oriental Languages at the University of California,

Berkeley. After receiving full ordination in the Mahayana tradition of Chinese Buddhism he commenced a "three steps, one bow" pilgrimage. With a fellow monk, he traveled up the California Coastal Highway from South Pasadena to Ukiah, a distance of more than eight hundred miles, making a full prostration to the ground every three steps. The two closed each day of their pilgrimage with a dedication of their efforts to world peace. The spiritual journey took over two years and nine months  to complete, as the two monks arrived at their destination in Northern California in November of 1979. Throughout the pilgrimage and for three years following, he observed a practice of total silence.

Rev. Sure currently serves as Director of the Berkeley Buddhist Monastery and holds a Doctorate in Religion from the Graduate Theological Union, Berkeley, California, where he co-teaches a class on Buddhist-Christian Dialogue. He has represented Buddhism on the Global Council of the United Religions Initiative and has served on the Board of Directors of the Interfaith Center at the Presidio, has been a Buddhist delegate to the Parliament of World Religions Capetown, South Africa in 1999, Parliament of World Religions, Barcelona, Spain, 2004, Parliament Assembly, Montserrat, Spain, 2004, and

Parliament of World Religions, Melbourne, Australia, 2009 . Rev. Heng Sure is fluent in Mandarin Chinese, French and Japanese. He speaks around the world on topics as diverse as human values in the hi-tech world, eating a harmless, plant-based diet, and translating Buddhist music into the West. An accomplished folk musician and storyteller, Rev. Sure interprets traditional insights for contemporary seekers of the path to liberation.

Rev. Sure is also involved in the on-going conversation between spirituality and technology. He has used Macintosh computers since 1989 to translate ancient wisdom texts from Chinese into English. He uses Chinese language word processors and layout programs in this work. He has reviewed Asia-related software for the Berkeley Mac User's Group (BMUG) *Newsletter*. He has also been contributing to the establishing of a website for his parent organization, the Dharma Realm Buddhist Association, (http://www.drba.

org). Rev. Sure is also a composer and performer of contemporary and traditional Buddhist music; he has published two music CDs: *Paramita: American Buddhist Folk Songs*, and *Buddhist Stories for Awakening*, which are available through iTunes and CD Baby.

Some of Rev. Sure's publications include: *Sacred Literature Into Liturgy: Jingyuan (1011-1088) And the Development Of the Avatamsaka Liturgy In Song China*, Ph. D., Dissertation, Graduate Theological Union, 2003; *Buddhist Dreams and Emptiness: An Annotated Translation and Partial Analysis of Three Passages from the Ta Chih Tu Lun (T.1509)*, Master Thesis, University of California-Berkeley, 1976;

Heng Sure, Preface to *Jizo Bodhisattva : Modern Healing and Traditional Buddhist Practice* , by Jan Chozen Bays Roshi, Tuttle, 2002; Heng Sure, "Filial Respect and Buddhist Meditation" in *Purity of Heart and Contemplation: A Monastic Dialogue Between Christian and Asian Traditions,* edited by Bruno Barnhart and Joseph Wong, Continuum Press, 2001.

James A. Swan, Ph. D.

Dr. James A. Swan was a moderator for the first and second symposiums of the International Association of Sufism.

James grew up on a 10 mile-long cigar-shaped island in Lake Erie, Grosse Ile, where he spent countless hours on Lake Erie. Moved by his love for nature and growing up downwind and downstream from Detroit, where oil spills from factories polluted the water and clouds of irritating smoke from mainland factories often filled the air, he chose a college major in conservation at the University of Michigan, where he also played intercollegiate football and rugby (leading scorer, 1963), until knee injuries put him on the sidelines.

James received his B.S. in Conservation Education, an M.S. in Resources Planning, and in 1969 a Ph.D. in environmental psychology, the first such Ph.D. granted by the University of Michigan. He is one of the original founders of the Division of Environmental Psychology in the American Psychological Association.

In 1969, James wrote and hosted two documentaries, *Poisoned Paradise: Pesticides*, and *Up in Smoke: Air Pollution*, for the University of Michigan-T.V. Center that were transferred to film and distributed worldwide. James was one of the producers of the nation's largest college Earth Day 1970 teach-in that drew 50,000 people. That same year he appeared at 22 teach-ins across the

US, speaking and playing music for audiences of up to 4,000 people.

From 1969 to 1978, James was a college professor, teaching both psychology and environmental studies at the Universities of Michigan, Western Washington State, Oregon and Washington.

In 1975, at the University of Oregon, he produced a National Endowment for the Humanities-sponsored symposium on the spiritual aspects of sports that included a 5,000-person Professional Track Association Track meet. Michael Wiese's documentary, *Extraordinary Powers*, is based on this conference.

From 1974-1982, James practiced as a coach, with training from Cold Mountain Institute and the Esalen Institute. During this time, he first became aware of Sufism through the writings of Robert Ornstein about the bi-lateral hemispheres of the brain, which led him to study the writings of Idries Shah. While practicing he worked with a number of national and world-class athletes.

From 1979 to 1982, he directed a holistic health clinic in Seattle and produced a number of lectures and workshops featuring a wide-range of holistic health practitioners.

In 1984, he was a featured speaker at the First World Congress on Cultural Parks, held at Mesa Verde National Park, where he presented a typology of sacred places that is used world-wide today in heritage preservation.

In 1985, James produced the world's first symposium on the "Gaia Hypothesis" that earth is a living organism for the National Audubon Society at the University of Massachusetts in Amherst.

From 1988 to 1993, James and his wife, Roberta, produced five landmark Spirit of Place symposia in the U.S. and Japan, seeking to explore the modern significance of ancient wisdom about the unique qualities of place. These programs attracted 10,000 participants, featured 375 speakers, and performances by Paul Horn, Anna Halprin, R. Carlos Nakai, Steven Halpern, and the Japanese rock band Earth Spirit, as well as participation from members of 20 American Indian tribes, Inuit, African, Australian and Asian traditional cultures. The 1991 Spirit of Place symposium held in Sendai, Japan, was the largest environmental conference held in Japan that year, attracting 5,000 attendees.

For 1990 Earth Day, he created a county-wide contest for choosing a recycling mascot for Marin County. Using the winning drawing of an eight year-old boy, George Lucas' Industrial Light and Magic made a full-body costume for "Recycleman," which James wore. From 1990-93 he performed as "Recycleman," the rock and roll recycling clown, both alone and with an all-star band Muruga Booker (Stevie Wonder) on drums, James Gurley (Big Brother) on lead guitar, and Jack Prendergast (Buddy Rich) on keyboards; opening for Jesse Collin Young, Pride and Joy and Gary Lewis and the Playboys.

James' screen acting career began in 1988 as an extra in the movie *Tucker: The Man and His Dream* in which he was placed in a scene with Martin Landau. Landau encouraged him to pursue acting, and he soon joined Screen Actors Guild for work as "Coach Black" in *Angels in the Outfield*. His favorite roles have been as Kevin Bacon's Alcatraz escort guard in *Murder in the First* and as Patrick Stewart's photo double in *Star Trek: First Contact* – hunting The Borg on the hull of the Enterprise.

In addition to appearances in 20 films and the *Midnight Caller, Jesse Hawkes*, and *Nash Bridges* dramatic TV series, James has appeared in over 40 commercials, industrials and print ads. From 2006-2008, he was a member of the Northern California Executive Council of Screen Actors Guild.

James has been a featured guest on the *Donahue Show* and *Good Morning America* in the US, and CBC and NHK. He is the author and co-author of 10 popular non-fiction books and one novel that have sold well over 250,000 copies worldwide, include the Book-of-The-Month Club selection *Sacred Places: How the Living Earth Seeks Our Friendship*. He has published over 300 articles in popular magazines, and was a Senior Columnist for ESPNOutdoors.com for a decade. Today he is a columnist for *The Outdoor Hub* online magazine. He has been a writer/consultant and on-camera expert for the *NOVA, Sightings, Modern Marvels, Ancient Mysteries* series, and ESPN and Sports Afield TV, as well as over 100 outdoor sports shows on the Outdoor Channel and Versus.

In 2002, James, Roberta and their son, Andrew, founded Snow Goose Productions, LLC as a full-service video and film production company. They have produced several documentaries on outdoor sports and a feature-length documentary, *Endangered Species: CA Fish and Game Wardens*. This documentary was an inspiration for the reality series "Wild Justice" on the National Geographic Channel that premiered in 2010 to the largest audience for a reality series premiere in the history of the channel, with 3.2 million viewers. James is Co-Executive producer for the *Wild Justice* series.

His primary focus these days is as a producer of films and TV and a writer and screenwriter.

Charles T. Tart, Ph.D.

Charles T. Tart, Ph.D., Executive Faculty at the Institute of Transpersonal Psychology (now Sofia University), and Professor Emeritus of Psychology at UC Davis, is internationally known for his research with altered states of consciousness, transpersonal psychology, and parapsychology. His books include two that have been called classics, viz., *Altered States of Consciousness* and *Transpersonal Psychologies*, as well as 11 others dealing with states of consciousness, marijuana intoxication and parapsychology. His 1986 *Waking Up: Overcoming the Obstacles to Human Potential* synthesized Buddhist and Sufi mindfulness training ideas transmitted by G. I. Gurdjieff with modern psychology, as did *Living the Mindful Life*. His book, *Mind Science: Meditation Training for Practical People* (2000), further explores the possibilities of awakening. His LATEST, *The End of Materialism: How Evidence of the Paranormal is Bringing Science and Spirit Together* was published in 2009.

He has been a student of Aikido, Buddhist meditation, Gurdjieff's work and of other psychological and spiritual growth disciplines. His primary goals are to build bridges between the scientific and spiritual communities and to help bring about a refinement and integration of Western and Eastern approaches to personal and social growth. Full information is available at blog.paradigm-sys.com. Dr. Tart has presented a culmination of decades of research into the self, including his research on altered states, transpersonal psychology and parapsychology. He said that one of the major problems that hinders self-discovery is the perceived conflict between science and spirituality, which is really a conflict between second-rate science, scientism, and second-rate spirituality, dogmatism. He describes both faith and doubt as human attributes that have healthy and pathological forms. He describes his project, in which he is gathering reports of scientists' transcendent experiences, in TASTE (The Archives of Scientists' Transcendent Experiences, www.issc-taste.org). He shares his belief that it is possible to bridge the gap between real science and real spirituality.

Devi Tide

Devi Tide was born in New York City. She received her early schooling in New York, is a graduate of the University of Florida, and has a further degree in Counseling from the University of Oregon. Her training in yoga began in 1970 at the Integral Yoga Institute in New York City. She continues to teach yoga as part of her offering for those on the path of healing and transformation.

Devi began her training in Sufism with Pir Vilayat Inayat Khan as part of the Sufi Order International in 1976. She has been a teacher of Sufi practices since 1981 and has specialized in healing meditations, practices and retreats since 1997. Her training in Sufism is in the lineage of the Chishtiyya of India and the teachings of Pir-o-Murshid Inayat Khan as they have been adapted to the needs of the Western world. She has also studied, with Pir Vilayat Khan, the light practices of the Shihabuddin Suhrawardi. In 1994, Devi became the Secretary General of the Sufi Order International in North America, and in that capacity began teaching, speaking and offering retreats worldwide.

Devi became the Head (*Kefayat*) of the Sufi Healing Order in North America in 2004. She began offering seminars, lectures and retreats on healing worldwide, and continues this today. With training and practice that spans over thirty years, she is a master of meditation and meditative healing practices. As an internationally known speaker, Devi has offered programs for medical professionals, educators, sociologists, and laypeople in Australia, New Zealand, India, Europe and North America, and has spoken in places such as the Harvard Mind Body Institute and the University of Washington Medical School. She was the first woman to speak at a Sufi Symposium in Hyderabad, India and was an invited delegate to the United Nations Millennium Peace Summit. As a retreat guide and teacher of meditation, she offers individual and group retreats oriented toward inner awakening and unfoldment, as well as healing of the body, mind, heart and soul.

The purpose of the Sufi Order International is to offer tools of awakening to develop the breath, heal the heart, and awaken the individual to divinity within them. One of its goals is to support the emergence of beauty and harmony in the world. Its foundation rests on a bedrock of the unfoldment of the heart and the awakening of the soul to its nature and its purpose in life. The mission of the Sufi Healing Order is to facilitate and support access to inner resources that develop the innate healing capacity within each of us. When one is awake to the power of the Divine spirit to heal, one is more able to serve one's purpose in the world.

Devi trains specialists in the skills necessary to guide healing retreats and also individual healing sessions. She teaches the meditative skills that provide guidance to those on the spiritual path and those in need as they go through the challenging transitions of life. Devi offers classes and healing meditations via the web, cds, video and written media. Her private practice offers meditative healing skills to people receiving ongoing medical care and those interested in a whole-being approach to health. These skills use the tools and ancient healing practices of the Sufis and the Yogis, and are easily learnable non-medical meditative healing practices. They help one grow in inner and outer capacity, strengthen one's focus, open and awaken the heart and develop new habits of perception.

The essence of Devi's teaching now orients people to the natural inner processes that lead them toward wholeness, awakening and healing. This creates a context from which one can integrate and actualize those inner resources of awakening, deepened insight, and developed intuition and confidence.

Earlier in her career, Devi was a student and later a teacher of Polarity Therapy. She was trained and later offered non-force chiropractic treatments and taught Communications and Public Speaking at the college level. Her skills in mediation and insight brought her into the business environment as a consultant in the areas of personnel relations and management working for such companies as Mannesmann Tally, Execusearch, and Education Management Corporation.

Devi is a Murshida in the Sufi Order International, a mureed of Pir-o-Murshid Inayat Khan, Pir Vilyat Inayat Khan and Pir Zia Inayat-Khan.

Pir-o-Murshid Inayat Khan was initiated into the Chishti, Naqshabandi, Suhrawardi and Qadiri lineages of India.

Devi is also the Vice President of the Art of Healing Foundation. She is the senior editor of the Dynamics of Healing book series that, to date, has published three books – *Magnetism*, *Secrets of the Heart* and *The Heart of the Healer*. Devi is also senior editor and a contributor to the *Healing Conductor Manual* and *A Manual for Healing Retreats*. You will find articles from Devi in books and periodicals on healing or meditation.

Sheikh Ahmed Tijani

Sheikh Ahmed Tijani was born in Ghana, West Africa. He specialized in Islamic Law and Jurisprudence, studied and became a Master of Comparative Religion. Sheikh Tijani also studied Astronomy, Spiritual Science and Healing, Divine Poetry and Chanting, Singing, Fine Arts and Culture. He focused on Arabic and Islamic Studies at the Kulliyat Athakaffah Al Arabiyah in Ghana, studied and mastered Biblical Science and History through the Methodist Missionary High School in Ghana. Sheikh Tijani also specialized in Media Broadcasting and Mass-communications. He studied and memorized the Holy Qur'an at age 15 and the Holy Bible at age 20. Shaykh Tijani has served as Secretary General of the African Muslim Organization in Africa; Director General Ghana National Council for Islamic Celebrations; Director Qur'anic Institute Lagos, Nigeria; Religious Education Broadcaster Nigeria Radio and Television; Imam Islamic Educational Congress USA; member International Organization of Journalist; consultative with Economic Social Council United Nations and UNSECO; Educational and Religious Editor West Africa Press Syndicate; National Advisor International Association of Sufism USA; Advisor Islamic Studies and Research Association ISSRA USA; President and Imam Universal Islamic Center USA; member of the World Council of Religious Leader under the auspices of The United Nations Millennium World Peace Summit. Ahmed Tijani Ben Omar advocates spiritual and interfaith interactions from a global perspective. He has travelled to over 105 countries worldwide giving numerous lectures and presentations at conferences, universities and public gatherings around the world. Hosted and directed several national and international Islamic conferences for peace.

Yannis Toussulis, Ph.D.

Yannis Toussulis, Ph.D. is the primary successor of Mehmet Selim Ozic of Istanbul and a traditionally authorized *murshid* in the lineage of Pir Nur al-Arabi, the Nuriyya-Malamiyya. He is an inheritor of six lines of ascription from the following Sufi Orders: Naqshbandi, Qadiri, Rifa'i Khalwati, Mawlawi, and Uwaysi. Dr. Toussulis is also the sole surviving successor of the late Hasan Sari Dede (d. 1997), a Qadiri-Rifa'i Shaykh and a great lover of Mawlana Jalaluddin Rumi.

Author of *Sufism and the Way of Blame: Hidden Sources of a Sacred Psychology* (Quest Books, 2011), Dr. Toussulis serves as the spiritual director of the Itlaq Foundation which was named after the spiritual approach of Hasan Lutfi Susud, a malamati Sufi who influenced the later work of J.G. Bennett.

Dr. Toussulis' formal education includes an M.A. from Lone Mountain College in Existential Counseling Psychology (1977) and a Ph.D. in Psychology with an emphasis in human science research from Saybrook University (1997). Dr. Toussulis' doctoral thesis examined the faith experiences of a Sufi Shaykh, Hassidic Rabbi, and a Catholic monk while pioneering the use of Dr. Amedeo Giorgi's "empirical-phenomenolagial" method as applied to the psychology of religious experience. While at Saybrook University, Dr. Toussulis also studied hermeneutics and critical theory having been prompted to do so while serving briefly as a research design and program development specialist at The Sadat Peace Foundation between 1983-1984.

Both before and after receiving his doctorate, Dr. Toussulis taught graduate and undergraduate courses in psychology for over 35 years. Between 1975-1989 he taught graduate courses on psychology, religion and comparative mythology at Antioch University/West and directed its graduate program in Consciousness Studies. Alarmed by increasing conflicts between "Islam and the West," Dr. Toussulis served as an adjunct professor in cultural psychology at the Monterey Institute of International Studies between 1996-2008. While at that institution, he focused on the psychology of intercultural conflict and democratization processes throughout the greater Middle East.

During the same period, Dr. Toussulis was a key speaker at the UNDP's "Conference on Good Governance, Empowerment, and Participation" (2005), and he lectured on "Cross-Cultural Negotiation in Muslim Majority Nations" at the Inaugural Conference of the Global Majority (2007). He was also a key presenter at "Religion and Society: A Dialogue between Indonesia and the United States," a seminar co-sponsored by the U.S. Department of State and Legacy International. During the same time, he co-authored an article for the Journal of Policy Studies on "Religion and Conflict" that was subsequently published in the anthology, *Islam and Tolerance in Wider Europe* (Budapest: Open Society, 2007).

Dr. Toussulis' attraction to Sufism resulted from his parental upbringing. Both sides of his family included ethnic Greeks from Anatolia, and he became fascinated with the Middle East in his childhood. His mother was born in Izmir and his father in Istanbul. The paternal side of Dr. Toussulis' family included minor Byzantine nobles who served as functionaries in the Ottoman Empire after the fall of Constantinople. On his maternal side, the family originated in Cappadocia, a center of early Christian monasticism and qalandari Sufism in central Turkey. While first reading Idries Shah's *The Sufis* in 1968, Dr. Toussulis immediately recognized a familial resonance, and after a brief hiatus in which he studied the comparative practices of Advaita-Hinduism, Buddhism, Christianity and Judaism, Dr. Toussulis traveled to Turkey in 1978 and met Hasan Lufi Susud who encouraged further studies in Sufism. Returning to the United States, Dr. Toussulis met and studied with Dr. Javad Nurbaksh. After spending two years with the latter as a novice dervish, Dr. Toussulis became the dedicated *murid* of a Syrian-born professor of international relations who was also a Rifa'i Shaykh. The latter (who shall remain unnamed) was associated with a circle of Qadiris, Naqshbandis, and Rifa'is in Damascus who focused on the study of Muhyiddin Ibn al-Arabi. Having practiced with this Shaykh for eight years, Dr. Toussulis was instructed to work with *tariqas* arriving in the United States to help them to adjust to the cultural psychology of Americans. In 1991, as part of his preparation to fulfill this aim, Dr. Toussulis traveled to Turkey where he was appointed by the Board of Directors of the Ayni Ali Baba Tekke to serve as a *khalifah* of the Qadiri-Rifa'I Order in the United States. He served in that capacity for the next four years.

In 1995 Dr. Toussulis met his current Murshid, Mehmet Selim Ozic, and the latter advised him to step down as a formal Shaykh and work on a *malamati* (or "blameworthy") approach that was better adapted to a secular environment. This approach, which emanated from Pir Nur al-Arabi (d. 1878), led to an Akbarian "school" which had undergone modernizing reforms after the formation of the Republic of Turkey.

As a result of his fifteen-year-old collaboration with Mehmet Selim Ozic, as well as his professional academic research and teaching, Dr. Toussulis restricted his activities as a *murshid* to a small circle of students in the greater Bay Area and in Istanbul. The focus of this pilot group was to gradually synthesize the findings of human science with those of the classical Sufi tradition and to offer that combined approach to those who were best suited for it.

While focusing on the Akbarian tradition of Ibn 'Arabi, Dr. Toussulis discovered that the methods used by *malamatis* in Turkey and the Balkans were directly derived from the Khwajagan-Nashbandiyya of Central Asia. This hypothesis had already been proposed by Hasan Lutfi Susud, but Dr. Toussulis wished to confirm it for himself. Conducted with the help of Robert "Abdul Hayy" Darr, the resulting research that confirmed this hypothesis is presented in Dr. Toussulis' book, *Sufism and the Way of Blame*.

While focusing on the methods of the *malamatiyya* who were influenced by the Khwajagan, Dr. Toussulis co-developed a streamlined approach to Sufism with Mehmet Selim Ozic. This approach combines the insights of Western psychology with "bare-bones" Sufism. Although seemingly novel, Dr. Toussulis stresses that his work is a continuation of the two hundred year old legacy that was passed down from Pir Nur al-Arabi, through Hadji Maksoud Pristinevi, to Hasan Lutfi Susud, and thence to Mehmet Sadettin Bilginer and Mehmet Selim Ozic. The combined legacy of these *murshidun*, moreover, link back to the earlier *malamatis* of Anatolia, Central Asia, and ninth-century Khorasan.

Dr. Toussulis maintains that classical Sufism is a dynamic and unfolding tradition that is capable of adapting to conditions of globalization and "post-modernity" without losing its inner substance. His next book will be dedicated to exploring that approach in detail. In the meantime, Dr. Toussulis continues to conduct a part-time practice in family psychotherapy (MFT #11962) as well as working as a lecturer and occasional adjunct professor. Several of his earlier articles on Sufism were featured in *Gnosis Magazine* in the late 1980s and early 1990s during which time he lectured at the Egyptian Scientific Society in Cairo and the International Association of Sufism's Annual Symposium.

Frances Vaughan, Ph.D.

Frances Vaughan, Ph.D. is a psychologist, educator, and author of books, chapters and articles on psychology and spirituality. Her books include: *Awakening Intuition, The Inward Arc: Healing in Psychotherapy and Spirituality*, and *Shadows of the Sacred: Seeing Through Spiritual Illusions*. With her husband, Roger Walsh, she is coeditor of *Paths beyond Ego: The Transpersonal Vision*, and *Gifts from A Course in Miracles*.

As a pioneer in transpersonal psychology, Dr. Vaughan was a founding faculty member of the Institute of Transpersonal Psychology. Later she joined the clinical faculty at the University of California Medical School at Irvine. At present she is a founding faculty member of the Metta Institute.

Dr. Vaughan has served as President of both the Association for Transpersonal Psychology and the Association for Humanistic Psychology, and she is a Fellow of the American Psychological Association. She is currently a trustee of the Fetzer Institute. She has served on the board of directors of several non-profit organizations and on the board of editors of several journals.

Dr. Vaughan holds a Ph.D. in clinical psychology and has been a practitioner of meditation since 1972. She has studied and practiced Buddhist, Sufi and Hindu spiritual traditions in addition to deepening her understanding of Christian mysticism. She has lectured and conducted workshops throughout the U.S. and in Europe, Asia, Australia, and Latin America. She graduated from Stanford University and was elected to Phi Beta Kappa. She has two children and five grandchildren. She lives with her husband in Marin County, California.

Llewellyn Vaughan-Lee, Ph.D.

Llewellyn Vaughan-Lee, Ph.D. is a Sufi mystic and lineage successor in the Naqshbandiyya-Mujaddidiyya Sufi Order. He is an extensive lecturer and author of several books about Sufism, mysticism, dream work and spirituality. Born in London in 1953, he began following the Naqshbandiyya-Mujaddidiyya Sufi path at the age of 19, after meeting Irina Tweedie, author of *Daughter of Fire: A Diary of a Spiritual Training with a Sufi Master.* He became Irina Tweedie's successor and a Sheikh in the Naqshbandiyya Sufi Order. In 1991 he moved to Northern California and founded The Golden Sufi Center to help make available the teachings of this Sufi Lineage (see www.goldensufi.org).

Llewellyn Vaughan-Lee has also specialized in the area of dream work, integrating the ancient Sufi approach to dreams with the insights of Jungian Psychology. Since 2000, the focus of his writing and teaching has been on spiritual responsibility in our present time of transition and an awakening global consciousness of oneness. More recently he has written about the feminine, the world soul, the *anima mundi*, and the emerging field of spiritual ecology (see www.workingwithoneness.org and www.spiritualecology.org). He has also hosted a number of Sufi conferences bringing together different Sufi orders in North America (see www.suficonference.org).

Llewellyn Vaughan-Lee's initial work from 1990 to 2000, including his first eleven books, was to make Sufi teaching more accessible to the Western seeker. In particular, he was exploring the processes of inner transformation, both spiritual and psychological, as experienced on the Naqshbandi Sufi path. The second series of books, starting from the year 2000 with *The Signs of God*, are focused on Sufi teachings about oneness and how to bring them into contemporary life. The final book in this series is *Alchemy of Light*. He has written two autobiographical books on the subject of the mystical journey: *The Face before I Was Born: A Spiritual Autobiography*, and *Fragments of a Love Story: Reflections on the Life of a Mystic*. His most recent books are *The Prayer of the Heart in Christian and Sufi Mysticism* and *Spiritual Ecology: The Cry of the Earth*. He has also been interviewed by Oprah Winfrey for *Super Soul Sunday*, and been featured on PBS in the *Global Spirit* series.

Swami Vedananda

Swami Vedananda is a monk of the Ramakrishna Order of India, and is associated with the Vedanta Society in San Francisco, living primarily at the Society's retreat at Olema in West Marin. He has been associated, almost since its inception, with the "Building Bridges of Understanding" group that plans interfaith conferences.

Neill Walker

Neill Walker is the principal Founder and Director of the Edinburgh International Centre for World Spiritualties, EICWS (www.eicws.org), 1995-2008; the Co-Founder and the Co-Director of the annual, Edinburgh International Festival of Middle Eastern Spirituality and Peace, MESP (www.mesp.org.uk), 2004-Present; Co-Founder and Director, The Middle Eastern Film Festival, MEFF, 2004-Present (www.filmhousecinema.com); and the Co-Founder and the Co-Director and Executive Secretary of the Edinburgh International Centre for Spirituality and Peace, EICSP, Scottish Charity, SC038996 (www.eicsp.org), 2007-Present.

Roger Walsh, M.D., Ph.D. DHL

Roger Walsh, M.D., Ph.D. DHL graduated from Queensland University with degrees in psychology, physiology, neuroscience, and medicine and then came to the United States as a Fulbright Scholar. At Stanford University he passed licensing exams in medicine, psychology, and psychiatry, and then moved to the University of California at Irvine where he is currently professor of psychiatry, philosophy, and anthropology, and a professor in the religious studies program.

Roger's 250 publications include investigations of neuroscience, clinical psychiatry, exceptional psychological health and wellbeing, virtues such as ethics and love, meditation and contemplative practices, and the psychological roots of social and global issues. He recently edited the book The

World's Great Wisdom which is a cross-cultural survey of the understanding and cultivation of wisdom. His writings and research have received over twenty national and international awards and honors, while his teaching has received one national and seven university awards. At the University of California at Irvine he received the Edward Berk Medal as Outstanding Physician and was named the University's Distinguished Writer.

In his other lives, Roger has been a student, researcher, and teacher of contemplative practices for three decades. In his youth he worked as a circus acrobat, and he recently graduated from the San Francisco Comedy College and tried his hand, rather unsuccessfully, at stand-up comedy.

Nikos Yiangou

Nikos Yiangou was born and raised in South Africa, a son of Cypriot immigrants. He received his B.A. in Developmental Psychology at the University of Sussex in England. While living in the U.K., he met the founder of the Beshara School, Bulent Rauf, and was introduced to the principles and teachings of the School that are steeped in the way of oneness and unification. Here he received his core spiritual education that was to become a life-long involvement. At the Beshara School, Nikos completed an eight-month Introductory Course and a six-month Advanced Course, and continues to this day as a student of the School.

After immigrating to the United States, Nikos became involved in the Ibn 'Arabi Society, dedicated to promoting the teachings of this great master. He sits on the Board of Directors and has participated in organizing over twenty conferences. The Society publishes a journal twice annually, and has been pivotal in bringing the work of Ibn 'Arabi to a western audience.

Nikos holds a Master's degree in Transpersonal Psychology and writes and speaks on topics related to personal growth and transformation. He hosts workshops and study groups in the Bay Area. He works as an IT manager in a Fortune 500 software company and has an abiding fascination with the convergence of contemporary trends in culture, spirituality and new media and their intersection with the evolution of human consciousness.

Salman Baruti

"The journey begins with awareness; awareness implies that one has some knowledge of the goal you are pursuing." –Dr. Nahid Angha

More than twenty years ago, the hand of destiny led me to the door of a Berkeley-based bookstore searching for the book, *The Signs and Symbols of Primordial Man.* I did not know it at the time, but that search would change my life forever. At the bookstore I struck up a conversation with Martha Burke Murshida Batul who worked at the store. She told me she was a student of Sufism and inquired whether I would be interested in meeting her teacher. Although I had never heard about Sufism, something about what Martha said intrigued me and piqued my interest. After meeting another student who explained more about the teacher and the group, I was invited to a gathering at the teachers' home in San Rafael.

The night before the gathering, I had a dream that I still remember to this day. In the dream, I saw myself knocking on the door of a house and when it opened, I saw the teacher and a group of students sitting on the floor. The next evening when I went to the house of the teacher, I was astonished to witness the same scene that I had dreamed about the night before. Something about that night told me that there was something very special about the gathering and the teachers that I met that evening.

Prior to meeting Seyyedeh Dr. Nahid Angha and Shah Nazar Seyyed Dr. Ali Kianfar that fateful night many years ago, I considered myself as one who was attracted to the idea of religion, history and philosophy. As a part of my quest, I spent years of wandering and searching several different religions, philosophies and spiritual paths without really knowing what I was searching for. The poem "Door of the Heart" by the great 20th century Sufi, Moulana Shah Maghsoud, translated by Seyyedeh Dr. Nahid Angha, summarizes my search:

Last night I knocked on every door to ask within for a cup of wine
All doors were locked except the door of the heart.
Before its house I stood and heard, you've searched in vain before false doors
There is no door except the door of the heart.

I am eternally grateful that Allah (SWT) guided me to the heart of Islam under of the guidance of two wise and compassionate teachers, for it truly was the beginning of a new phase of awakening in my life.

My life changed dramatically after meeting Seyyedeh Dr. Nahid Angha and Shah Nazar Seyyed Dr. Ali Kianfar. I have been truly blessed to gain a deeper understanding of the meaning of religion as a personal quest to be discovered within my own heart rather than a set of laws and rituals to be followed blindly.

"Unless the reality of God is cognized by a human being, his religion is nothing but manipulation. The goal of the Sufi is to discover the reality of God."
--Shah Nazar Seyyed Dr. Ali Kianfar

I have also been taught by my holy teachers that the true meaning of life is to serve humanity, while remaining connected to one's heart. Since learning this valuable lesson, I have aspired to live and practice this goal in my daily work as a social worker in my interactions with clients and co-workers, and also with family and friends. Through the blessings of my teachers, I have learned many Sufi stories, metaphors and wise sayings and try as much as possible to use the spiritual wisdom I have learned from them to inspire youth, colleagues, family and friends.

At our Sufi gatherings, I have been given the honor to recite the *adhan (azan)*, or call to prayer and make *dua* or supplication after the *zekr (zikr, dhikr)*, and serve tea to the holy teachers. As a member of Taneen Sufi Music Ensemble, I have discovered a love of devotional singing and have sung in concerts both nationally and internationally. As part of the International Association of Sufism's Prison Project, I have written to thousands of inmates in many states and shared the wisdom of Sufi teachings with them. Through the blessings of Seyyedeh Dr. Nahid Angha and Shah Nazar Seyyed Dr. Ali Kianfar, I have also had the opportunity to meet and become friends with Sufis from around the world at the annual Sufism Symposium.

Although I did not know it at the time, or comprehend its profound value, I now know that the day I met my teachers, I received a priceless gift. I am eternally grateful that Allah (SWT) guided me to the doorstep of these two gracious, compassionate and wise Sufi masters. And I pray to Allah (SWT) that He will find me worthy to remain eternally under their guidance. *Subhan'Allah, Alhamdulillah, Allahu Akbar*

(Sheikh Salman Baruti, LCSW has been a social worker for more than 30 years. He is the Behavioral Health Care Manager at the Alameda County Child Guidance Clinic. He is a student of Sufism under the guidance of Shah Nazar Seyyed Dr. Ali Kianfar and Seyyedeh Dr. Nahid Angha.)

Zaheda Baruti

Zaheda Baruti, now a mother of three, joined the International Association of Sufism in 1987 and changed the course of her life and the path for the better. During her time as a student she made many accomplishments; she received her Bachelor's degree in Human Development in 1997, a certificate in Aging Studies, and accomplished the level Nikyu in Aikido. Currently retired from a twenty-one year career in social work, she is currently continuing her education in the area of nutritional counseling for wellness, and helping others in and around her community to make necessary changes and to live healthy active lifestyles.

Finding Sufism has been one of the biggest blessings in my life and has given me a perspective from which I can remain grounded and centered in this ever-changing landscape of the world we live in. In 1987, I was a single mom with one small child and another baby due and was in need of supreme guidance in my life. Although I was born into a Muslim family, I had lost my way, but remained an interested and longing seeker of a spiritual path to follow.

Thanks to a loving and caring friend at that time I was able to come into contact with Dr. Nahid Angha and Dr. Ali Kianfar, the founders of the IAS, who were teaching a small group of people dedicated to following a realistic path to the experience of the Divine. Since then this group has grown astronomically and has since become a center for people all over the world and from many cultures and through many creative forms of self expression to obtain the same goal of experiencing the Divine.

Because of my experiences growing up and finding myself in the role of peace-maker, it became my mission in life to help others and make a difference in their lives. Dr. Angha founded the Sufi Women Organization, which started as a group of women who wanted to address the specific issues of women of all faiths and especially to promote equal rights for women all over the world. One of the SWO's many projects and programs over the many years was the Prison Project, for which I volunteered eagerly and became the coordinator of that project.

The Prison Project was created with a small group of volunteers, members of SWO, with a compassion for one of the most neglected populations of the world, women in prison. Incarcerated women all over the world are our forgotten sisters, mothers and daughters. Our volunteers came with credentials in social work, human services, psychology, sociology, and teaching, as well as extensive life experience. We had also been students of the spiritual path of Sufism for many years.

My involvement in the prison project has forever shaped my way of relating to women less fortunate than myself and helped me to be even more compassionate. One of the first things we discovered in our work with the women was that they were made to be extremely deprived of sensory experiences. On our first outing we held a stress reduction/breast cancer awareness workshop that was held in one of the Federal Women's Prisons, FCI Dublin, in Dublin, CA. Our group of volunteers embarked on our journey with great excitement and a workshop agenda and plan that would surely melt hearts and open minds and teach self-awareness. We truly succeeded in our goal of first introducing our concept of breast cancer self-awareness and self breast exams by playing the recording, "Loving You" by Minnie Ripperton, a famous pop artist and early victim of breast cancer. After that we had them! The women inmates were all ears and found us to be an oasis of love and compassion in their harsh reality.

The prison project volunteers went on to create an award-winning series of workshops and classes at the Marin County Jail, teaching meditation starting out with familiar music that was calming to their souls, including some environmental sounds of which they were so deprived. This would always help to balance and center the women and remind them of times when their lives were more normal or of the good times they had. During this process we would invite them to practice meditation and breathing techniques. Our objective was to give them tools that they could use anytime they needed to find peace and to escape and "be free."

Our classes continued for several years and then blossomed to include correspondence and providing resources and literature to women and their children who visited them in jail. It became one of our goals to provide companionship to women inmates through letter writing and sharing Sufi perspectives and principles. With the help of the Spiritual Literacy and Library Project, we also donated of children's story books for the visiting families.

My involvement in the IAS and all its many avenues for spiritual growth and education have been a major source of inspiration in my life and my current endeavors. In my studies with my teachers and fellow students, I have found a way of experiencing this human life and a clear set of lenses to see the world and understand my existence. I am so glad to have had the experience of being a part of this incredible and life-changing organization. I continue to be a devoted and honored follower and student of the International Association of Sufism and pray that I may always and eternally be connected to our teachers and extended family and friends.

Mohammad Saeed Behjat

I was born on May 11, 1956, in Shiraz, Iran. I was raised in a simple middle-class family that practiced Islam based on tradition. My father taught me how to pray and advised me from time to time. I did not have any religious activity during my teen years. Thirty-three years ago, I married my loving and wonderful wife, Mitra Changizzadeh, and God gave us two beautiful children, who have become seekers of reality. I practiced my religion on and off, but my wife always encouraged me to keep my faith in any situation. I became busy with daily life, so that I did not pay attention to how fast my life passed me by. In 1997, we moved to the United States and started a new life. At the beginning, I was confused and stressed. With the responsibility of family and feeling my life changing, I did not know what to do. I asked God to help me and I started to search for a spiritual gathering in my area. I tried many places, but none of them gave me what I was looking for. On

a holiday related to Imam Ali I was listening to a poem about him. All of sudden I got up and looked in the Iranian yellow pages, and there was the International Association of Sufism's phone number that caught my attention. As soon as I called the number, Shah Nazar Seyyed Dr. Ali Kianfar, the co-founder of IAS, answered the call. He asked me some questions and directed me to a gathering that was held in Fremont, California. Before the first session while I was getting ready to go with my wife, I kept saying, "God is the light of heaven and earth" and during that gathering Dr. Kianfar talked about the same verses of the holy book. I was shocked. I listened to Dr. Kianfar's spiritual teachings and began to practice Sufism in my daily life, trying to connect to the heart of the universe. We then had the privilege of knowing Dr. Nahid Angha, daughter of Hazrat Moulana Shah Maghsoud the Pir of Uwaiysi, and learned in pure Sufi knowledge and wisdom.

Many years passed, and I witnessed how Dr. Angha and Dr. Kianfar worked hard to invite Sufi masters from all over the world to one place to share wisdom and friendship. To me this was the first miraculous gathering of so many Sufis gathering in one place, perhaps first in Sufi history. Every year Sufis' heart and soul became one at the symposium. I also witnessed how they have been active and concerned about interfaith over the years. This includes teachers from different faiths gathering in one place to express their thoughts and experiences. At the same time, participation is encouraged for humanitarian activity in the Bay Area and the world.

Even with such a busy life, Dr. Angha and Dr. Kianfar consult every one of us and solve our problems as needed. These are just hints of their great work and I am sure there are lots of things I have yet to discover. Only after attending gatherings and events have I realized what true faith and religion is, since my own personal insights have proved this to me.

Sufism has been critical to the evolution of my spirituality, and I want to express sincere appreciation to my true spiritual teachers in the pursuit to improve and purify oneself on the Sufi path. We are all blessed to be around our great Sufi family. The experience of being here continues to bring complete fulfillment in my life. God bless all of us.

Samiramis Behjat

I was born in Iran. My mother is Mitra Changizzadeh, and my father is Mohammad Saeed Behjat. Growing up in a family that has a strong sense of faith and spirituality, I had a longing to find a spiritual path and searched many different religions. Though I was born a Muslim, I did not always agree with what I had heard. Therefore, I explored my options by seeking other religions. My mother and father also had the longing and were always searching for the right path. My family was very fortunate  to join the International Association of Sufism in 1999, and I was very lucky to follow. The Quran states: "There is no coercion in religion." Such a truth should open up for us new doors to understanding religion. How can anyone be forced to be attracted to a beloved, and how can anyone become a follower of a principle, if the motivation is not already always present in his heart? I have had the honor and privilege of being under the guidance of wonderful Sufi Teachers Seyyedeh Dr. Nahid Angha and Shah Nazar Seyyed Dr. Ali Kianfar. As a teenager in my quest for knowledge, I met many wonderful spiritual people and had the honor of working alongside them on many projects. Our youth group created the Voices for Justice that over time became UNICEF's ambassador, and was nominated for the Heart of Marin Award. We worked together collecting knit caps for babies in Darfur, providing immunization for children in parts of Africa, collecting for UNICEF's Trick or Treat program, organizing a youth retreat, an Annual Peace Convention, and much more.

When I first met our wonderful teachers, I was lost like many other teenagers; things were not always as easy as they seem, and there were many roadblocks on the way. I always felt pulled towards my faith and that I could overcome any obstacle. I found that the teachings and help of Dr. Angha and Dr. Kianfar pulled me out of many hardships and put me on the right track. In the journey of life, I have gone through many ups and downs, and always turned to my inner faith and the guidance of my teachers. Without them I would not be where I am today. I went from studying political science to understand the world around me, only to be turned off by the devastations I saw before me, to pursuing a career in nursing.

Currently, I am working at the New York Methodist Hospital and now studying to become a nurse practitioner. I owe all of these new blessings in my life to the grace of God and the teachings of my wonderful and amazing teachers. They taught me to stand for my right, educate myself and serve humanity. I hope to make them proud with every move I make in every aspect of life. I wish to someday come back to California and to devote more of my time and heart to the wonderful cause and service Sufism always strives for towards humanity. Thank you for giving me the opportunity to be a part of this collective and wonderful book, next to such amazing people that I have had the pleasure of meeting throughout the years.

Kourosh Behzadi

After the revolution of 1979 in Iran, my comfortable life was shattered both in the U.S. and Iran. My outlook on the future became bleak and discouraging year after year. Prior to the revolution, I had a comfortable life and had never experienced hardship until the age of 22. I was looking for solace and truth from all directions but nothing was satisfying in a real sense.

I met Dr. Kianfar around 1984-85 in Los Angeles. There was a magnetism of power and strength in Dr. Kianfar that drew me to him. Dr. Kianfar became my source of guidance and strength. As years passed and IAS became an established entity, I became more and more interested in its events and seminars. Throughout the hardships of life, I realized that life could be complicated and also mysterious. It became obvious to me that in order to find the truth, spiritual guidance is needed. Hence my spiritual journey with Dr. Kianfar and IAS.

I started my career as a civil engineer in Los Angeles and later switched to a new career in law. I have been a lawyer for the past 22 years. I received my degrees from University of Southern California, Loyola Marymount University, and Golden Gate University Law School.

Sherri Brown

"The Divine message is within the nature of every human being. Your soul is longing for this. The goal is to receive wisdom and become tranquil."--Shah Nazar Seyyed Ali Kianfar

The desire for wisdom and tranquility has been a part of my life journey from the beginning; although, my conscious awareness of this longing has grown as the years have passed. As a child I experienced the sudden death of my beloved grandfather when I was six and my own dear father when I was eight. These two experiences were the beginning of a deep quest to find purpose and meaning in life. My mother was on her own search for security and comfort—so during my formative years we attended a variety of churches. For this I am thankful. I was able to learn about organized religion in its many forms and structures. These churches were places where the teaching of morals, ethics, service, and the search for God could take place. The wonders of the Divine became a part of my early understanding of life.

Watching the unfolding of nature, with its cycle of creation and destruction—birth and death—brought awareness of beauty and a sense that life follows rules and patterns. My mother and I often stood by the window at night, surrounded by darkness that was filled with glittering light of stars and moon. In the morning, that same window would radiate with the sunshine of a new day. Both were glorious and filled me with a sense of wonder. This image of wholeness has been helpful as other losses have occurred in my life.

As I grew to adulthood I discovered, through travel and books, the even wider world of religion than I had known in my youth. Each path, however diverse on the surface, seemed to be pointing in the same direction—discover the Divine within yourself. How to do this became my struggle and search. I explored many of the personality tools offered through classes and books—the Meyers Briggs Typology and the Enneagram were two that were helpful. I returned to school to study psychology, receiving an M.A. in Counseling Psychology. Professionally, I worked as a director of religious education in an Episcopal Church, a therapist, and teacher. After taking Hospice training I designed a curriculum and created programs to help children and adults who were in grief, and I volunteered in non-profit organizations in communities where I lived. All of these experiences led to my next step.

In the late 1990s I was introduced to Dr. Ali Kianfar and Sufism; my world greatly expanded! Dr. Kianfar had been invited to come to Seattle for a weekend program. For the first time, after years of searching, I was hearing Truth at a level beyond my mind. His words penetrated my heart and I knew that this was the wisdom that I had been searching for. From that moment forward, I have been focused on the principles of Sufism and the amazing teachings of Dr. Ali Kianfar and Dr. Nahid Angha. Following his visit, a Sufi group formed in Seattle. We worked on the International Sufism Symposium that was held for two years in the Seattle area. As a group we planned and participated in interfaith understandings through the Mystical Chant program and through educational offerings. We planned and attended retreats, gatherings, meditation groups, and classes both in Washington and California. There have been many programs offered to the public through IAS (International Association of Sufism founded by Dr. Ali Kianfar and Dr. Nahid Angha). All of these offerings are designed to guide us to return to ourselves—to find the rich treasures that are within each of us. This can be accomplished through the purification of the heart.

In the words of His Holiness, Moulana Shah Maghsoud Sadegh Angha, a 20th century Sufi Master and the spiritual teacher of Dr. Kianfar and physical and spiritual father of Dr. Angha:

"Understanding frees you from the bondage of attachments and guides your steps with certainty toward the reality of your truth. It is for us to open the gateway of knowledge to the human being, and so make knowledge the light of the way and understanding the light of the aware heart."

I live with deep gratitude to these teachers for this Holy wisdom. Without their knowledge and merciful guidance, this Reality would be unattainable for me.

Sanaa Joy Carey, Ph.D.

At age thirteen, a mystical experience set the direction for the rest of my life. Of course the experience is indescribable, but I knew I had been touched by the Divine because immediately afterwards, I went downstairs to apologize to my mother for my unpleasant attitude. For an arrogant and rebellious New York teenager, this definitely qualifies as miraculous.

Most everything I have done since has been motivated by a desire to understand or to re-enter the peace I felt that day so long ago. Seeking a way of making sense of what is beyond the senses, I turned first to the physical sciences and then to several social sciences. Once I ran out of academic degrees to pursue, I explored theology, meditation and ancient healing practices. I studied with Buddhist monks in Taiwan, Hindu gurus in India, Native Americans, and I became a certified "Spiritual Director" in the Christian tradition. All  wonderful learning experiences – bread crumbs along a mysterious path that was walking me….

Then through a series of circumstances that only God could arrange and I found myself living in a Sufi Muslim community in southern Virginia. With no conscious interest in Islam, I was suddenly surrounded by loving and dedicated Muslims for whom God was the center of life. Inspired by their gentle way of being, I began to read the Qur'an.

More than anything I had read before, the Qur'an helped me to understand what it means to be a fully functioning human being and a responsible member of society. But I did not find the peace I sought. I wanted to stay with these beautiful souls forever, but knew that I could not.

Then, the dreams started. Again and again, there was a man with a piercing glance who was saying something to me that I knew was important, but I couldn't quite make out what it was.

Not long after the dreams started I met this man that I had seen in my dreams. His piercing eyes were directed my way as I entered a hotel lobby for my first Sufi Symposium. Without knowing how I knew, I was certain that this man could teach me what I needed to know. The man was Dr. Ali Kianfar. My real spiritual journey was about to begin. Everything before that moment had just been preparation.

Eighteen years have passed, and not a day goes by that I don't thank God for the teachings, the guidance, and the selfless dedication of Dr. Kianfar and Dr. Angha. Their wisdom has touched every aspect of my life. Their inspiration and teachings infuse the Interfaith work I do, and the Qur'an and meditation Circles I facilitate. I pray that by God's Grace, I may be able to reflect a small part of their profound understanding of Islam in my role as Islamic advisor to Seattle University's School of Theology & Ministry, and as president of an Outreach Committee at a very large mosque in Washington State.

My husband's story provides an example of Dr. Kianfar's Divine giftedness. Samad, also a student of Dr. Kianfar and Dr. Angha, was diagnosed with several kinds of cancer. After a six and a half hour operation, the doctor's gave him from a few weeks to a few months to live. Dr. Kianfar worked with Samad intensely, enabling him to keep such a positive attitude that it inspired everyone around him. He maintained a heart connection with his teachers and a good quality of life till the very end. Samad died very peacefully five years later.

Nancy Carroll

I grew up in Detroit, Michigan as a middle child in a family with eight siblings. It was a chaotic experience without much guidance. I like to think of it as "survival of the fittest." My parents were raised Catholic, and so we all piled into a station wagon and went off to church every Sunday, until one day my parents mysteriously did not go to church any longer. I was 12-years-old and that was the end of my religious training. I could not wait to get out of the household at 18, when I then went directly into the workforce doing secretarial work. I was always very proud that I could make it on my own but felt there was something better in life and had this nagging feeling deep inside me that something was missing. I left Detroit for San Francisco, California where I essentially worked, got by, and led a life of spiritual ignorance. After a failed marriage, I moved to the other side of the Bay and settled in Berkeley. I still had a continuous gnawing feeling that my life was headed in the wrong direction.

I attempted to straighten out through twelve step programs. I learned I needed to first make a decision to turn my will and life over to the care of God, as I understood God, and to seek this through prayer and meditation to improve my conscious contact with God. I prayed only for his knowledge

164

and his will and the power to carry out my hopes. But I couldn't do it on my own and found that the twelve step meetings were not where I could go to find peace and solace. I needed guidance; I needed a teacher.

A turning point came walking into my life, and his name is Tony Roybal. When I was at work I would occasionally see Tony at a coffee shop on a break. There was something I was drawn to in Tony. He had a calmness and confidence about him. We became friends and fell in love. I came to find out that he is a Sufi student under the guidance of the honorable Seyed Dr. Nahid Angha and Shah Nazar Seyed Dr. Ali Kianfar.

Taher (Tony's Sufi name meaning "pure, chaste, and clean") is part of a Sufi musical ensemble called Taneen. I would periodically go to events where Taneen would play. I was immediately drawn to the music and the words that tugged at my heart. I went to see Taneen play at the end of a Sufi Symposium in 2011. My life completely changed ever since that day when Taher introduced me to his spiritual teachers, Dr. Ali Kianfar and Dr. Nahid Angha. I felt as if I was being seen through, and that they could see something I could not. At the invitation of the teachers, Taher took me along to their "gatherings" wherein under the guidance of the teachers, the students practice meditation and pray.

I have learned that we carry in ourselves our own culture we were born with, but opportunity leads us to find our own religion, which is inside us. This is what Sufism is to me: we begin as a small seed and we meditate so the seed can open up and find suitable ground. The seed is your heart. Once the seed is open it needs to exchange information. It is here that Sufism comes into place to create the suitable ground. If a human being is truly seeking, then you will find: "what and where is me?"

In the course of these few years of being a Sufi student, I have become involved with the Sufi Women Organization -- a department of the International Association of Sufism founded by Dr. Nahid Angha in 1993. The Sufi Women Organization gathers women together from all around the world who share goals of creating a world where we can help with human rights, especially women's rights, education, and social awareness.

I have also worked at the International Association of Sufism's yearly symposia and festivals by greeting participants and with registration. I also participated at the festival in a luncheon/fashion show hosted by the Sufi Women Organization with all donated items being sold at auction.

I truly offer thanks from the bottom of my heart to my teachers who have allowed me to learn from them and embark on this journey. Bismillah ar-Rahman ar-Raheem.

Ana Marcelina Castillo

I was born in Quezaltepeque, Dpto. La Libertad, El Salvador, Central America. I obtained my high school diploma in Arts and Science in 1970, married in 1972 to Lic. Misael Armando Tejada and had my daughter. I attended the National University of El Salvador, studying Psychology and Linguistics for three years; unfortunately I did not complete my degree. I emigrated from El Salvador to the United States. With my faith and my toddler we set forth on a new journey. We landed in San Francisco, moved around in Sutter County, but eventually headed back to the Bay Area.

In the early 1980's it was my good fortune to take a meditation class, taught by one of Shah Nazar Seyyed Dr. Ali Kianfar's students. I had no knowledge about Sufism but I had a beautiful dream during this time. I saw people in white clothing, whom I later understood to be "Sufis," and I heard the word "*Alhamdulillah*," which I kept in my heart, and it constantly resonated in my mind. I yearned to know its meaning. Shortly after that dream, I was invited to Seyyedeh Dr. Nahid Angha and Shah Nazar Seyyed Dr. Ali Kianfar's gathering to learn about Sufism.

My life has been forever changed by the teachings of Moulana Shah Maghsoud, his daughter, Seyyedeh Dr. Nahid Angha, and Shah Nazar Seyyed Dr. Ali Kianfar. I have been with The International Association of Sufism (IAS), since the beginning stages in 1983 when it was formed. Throughout the years I have been involved with various events conducted by International Association of Sufism, including collating the *Sufism an Inquiry* journal, preparing mailings for events, Sufi Women Organization (SWO) fundraisers, and assisted during IAS's Annual Sufism Symposia. I am grateful for the teachings of the Uwaiysi Tarighat. I would like to extend my appreciation to Seyyedeh Dr. Nahid Angha for the opportunity to accompany her mother Mah Talat Etemad Moghadam Angha (PBUH) during the annual Sufism

Symposia, as this had been my honor for several years. I also offer gratitude to Shah Nazar Seyyed Dr. Ali Kianfar for his guidance through the years.

Neda Ana Tejada Castillo

Bismillah ir-Rahman ir-Rahim.

First I would like to thank my teachers, Seyyedeh Dr. Nahid Angha and Shah Nazar Seyyed Dr. Ali Kianfar for this humble opportunity to be a part of the International Association of Sufism's history and for the blessings derived from the teachings of Hazrat Moulana Shah Maghsoud. I would also like to acknowledge the contributions of Mah Talat Etemad Moghadam Angha throughout her lifetime of service, as well as her granddaughters, Seyyedeh Hamaseh Kianfar and Seyyedeh Sahar Kianfar.

I am the daughter of Ana Marcelina Castillo, born in El Salvador, and a member of the International Association of Sufism (IAS) since its inception in 1983. I recall the meeting being held at the office of our teachers, Seyyedeh Dr. Nahid Angha and Shah Nazar Seyyed Dr. Ali Kianfar, when the initial planning, organization and commitments were being discussed around the conference room table, for future Sufism Symposia conferences. I was all but 11 years old, assigned the responsibility of distributing the program flyers for the symposium, eventually graduating to registering the panel speakers and conference attendees as I got older. It has been my honor to have been a part of the registration process for so many years. I've had the pleasure of introducing some of our guest speakers and appreciate the exchange of dialogue amongst our interfaith family.

As a member of Sufi Women Organization (SWO) I have supported ongoing projects and joined in fundraising events. In another department of IAS, Voices for Justice (VFJ), under the direction of the Founder and Chair, Seyyedeh Hamaseh Kianfar, I have been involved in numerous projects, with the aim of advocating for the rights of children. VFJ has been recognized as an Ambassador to UNICEF, and we have participated in annual food drives, a baby knit cap project for Malawi, and collecting school supplies for children in Central America, as well as collaboration with other organizations.

I hold a Bachelor's degree in Psychology from Mills College and a Master's degree in Public Administration from California State University East Bay. I currently live with my daughter, Suhaila Misia Tejada, in Alameda County. In my personal and professional life, I seek to be of service to the international community, for all the grace that Allah has bestowed upon my family, with much gratitude to the path and the teachings of the Uwaiysi Tarighat.

Sara Changizi

I was born in a traditional and religious family in Iran. Before I was married, for sixteen years I was under the guidance of my kind and devoutly religious mother who lovingly introduced and taught me the principles of Islam. After my marriage I entered a new chapter in my life with my husband's family in a new city and new environment. I was able to keep up my prayers on a daily basis, even though their Islamic practices differed. My husband was very kind, generous and a man of true faith; our family grew and I now have three sons, three daughters and eleven grandchildren. Many times in my life, I wanted to ask about prayers and so from a true Muslim, deep down in my heart I felt a direct connection to God. Each day I would find peace and tranquility in my prayers and *zikrs (dhikr, zekr)*.

In 1985, I immigrated with my husband and two of my daughters, with great difficulties, to the United States of America. In the first few years I was unsure whether I would be able to teach my young daughters Islam with my limited knowledge. This was a great responsibility in my mind that I tried to accomplish by finding many Persian families and friends to surround my daughters with. The first gathering of good folks I found were a group of Persian Christians. They insisted that I become a Christian in order to be a better human being. Even though I love and honor Jesus Christ, I always felt deep in my heart that there is only one God, and all mosques, churches, and synagogues belong to Him. I saw no basis for changing my religion, especially when I saw no satisfying answers to my questions until 1999 when I was introduced, through my daughter and son-in-law, to Sufism under the direction of Seyyedeh Dr. Nahid Angha and Shah Nazar Seyyed Dr. Ali Kianfar. I was happy and honored to be able to attend their classes, and to find answers to my questions and experience my heart as closer to God Almighty. I thank God so much that he sent the best teachers that any one could ask for. From then on all my ideology and my thoughts were changed. After 50 years of prayers, I finally found the true meaning of Islam. The holy Quran is no longer just another book in my house, it has become my lifeline and the guide to all my questions. Dr. Nahid Angha and Dr. Ali Kianfar are messengers of our times and they give me and my family guidance in our religious and spiritual lives. These two true teachers, under the guidance of Moulana Shah Maghsoud and his devoted wife Mah Talat Etemad Moghadam Angha, learned the Uwaiysi teachings and have continued its tradition. I have been blessed and honored to be part of The International Association of Sufism and happy that I was able to attend the symposia and retreats where I was able to meet many wonderful Sufis from around the world.

I am honored to be part of the Sufi Women Organization (SWO) which through the support of Sufi sisterhood has helped the Muslim women of the world achieve equality and Human rights. We held many educational sessions in South Bay for the prevention of domestic violence, advocating for women's rights. The biggest honor for me has been to meet the holy, kind mother Mah Talat Etemad Moghadam Angha, for without her support, this school of thought would have perished.

Mitra Changizzadeh

I was born in Abadan, Iran, and grew up in a modern family with spiritual ideals. I started practicing my religion in the traditional way my mom taught me, which played an important role in my life. I had lots of questions about everything I was doing in prayer and worship, but no one had the answers. Even when I married and had children, I was always searching for the right path to find the Divine.

My life had many interesting twists and turns but the most significant moment was the time that I had to make the difficult decision to come to America. I prayed to keep my relationships and connections strong with my blessed family. In 1997 I arrived in San Jose, California and got busy in life. For two years I participated in many local Islamic centers for worship. I could not find the right organization to develop my spirituality for personal growth. Finally, one day I asked God to put me in the right place. The critical moment came when my husband told me he found an advertisement in an Iranian newspaper for a Sufi gathering in Fremont. It was organized by the International Association of Sufism, co-founded by Dr. Seyyedeh Nahid Angha, daughter of Hazrat Moulana Shah Maghsoud the Pir of Uwaiysi, and Shah Nazar Seyyed Dr. Ali Kianfar. When we first attended, and as soon as Dr. Kianfar began teaching the group, it was as if he was answering my questions. At the end of the class, I asked him how he knew my questions before I asked him. He told me, "If the teacher does not know what is in their students' heart and mind, he or she should not call themselves teacher." I knew this was a sign that my prayers were met in 1999 and I found my teachers.

From that moment my life changed and I realized religion is a personal matter. Only with my own practice under the guidance of true teachers, would I be able to improve myself and know the Divine. In the past fifteen years I have been to many gatherings, retreats, and symposia and was truly impressed at the professional scholarship of the interfaith community worldwide. I have also been honored to be part of the Sufi Women Organization founded by Dr. Angha, to help establish a voice for Iranian women in the Bay Area. Dr. Angha helped me to become a great Sufi woman and a strong mother for my children. Once she said, "In order to help others, you must first educate yourself and be confident in what you do."

As examples, Dr. Angha, Dr. Kianfar, and their children became great role models in my social and spiritual life. They always encourage me and my children to make positive contributions and to attain higher education to help the future generations of humanity. That is why I returned to school to pursue my degree in ultrasound technology to support my children's goals. I am eternally thankful for my teachers and all my brothers and sisters whom I have had the privilege to meet, and look forward to expanding my faith for enlightenment.

Soraya Chase Clow, Ph. D., Uwaiysi Tarighat

Bessmillah ar-Rahman, ar-Raheem.

With unbounded gratitude to my teachers, Shah Nazar Seyyed Dr. Ali Kianfar and Seyyedeh Dr. Nahid Angha.

Born August 11, 1963 in Aspen, Colorado, the third and last child of James C. Clow and Susan B. Merwin, I was named Marian Chase Merwin Clow at birth. I inherited the name Marian from my great aunt and Chase from my grandfather. My parents chose to call me Chase, unusual for a girl, and this seems to have defined my personality, as I was always chasing after something, including spiritual insight. This has been my primary ambition throughout my life: to know who I am and why I exist and to directly cognize the greater reality, of which this physical world, particularly the human-made world, seems but a dark and slippery shadow. Deep within me, but not yet manifest, was Soraya.

The spirit of longing and inquiry was nourished by the wide spaces, open skies, and deep silence of the American West, where I resided throughout my youth. My father, who has since passed away, was a cattle rancher and my mother is an artist and scholar who has lived in relatively small towns surrounded by open space. Both well-educated and appreciators of the natural world, they inculcated in me a deep love of books and of nature. I spent much of my youth alone – reading, drawing, hiking or horseback riding, exploring for miles while carefully observing plants, animals, birds and insects and simultaneously contemplating the reason for existence and the vastness of this complex and beautiful universe.

Although I was not raised with religion, my parents instilled in me a strong ethical rudder and a respect for others. I always felt connected to a greater whole and perceived a benevolent, unseen spirit guiding me. Up until the age of twelve or thirteen, I had several profound experiences of seeing and/or intuiting events before they occurred. I felt a desire to further hone these skills, but did not know how. By the age of fourteen I began longing for a spiritual teacher.

At the age of nineteen I moved to Berkeley, California and strongly sensed my teachers were near, but didn't know where to look. I had been seeking for five years and, despite having attended many different religious organizations and spiritual gatherings, I was disappointed at not having found the one with the key to my heart. Soon thereafter I met my beloved teachers, my spiritual parents, Shah Nazar Seyyed Dr. Ali Kianfar and Seyyedeh Dr. Nahid Angha, both of whom are students of my grand master, the great twentieth-century Persian Sufi, Shah Maghsoud Sadegh Angha. I knew I found my home because, for the first time I was directed toward my heart and when asked why I was seeking I replied, "I want to learn how to love," which was a great surprise to me. I always thought I was looking to hone my sixth sense, but the truth of that statement, which quickly rose uncensored from my heart, was sure and unwavering. My path was further confirmed that evening when, upon practicing a heart-based meditation given to me that day, I clearly heard within me a voice saying, "I am the way." I thought, "*You* are the way?" and then heard, "No, *you* are the way." A great question arose within me as to what exactly that meant and with whom I had had this exchange.

There began what has now been over a thirty-year practice of learning how to love and of collecting all the scattered bits of self into a coherent whole, a self capable of journeying on the way. This has meant allowing the qualities and habits that prevented me from experiencing love to be peeled away, sometimes painfully, by my teachers and of disciplining my mind and heart to allow their love to grow within me and bring forward a shining star, a quality they saw hidden within me under many layers of unhealthy, untamed mental and behavioral qualities. Through them I have witnessed the light of love, the foundation and essence of all being.

By their invitation, I have the honor of being a founding member of the International Association of Sufism, which I have served in a number of capacities. I became a graphic designer and produced many designs for IAS, including the print journal, *Sufism: An Inquiry*. In the early years, I handled registration for the Sufism Symposia. I also was directed to become a founding member of Taneen Sufi Music Ensemble as a singer/song-writer and under its guise have helped lead *zekr (zikr, dhikr)* in our gatherings as well as represented IAS at events nationally and internationally. We have also recorded our music, helping to spread the beauty of Sufi wisdom and poetry through original prayer-and-meditation-inspired heart-opening music.

My teachers have guided my entire adult life. They have shaped every aspect of my being. They have opened more doors than I could have imagined and gently pushed me to walk through even when I didn't believe I was capable. I pursued first my bachelor's, then my master's, and now my doctorate due to their encouragement. I have raised two gracious, confident, and kind daughters, Rabea and Ameneh McCullough, under their careful tutelage. I have a solid and wonderful career as a university educator and administrator solely because they believed in me and guided me to this point. Although my first marriage to another founding member of IAS, Jeff McCullough, was not a success, I have a loving, healthy, respectful relationship with my second husband, Lorin Spaulding. These are only a few of the unbounded blessings.

I long for and strive to be a worthy student of these two gracious Sufi masters, a student deserving of their love, support and guidance, and one who will be able to carry their teachings forward, *ensha-Allah.*

Matthew Evan Joseph Davis

A student of Sufi Masters Dr. Nahid Angha and Shah Nazar Seyyed Dr. Ali Kianfar, with the living practice of being an ever-refining reflection of their light. As Jesus spoke in *The Sermon on the Mount,* "When thine eye be single, thy whole body will be full with light." And so it is that ten centuries later it was noted in the *Mysteries of Unification* that the Sufi Master and poet Abu Sa'id admitted in the illumination of his heart that, "I am nobody, son of nobody." Along the wave between eternity and eternity, how can it be that any existence can claim so small a title as to be named in separation from the source of all that is? Even words float and then dissipate as nebular echoes in the hidden hall leading to the secret garden in which there is the fountain of our origin. Alhamdulillah, may all find a living guide to show them the way of unveiling through the cosmos.

Hamid Edson

Bismellah-i Rahman-er Rahim.

Hamid Hank Edson was born in San Francisco in 1967 and grew up in Marin County, a child of the positive ideals of the 1960's, which were reinforced by the community of the local Unitarian church, and the good schools and engaged neighbors where he lived. He was and continues to be also greatly nurtured and influenced by his life-long connection to a small section of forest-land owned by his father bordering a lake in Northern Wisconsin. Graduating from Stanford University with a degree in English literature, Hamid aspired to be a writer, spending time living abroad, before becoming a public school teacher. During his time abroad, Hamid experienced an awakening embrace of life's spiritual dimension and upon his return home he first encountered the world of Sufism and the great Sufi Masters, Dr. Nahid Angha and Shah Nazar Seyyed Dr. Ali Kianfar. Under the guidance of these two teachers, Hamid's character and being grew stronger and straighter, and many times the protection of his teacher's wisdom prevented him from falling into all kinds of error. Hamid went back to law school in his 30's and eventually self-published a volume of poetry, *A Brave New Worldview;* an illustrated poem, *The Deer;* a political treatise, *The Declaration of the Democratic Worldview*; and a work of political non-fiction, *Radical Equality.* In all of these books, much of what is best achieves what it does by virtue of the influence of his Sufi teachers and their teacher, Moulana Shah Maghsoud.

During his 40's, Hamid married Ingrid Catherine Rulifson, a scientist, and together they had a son, Wyatt Henry Edson. Hamid, Ingrid and Wyatt then moved to Palo Alto, started a garden and were exceedingly happy to have set down roots in a wonderful community. Hamid opened his own business as a family law mediator called Family Tree Mediation. His wife, Ingrid, continued her impressive career as a principal scientist running a diabetes research lab at the biotech firm, Amgen. At the time of this writing, Hamid and his family enjoy these great blessings and strive and seek to build a wholesome, stable, and spiritually connected home and life for each other, their community and their world.

174

Looking back on nearly 20 years of blessings as a student of Dr. Angha and Dr. Kianfar at this time, Hamid is grateful for the countless opportunities they have given him to be a participant in the great effort of service Dr. Angha and Dr. Kianfar have advanced through their organization, the International Association of Sufism. To Hamid, the wisdom and guidance of Dr. Angha and Dr. Kianfar very much possess transformative power of alchemy. His world has been irreversibly improved by the experience and understanding they have provided. Peace, beauty, intention, patience, discipline, honesty, purity, balance, knowledge, love and service are just some of the most important elements of the spiritual path Dr. Angha and Dr. Kianfar have taught and helped Hamid to strive to embody. By divine grace and the light of these teachers, may Hamid become a true Sufi, a true servant of God, and an honorable testament to the profound legacy of Dr. Angha, Dr. Kianfar, Moulana Shah Maghsoud and all the masters of the Uwaiysi school of Sufism.

Lorne Falk

Lorne Falk is a Five College visiting associate professor of contemporary art, theory, and criticism who teaches courses at Hampshire College and Amherst College in Western Massachusetts. He has worked in the arts and education for 40 years. His experience is international, interdisciplinary and transcultural. His interests include the contemporary visual and media arts, digital culture, cultural theory and criticism, and curatorial practice. Among the issues that burn brightly for him now are the challenges of interdisciplinary research and creation, ethical imagining, our relationship to the environment, the generation of strong local communities in global culture, the creative application of compassion, generosity and serious play, and the instrumental role of the liberal arts in all of these domains.

Lorne has written and published more than 60 essays and produced 19 catalogues and books. He has curated more than 150 exhibitions, including 8 major projects. He was Dean of Faculty at the School of the Museum of Fine Arts (SMFA) in Boston from 2001 to 2008. From 1997 to 2000, he was Associate Professor (design theory and criticism) at the School of

Design, the Hong Kong Polytechnic University. From 1989 to 1994, he was a Program Director at the Banff Centre for the Arts, where he created and directed an international multidisciplinary residency program for artists and scholars with themes such as Rhetoric Utopia and Technology, Nomad, and Living at the End of Nation States. From 1978 to 1985, he was Director and Chief Curator of the Walter Phillips Gallery at The Banff Centre for the Arts in Canada. He was Director-Curator of The Photographers Gallery in Saskatoon, Canada from 1973 to 1977.

Susan Ferdowsali

Susan Ferdowsali was born on August 12th, 1965 to Seyedeh Sorror Aghdas Safavi Eghtedar and Mohammad Kazem Ferdowsali in Shiraz, Iran. She was born to family whose ancestral roots can be traced back to the Prophet Mohammad (PBUH) and the Safavid Dynasty. Growing up in Shiraz, Susan was exposed to the poetry and teachings of Hafiz, Saadi, Rumi and Khayyam. She became enraptured by the beautiful words of these great masters and began her quest to understand what exactly this Divine ecstasy was that had so moved these great men, what kind of longing they were talking about that even the king's presence paled in comparison. Susan left Iran at the age of ten, and eventually immigrated to the United States, where she put herself through school, never ceasing her search for the Beloved. She married and has two beautiful daughters, Rosheen and Sarveen. Susan then went back to school and gained her B.A. in Psychology from Dominican University of California. It was during her time in Marin County that Susan became exposed to International Association of Sufism.

It was with the International Association of Sufism that Susan began to find her spiritual path to the Beloved, finally beginning to clearly understand what the poets of Shiraz were describing. She had learned only the superficial meanings of the poems until she found the Quran in San Rafael and the direct instructions of how to fulfill this longing through the guidance and teachings of her Holy Masters Seyyedeh Dr. Nahid Angha, Shah Nazar Seyyed Dr. Ali Kianfar and Moulana Shah Maghsoud of Uwaiysi Tarighat. It was only then that she began to understand the depth and teachings of these great Sufi Saints, through the verses of the Holy Quran, that constantly instruct one to return back to oneself.

Invigorated by this understanding, and with the help of her Holy Teachers, Susan helped found the Persian American Association of Northern California (PAANC), with the goal of bridging the gap between Persian-American youth and their heritage. It is her ultimate goal to share her knowledge and culture with generations to come. She continues to work for and support the PAANC and IAS and is relentless in her pursuit to understand Allah.

Leili First, Ph.D.

Who I Am and What I Do

From my earliest memories, I understood that ultimately my own value would be based on what I do with my life, especially in terms of career choices. I learned from my parents, by their words and examples, that it is important to be honest and work hard, to follow the rules and pick up after myself. As a young student I knew that I needed to do well in school, that academic subjects were more important than sports and electives, and that social activities and playtime were secondary to work and study. My early education and training prepared me well for what I do, but who I am remained largely a mystery, and I was without the tools or direction for this discovery.

A great gift and blessing brought me to the path of Sufism, at a time in my life in which I felt as the lowest of the low, following all the rules and instructions of my childhood, yet feeling lost and lonely. My search for religion had led me to a church – I appreciated the rituals and the fellowship, but it didn't extend far beyond a few hours on Sundays, and the teachings did not satisfy either my intelligence or the longing in my soul. The separation of church and state continued all the way to a separation between religion and state of being. Like so many others, I had become accustomed to living my life in separate, disconnected compartments for each type of activity.

In our modern society filled with consumerism, competition and comparison, the beauty of creation and the treasure of human beings are easily overwhelmed, hidden under desires for transitory goods and fleeting fame and fortune. So often the lessons we learn at home, in school, and from examples in our ever-present media focus on how to succeed in the sense of having more prestige, money, and stuff. It is no wonder I felt empty and alone, and without direction.

Following the Sufi path to wisdom and becoming a member of the International Association of Sufism (IAS) have changed the way I know myself and the way I see the world and my place in it. Giving primacy to my quest for knowledge of who I am allows the wisdom of the universe to unfold within me, providing a new perspective.

For many years I have been under the guidance and direction of Seyyedeh Dr. Nahid Angha and Shah Nazar Seyyed Dr. Ali Kianfar, co-founders and co-directors of IAS. During this time I have been inspired by their examples of wisdom, love and dedication in action. Through their lives they are examples of people elevated to the status of true human beings. As some of their behaviors and knowledge have transferred to me, I began to understand the need and gift of service.

All of the works of IAS are built upon the principles of Sufism, celebrating the gift of human life by providing examples and opening conversations on how we might all move towards raising the level of civilization, individually and collectively. IAS honors believers of all kinds, and those who give service for humanity. I have been privileged to take part in IAS seminars, conferences and programs emphasizing the uniqueness and value of each person, and speaking out against injustice, standing for the rights of those who are oppressed, especially women and children. I have been deeply touched as I observed individuals come to accept themselves. I have been in rooms with diverse people who would not ordinarily come together; however, in the context of an event such as the Sufism Symposium, the atmosphere of respect for all generates fruitful discussion. The knowledge and opportunities for service that I have received have instilled in me both a desire and an obligation to share with others. I have discovered that the more I invest my energy in service to humanity, the more I receive.

How much I have grown and learned since my childhood days! Most importantly I have learned that a human being is inherently valuable, and that I improve my own sense of self-value by increasing my self-knowledge. One challenge that has been especially difficult has been controlling my mind and teaching it that it cannot be in charge – it must be under the control of the wisdom of my heart. As I was brought up with a strong emphasis on the rational and intellectual, it has also required a concerted effort to accept the whole of myself, learning to appreciate beauty, music, movement, and friendship. Without diminishing my intelligence, I have found great joy in other creative aspects within me and I have come to experience my connections with other people and the whole world. I have discovered gratitude. I know the changes within myself have effected positive changes in those around me.

I have become a generous and compassionate daughter and friend. I strive not to stand in judgment, of myself or of others. I appreciate the gift of my life, and enjoy the time I spend investing in myself and improving my surroundings. I continue in my life-long quest for self-knowledge, with faith that this is possible and hope that I will achieve it in my lifetime. I am learning to distinguish between my ego-self and essential-self, and to trust the latter. I work towards a deeper kind of honesty, seeing myself as I am so I can nurture the better qualities in me and correct the lesser ones.

At this time, I am free from career obligations, and free to choose how I spend my time. Rather than worrying about fame and fortune, my time is better invested focusing on who I am, and from this what I do will follow naturally and harmoniously.

Heidi Gilpin, Ph.D.

Heidi Gilpin is an Associate Professor of German, European Studies, Architectural Studies, and Film and Media Studies at Amherst College in Amherst, Massachusetts. She has served as chair of the program in Architectural Studies, chair of the program in European Studies, and chair of the department of German, as well as co-chair of the Five College Architectural Studies Council. She has taught as an associate professor of Comparative Literature and Cultural Studies at the University of Hong Kong, and as an assistant professor of Dance History and Theory at the University of California-Riverside. She holds a Ph.D. and M.A. in Comparative Literature from Harvard University, and has lectured and published internationally on perception, memory, trauma, movement, and performance in literature, dance, film, electronic and visual arts, and architecture. Her book *Architectures*

of *Disappearance*, and her edited book *The Senses in Motion*, are both forthcoming from The MIT Press. Since 1984, she has been a member of the International Association of Sufism and a student of Sufism under the guidance and wisdom of Sufi masters Shah Nazar Seyyed Ali Kianfar, Ph.D., and Seyyedeh Nahid Angha, Ph.D., of the Uwaiysi school of Sufism, in the lineage of Hazrat Moulana Shah Maghsoud Sadegh Angha, 20th century master of the Uwaiysi school of Sufism. A member of the Sufi Women Organization since its founding in 1993, she has assisted with many issues of the journal *Sufism: An Inquiry* since its beginnings in 1987, and has served as a moderator for nearly all of the IAS Sufism Symposia since the first symposium in 1994.

Jamal Lawrence Granick, Ph.D.

Jamal is a student of Sufism, a psychotherapist, and an educator. Originally from New York City, he moved to California in 1982. His first career was as a cook in upscale boutique restaurants in New York and the Bay Area, switching careers midlife to pursue his profession as a therapist.

Jamal was initially introduced to Sufism through the Mevlevi practice of turning in 1971, as part of an eclectic spiritual group in New York that also offered the teachings of both the Shankaracharya Advaita Vedanta tradition from India, and those of the Russian mystical philosopher P.D. Ouspensky. He met his Teachers, Seyyedeh Dr. Nahid Angha and Shah Nazar Seyyed Dr. Ali Kianfar in 1994, under whose guidance he has been a student of Uwaiysi Sufism since. Under their direction, he has participated in the activities of the International Association of Sufism, as a member of the Executive Committee, a co-director of the Sufism and Psychology Forum, and most recently, a facilitator of the 40 Days: Alchemy of Tranquility® program for psycho-spiritual Self development. He has also presented at the Annual Sufism Symposia, both in the United States and internationally, in Barcelona and Edinburgh.

Jamal has been a licensed Marriage and Child Therapist since 2001 practicing in the San Francisco Bay Area. His approach to therapy is integrative and holistic, focusing on clients' optimal development as whole persons, including mind, body, and spirit. Deeply influenced by the teachings of Dr. Angha and Dr. Kianfar, he sees his clients as more than "the sum of their parts" whose potential far exceeds the normative conception of human development in traditional Western psychology. Recently, his work has also been guided by somatic approaches that track subjective experience through its non-verbal, as well as verbal, communication, and help to achieve resolution of historically habituated maladaptive patterns by bringing awareness to their expression in the present moment.

Subsequently he obtained a Ph.D. in Transpersonal Psychology from the Institute of Transpersonal Psychology in 2011. His doctoral research focused on the presence of the psychotherapist as a factor in effective therapy. A significant finding of his research was that clients who perceive their therapists as highly present can experience pivotal moments in therapy in which the therapist's presence can evoke optimal states of healing. After graduating, Jamal accepted a position as an Assistant Professor at ITP (now Sofia University) in the Masters in Counseling Psychology program. He specializes in teaching classes in fundamental counseling skills emphasizing therapist presence.

Jamal also has a 30+ years martial arts practice, focusing primarily on Aikido, and including Chinese internal arts. He has studied with many teachers, both in New York and California, and has obtained the rank of 4th degree black-belt in Aikido. Jamal lives with his wife, Mary, who is also a student of Sufism and a psychotherapist. He met her and her two sons, Jonathan and Colin, then 10 and 12, in 1997. Both boys have grown into fine young men who currently live in New York.

Mary Toth Granick

Mary is a student of Uwaiysi Sufism and a member of the International Association of Sufism. She has contributed articles in the *SPF Newsletter* and the journal, *Sufism: An Inquiry*. She is one of the co-authors of the book, *Human Self, Volume 1:Body*. She has also presented her work with Sufism and Psychology at various retreats in the Bay Area.

Mary was born and raised in the Chicago area, and she lived in Illinois until 1990, when she moved to California. She became interested in and

drawn to work with a mission towards social justice and serving humanity from the time she was in high school. When she graduated from college, she'd had a variety of work experiences, including community organizing in Chicago and working in various social service agencies. She went on to pursue her Masters Degree in Education and worked as an educator, teaching English composition and literature in high school and community college settings for many years.

After her move to California, and while raising her two sons, Mary became interested in psychology. In 1994, she went back to school to get her second Masters Degree, this time in Counseling Psychology. She then continued working towards her licensure as a Marriage and Family Therapist, and has been practicing as a licensed clinician since 2000. She currently maintains a private practice with offices in San Francisco and Albany, where she works with individual adults, couples, adolescents, and their families. She also has extensive experience and a background in school-based counseling services in various settings in the Bay Area.

Mary has had a lifelong interest in spirituality, beginning with her Catholic upbringing and education in parochial schools throughout high school. She attributes her passion for social justice and the opportunities for service in part to both her family life and education. In her early 20's, her spiritual quest deepened, and she spent a year studying the Bible and growing in her Christian faith. Mary was introduced to Uwaiysi Sufism and her teachers, Dr. Nahid Angha, and Dr. Ali Kianfar, by her husband, Jamal Granick, who was their student. She is grateful for the opportunities to serve on various committees and programs for the International Association of Sufism, and for the wisdom and dedication of her teachers, who for her, are the perfect mirror of living a life dedicated to humanity and a love for the divine.

Ali Haji

Ali Haji was born and raised in Karachi, Pakistan. After completing high school in Karachi, he moved to the United States in 1984 to pursue higher education, earning his Undergraduate Degree from the Wharton School at the University of Pennsylvania in 1988 and his MBA from the Anderson School at UCLA in 1999.

Ali is a student of the Uwaiysi School of Sufism under the guidance of Sufi Teachers, Dr. Nahid Angha and Shah Nazar Seyyed Dr. Ali Kianfar. He is a member of the International Association of Sufism and an Executive Committee member of the Institute for Sufi Studies. Ali has served as moderator at IAS's annual Sufism Symposia. He has also participated in local poetry readings of classical Sufi poetry in the Marin County community as well as at Dominican University.

Ali is an insurance professional with 20 plus years in the insurance industry. He was recently the Vice President of Commercial Program Business at Fireman's Fund Insurance Company.

In his free time, Ali is an avid tennis player and has served on the Rolling Hills Tennis Board and the Pioneer Park Tennis Board, both in Novato, California. He is married to Nafisa Haji, writer and educator. With their son, Khalil, they live in Bodrum, Turkey.

Nafisa Haji, Ed.D.

Nafisa was born and mostly raised in Los Angeles—mostly, because there were years also spent in Chicago, Karachi, Manila, and London. Her family migrated from Bombay to Karachi in 1947 during Partition, when the Indian Subcontinent was divided into two states. In the late 1960s, Nafisa's parents came to the United States, shortly before she was born. When she was six years old, her parents stuck with their original plan of "going back home" and moved to Karachi. In less than a year, they knew that they had become more American than they realized and came back to Los Angeles.

Nafisa studied American history at the University of California at Berkeley, taught elementary school in downtown Los Angeles for seven years in a bilingual Spanish program (she speaks Spanish fluently), and earned a doctorate in educational leadership from the University of California at Los Angeles with a dissertation that involved research on caring, long-term relationships between teachers and students.

With an unfinished novel left long behind, she seized upon the birth of her son—when she decided to stay home full-time—as an excuse to go back to writing, learning to use nap times and weekends very efficiently. She started writing short stories at first, which then developed into an idea for her first novel.

Nafisa has represented the International Association of Sufism on the board at the Marin Interfaith Council, serving one year as Board President. She has also served on the board of Freedom Forward, an organization working to ensure the alignment of American ideals of freedom with the reality of American foreign policy. Nafisa is the author of two novels, *The Writing on My Forehead* and *The Sweetness of Tears*, both published by HarperCollins, and is hard at work on several more. Her work has been translated into more than 20 languages.

Nafisa is honored to be a student of Sufism under the guidance of her teachers, Seyyedeh Dr. Nahid Angha and Seyyed Shah Nazar Dr. Ali Kianfar. She currently lives in Turkey with her husband and son, but maintains close ties in Pakistan and California, traveling to both places regularly to visit family.

Arife Ellen Hammerle, Ph.D., MA, LMFT, JD

Dr. Arife Hammerle is a student of the Uwaiysi School of Sufism, as guided by Sufi Teachers Seyyedeh Dr. Nahid Angha and Shah Nazar Seyyed Dr. Ali. Kianfar. She is a member of the International Association of Sufism and Sufi Women Organization. She sits on the Executive Committee Board of the Institute for Sufi Studies where she teaches classes in Meditation, Psychology, Stress Management and Workshops with the 40 Days Alchemy of Tranquility® Program. Her spiritual practice and teaching are integral aspects of her work as a psychotherapist and Director of social services programs. Dr. Hammerle is a licensed Marriage and Family Therapist who holds a Doctorate in Clinical Psychology and is a psychotherapist with the Community Healing Centers, an integrative psychotherapy non-profit organization. She specializes in work with clients with psycho-spiritual issues. She co-founded Community Healing Centers which provides psychotherapeutic services to individuals, couples and families while overseeing psychotherapeutic interns pursing licensure. She started this practice and obtained non-profit status for it to provide low fee services to clients and develop an internship program for advanced level professionals sustaining an integrative psychotherapeutic treatment approach. Her oversight of program performance and management goals has allowed her to develop a fiscally viable and effective program that supports healing through a psychotherapeutic approach that effectively brings together psychology and spirituality.

Her knowledge, skills and abilities include work experience in the fields of community mental health, teaching experience and academic achievement of a Master's and Doctorate in clinical psychology. She is also skilled in managing long-term relationships, working effectively to build collaborations and negotiate for positive social change. Dr. Hammerle has developed strategies on HIV/AIDS issues and problems allowing her to become capable of complex negotiations. She has supervised Masters and Doctoral level students in their licensure process and taught academic classes to a diverse range of students. She is capable and comfortable working with diverse populations with confidence, confidentiality and the ability to work on multiple projects at a time to advance health care and positively impact the homelessness and lives of her students, staff and clients.

She has served on the Pro Bono Committee following her work serving on the MCAMFT Board for several years as the Board Secretary. Dr. Hammerle is a published author who has completed research linking psychology and spirituality. She is frequently called upon to give lectures and lead workshops in psychology and spirituality. Dr. Hammerle has extensive training and experience in managing Non-Profit Community Based Organizations with a specialization in the area of homelessness, women and families, and HIV/AIDS treatment and prevention. She is knowledgeable about building training programs and psychological healthcare infrastructure in resource constrained environments. As Division Director for Catholic Charities, she has worked tirelessly for over fifteen years in developing, overseeing and monitoring program development and special projects. The primary populations she has worked with are underserved, impoverished, homeless, multiply diagnosed, racially and culturally diverse HIV positive women living in San Francisco. During her tenure, she has cultivated collaborations with Doctors, Nurses, Psychotherapists and resource partners in the San Francisco HIV/AIDS services community to build resources for positive women and their families. Her programs serve as integral partners with the Centers of Excellence and Family Service Network Collaborative. Her work has been dedicated to develop successful intervention strategies to sustain programs and services through planning and revenue strategy development, contract negotiations and overall operations.

Dr. Hammerle's law training and experience supports her current work by affording her an invaluable skill of diplomacy and critical thinking with an understanding of the legal process. During law school and post law school employment, she was responsible for investigating abuse and neglect, public policy and federal regulatory procedures. All of her legal work has been integrated into her experience as a Division Director and Psychotherapist. The current emphasis in her work is on the integration of Western Psychology and mystical wisdom teachings. Her practice is integrative of body, mind and spirit. She possesses a broad range of professional experience which enriches her psychotherapeutic skills. She has extensive experience working with stress management, communication skill development within relationships, mediation, meditation, chronic illness and parent-infant work. Dr. Hammerle specializes in working with individuals and couples to cultivate communication, healing and transformation. She has cultivated a balance between program operations, management, teaching and adherence to policy supported by her capacity for insight, empathy and compassion that education, spirituality and social service affords our community.

Said Hassan

I was born in Baghdad, Iraq, the youngest in a family with three children – a brother and a sister. I completed elementary and high school before leaving Iraq to come the United States to pursue higher education. I was nineteen when I left and had a working knowledge of the English language.

One of my fond memories from the years I spent in Iraq was listening to Qur'anic recitation on daily basis. In most Middle Eastern countries and in North Africa, Muslims watch on television and listen on the radio to live recitations and recordings of professional Qur'an reciters who use one of two

186

basic styles: tartil or tajwid. In tartil the recitation is restrained and without melodic elaboration. In tajwid the style is more expanded and flourishing. When the verse is too long, the reciter sometimes pauses between each breath before beginning another long breath of recitation.

My undergraduate studies ended after I received two BS degrees in engineering - one in Mechanical and the second in Electrical engineering. My first fulltime job in the US was with an electronic firm in Chicago, Illinois. It was in Chicago where I became a naturalized US citizen, and a year later got married there.

I left the company after ten years to join a multi-national diversified company located in Bloomington, Indiana, and a year later, I transferred to San Jose, California for a better job opportunity. My employment with this company also lasted ten years.

My third and last employer was a national research lab located in California, where I worked for eighteen years until retirement.

Throughout my adult life, I was always interested in reading topics related to economic issues, such as the role of the Federal Reserve System in controlling the pace of the economy, the benefits of international trade, the functions of the banking system, etc. I finally decided to go to night school and get an MA in Economics to understand the theories and principles used in macro and micro economics.

My earliest exposure to Sufism was when I was in Baghdad. Throughout elementary school years, my family lived about two miles from the shrine of the famous Sufi Master Shaikh Abdul-Kadir Gilani, who was born in Gilan, Persia and died in Baghdad (1077-1166 CE). I used to ride around the large complex on my bicycle as I watched buses full of happy pilgrims from many Asian countries excited to have finally arrived safely after a long and tedious journey from their home countries. Air travel was not widely used at that time. The Kadiriyya School of Sufism is well known in the Asian continent and has many ardent followers to this day. The Twentieth-century Sufi Master Bawa Muhaiyaddeen, who was born in Sri Lanka, belonged to the Kadiriyya School of Sufism.

Even though I lived close to a thriving Sufi community early in life, neither I nor my family practiced Sufism. We had superficial knowledge of this mystical core of Islam, and were not attracted to it. This attitude of indifference continued throughout most of my adult life in the United States.

This all changed about seventeen years ago when I was going through a period of doubt and self-examination. It was brought about by disenchantment with life in general, as I felt there was a lack of meaning and purpose of human existence. I began to read books and scriptures of world religions hoping to find satisfactory answers to my dilemma, "why are we here?"

After a few years of search and evaluation, which sometimes gave rise to unexpected intuitions, dreams and other experiences that cannot be explained rationally, I gradually began to feel a measure of comfort and satisfaction when I was reading books about Sufism, and especially about the lives and teachings of the great Sufi masters.

Every Sufi book I read mentioned the important role a spiritual teacher plays in guiding and inspiring a student on the inner journey. Without a teacher, the narratives maintained, a seeker stands little chance to make meaningful progress to reach the goal, namely nearness to the Creator.

One day I came across a blurb in the Saturday Religion edition of the San Jose Mercury News announcing a Sufi Symposium to be held in Newark on the following Friday, Saturday and Sunday. The name of the group sponsoring the symposium was the International Association of Sufism (IAS). I thought it would be an excellent opportunity for me to observe Sufis in action and, hopefully, get to meet a Sufi Teacher in the meetings.

I attended all three days of the Symposium and was impressed and inspired by the quality of the talks, the enchanting music of Taneen, and the friendliness and welcoming attitude of the participants. I also felt a great honor and privilege when I met my teachers Dr. Nahid Angha and Dr. Ali Kianfar on the second day. Since that first exposure to a Sufi gathering, I have attended every IAS Symposium held in the Bay Area.

The best way I can summarize my attitude toward Sufism now is that it is not a philosophy, not an organized religion, but a way of life. If one insists on calling it religion, then it can best be described as a religion of love. The Qur'anic verse the Sufis often cite reads, "He loves them, and they love Him" [5-54]. This leads to the notion that God is both the Lover of humanity and their Beloved. This in turn leads to the principle of Divine Unity (Tawhid), which is best described by the statement, "There is no god but Him", (La elaha ella Huwa) [3-18]. One can readily derive from this statement that all spiritual paths lead to One God.

I have heard several of my fellow students maintain that the universality and inclusiveness of the Sufi teachings is one of the attributes that attracts and inspires them. This quality is of great value, especially today, because it is a spiritual path for all peoples and cultures, and for all seekers of truth. It certainly fills the void in my life, which I felt before joining IAS, and adds meaning and purpose to human existence.

Sheikha Halima JoAnn Haymaker

Sheikha Halima JoAnn Haymaker is a member of the Uwaiysi Sufi Tarighat and a student of Seyyedeh Nahid Angha, Ph.D., and Shah Nazar Seyyed Ali Kianfar, Ph.D. She was introduced to her Holy Masters by her son, Hamid John Hank Edson, who had already become their student.

Sheikha Halima serves on the Executive Committee of the International Association of Sufism, headquartered in Novato, California. She is a member of the Sufi Women' Organization and leads interfaith meditation groups and retreats for women at the Institute for Sufi Studies. She has been a speaker at International Sufi Symposia and has made presentations on Islam and Sufism at schools, organizations, Rotary Clubs and churches in Marin and Sonoma Counties. Her articles have appeared in the journal *Sufism: An Inquiry* and the online journal of Grace Cathedral in San Francisco, www.grace.com in addition to the *Pacific Sun* and *News Pointer* newspapers.

She attended Radcliffe/Harvard and Northwestern Universities and received a B.A. and M.A. in English from the University of Pennsylvania. She received a National Defense Fellowship for three years of work toward a Ph.D. degree in English at Penn and completed all requirements except for the dissertation. She taught in the English Departments at Rochester (Minnesota) Community College Evening School, College of Marin, Indian Valley College and in both the English and Business Departments at Dominican University of California.

For 27 years she served as a Consultant in fund raising, organizational development, board and staff training, conference and event planning, grant writing and public relations for more than 75 non-profit organizations in Northern California. Previously she was an editor for a legal publishing company, served on the staff of several Marin County, California non-profit organizations, and worked for a County of Marin substance abuse treatment diversion program. She also worked for the Marin County Commission on the Status of Women. She has been a guest lecturer on grant writing and fund raising at San Francisco State and Sonoma State Universities. She has presented numerous workshops and training sessions at College of Marin and for the Marin Council of Agencies, the Non-Profit Management Association and the Volunteer Centers of Marin and Sonoma Counties. She has been a frequent speaker at churches throughout the area.

In addition to court ordered diversion groups for arrested drug and alcohol offenders, she has presented journal keeping workshops, groups for women, singles and cancer patients in Marin County churches, community centers, hospitals, counseling centers, drug and alcohol treatment centers and in the Marin County Jail. She was appointed by the Marin County Board of Supervisors to the Alcohol Advisory Board. She served on numerous boards of directors and received the Martin Luther King, Jr. Humanitarian Award from the Marin County Human Rights Commission for her work with the homeless through the Marin Interfaith Council and the Board of Directors of the Marin Housing Center (now Homeward Bound). She also received a Shining Star Award from Marin Services for Women.

Halima is married to Will Haymaker, has an elder son, Barton William Edson and two grandsons, as well as two step-children and two step-grandsons.

Sheikha Halima states: "Since becoming a Sufi student, the years have been filled with learning, gratitude and service. I have experienced many blessings in health, balance, peace and deep contentment. These blessings have extended to every member of my family. I have learned a new way of being in the world and what it means to be a Human Being. I was honored to receive from my Holy Teachers the name Halima, the name of the nurse to the Holy Prophet Mohammad, peace be upon him. And later I was deeply honored to be given the title of Sheikha. My goal today is to be worthy of my name and title and to grow into the embodiment of these virtues, with increasing gratitude and continued remembrance of and submission to the

Divine. With thanks to my Holy Sufi Masters for their patience, guidance, understanding, wisdom and love."

Emily Hedges, M. Ed., Et/P

Bismellah-i Rahman-er Rahim.
In the Name of God, Most Gracious, Most Merciful.
It is with deep gratitude and appreciation to Holy Teachers, Seyyedeh Dr. Nahid Angha and Seyyed Dr. Ali Kianfar for the opportunity to submit my biography to this beautiful book. By their direct guidance on the path of the heart, my life's journey is bountiful and full of transformative blessings. I experience unending, truthful teachings and divine guidance, by their dedication and sincerity towards humanity.

I remember the first time I met my Holy Teachers. I was a young child. My mother dressed me in a new white dress and to this day I can recall the joy and eagerness when experiencing their presence. The profound energy of love within my being at a young age is the same divine connection and yearning I treasure in the presence of my Teachers today.

I pleaded with my mother to attend Sufi Gatherings with her and to bring me into their presence again. My young and pure heart yearned to receive their teachings and light, thus I followed my mother very closely and traveled by her side on the path of the divine. Being raised in a Sufi family under the guidance and direct lineage of Uwaiysi Sufi Masters is an eternal appreciation that words cannot describe.

As a young student, I received the honor to participate in the International Association of Sufism's Sufi Children's Program. We were a group of young children that met regularly with Sufi leaders that guided us in service projects, discussions, and opportunities to share experiences of the heart.

Soon after, I had the opportunity to participate in two Departments of the International Association of Sufism that support children and youth globally through direct service, equity and justice programs, and international awareness. Sufi Youth International and Voices for Justice, founded and directed by Seyyedeh Hamaseh Kianfar, Ph.D. and Seyyedeh Sahar Kianfar,

JD, Ph.D. are programs dedicated to the well-being of children and youth locally and globally. As a member of the Voices for Justice Department, I worked with youth leaders to advocate for the rights of children by providing a forum for public awareness through: education, community service, events and programs so that every child and every young adult has the opportunity to fulfill his or her highest potential. I am deeply appreciative for each chance I have had to learn and be guided in service work through various programs and departments of the International Association of Sufism.

It is with sincere gratitude to Seyyedeh Dr. Nahid Angha that I express appreciation for her generosity and beautiful magnetic teaching of the heartbeat meditation: a practice that has transformed my personal practice and spiritual path. The beauty of being called to listen to my own heartbeat, to be appreciative for each breath, and each beat has guided me to become more peaceful, appreciative, loving, and focused. Dr. Angha has taught me that during each moment of our lives, we are creating our book. We never have the opportunity to take out a page. It is this teaching that guides my journey. Each day I set an intention to be truthful to myself and honest on my path, to create a book that is worthy of the opportunity I have been granted. The 40 Days Alchemy of Tranquility Program, guided by Shah Nazar Seyyed Dr. Ali Kianfar, has transformed both my physical and spiritual being and has provided me with the stability and understanding of a daily meditation practice. The generosity of my Holy Teachers and their Sacred Family is unending and I am eternally grateful.

Emily Hedges, M.Ed., ET/P, currently works as an early childhood educator in the San Francisco Bay Area and is a practicing Professional Educational Therapist. Her passion is advocating for children's rights and an equitable and safe education system for all children.

Munir Hedges

In the Name of Love, Most Gracious, Praise Be to Wisdom, Most Merciful

We participate in this magnificent library of life. Every human being is a book. Every book is worth reading. Every book is a life and every life is worthy of living.

--Teacher, Sufi Master, Seyyedeh Dr. Nahid Angha

With profound appreciation and heartfelt love I recall moments of awakening. As it is customary to be introduced to a Sufi Master by way of a deserving, entrusted student, when I was invited to attend a gathering to study Sufism the term, Sufism, seemed unfamiliar. As truth unfolded, the essence of the gift of light was planted in my heart before the stage of thought and my search for a way to be close, to become closer to myself, I was shown, had been a steady and driving thirst with no name.

When Beloved Sufi Masters, Seyyedeh Dr. Nahid Angha and Shah Nazar Seyyed Dr. Ali Kianfar opened the door of Sufism to my heart, each one readied my being and graciously adjusted my first steps onto the divine pathway of *Uwaiysi Tariqat*. There are no words great enough with which to express gratitude for the breadth of this holy family Sufi Lineage and their extremely devoted sacrifice of approving my longing and becoming my Beloved Masters.

Dr. Nahid Angha invited me into her sacred world of Sufi poetry. As a guidance and pure blessing, Dr. Angha instilled the majesty of poetry into my heart by educating my being with extreme patience and care. I studied and learned, striving to follow her exemplary guidelines, while reviewing and tending to a number of her scholarly works and influential books on the subject of Sufism, as sole translator and author. This was a glorious time that continues.

It is a divine privilege to have been a founding member of the scholarly Journal, *Sufism: An Inquiry*, under the guidance and leadership of Dr. Nahid Angha and Dr. Ali Kianfar, Editors. Since the publication of Volume I, Issue 1 was presented to the world, this endeavor has been a great teacher for me as a way of understanding Sufi discipline, divine ethics and the integrity of writing and publishing. At the present time, September 2014, the fourth Online Journal XVI.4 is nearing publication. It is an honor, with appreciation, to be a member of the Journal Board.

The first Annual IAS Sufism Symposium held in 1994 in San Rafael, CA was blessed with an atmosphere of energy and generosity for guests, speakers, and members. Preparing for the first IAS Symposium under Dr. Nahid Angha's guidance was a significant time of discovery and awareness on my Sufi journey. IAS is now preparing to present the 20th Sufism Symposium to be held in San Rafael, CA, March 28th, 29th, 30th, 2015 where guests from all over the world will join in celebration.

Guided by Dr. Angha's esteemed wisdom, like-hearted Sufi women gathered to compose and formally submit the Sufi Women Code of Ethics, honoring the rights of women and children by establishing and conveying ways in which women may engage in outreach safely, securely and honorably as shown by Prophet Mohammad's example, pbuh. I am completely devoted to the educational rights of every woman and child. This right and expectation is a teaching instilled in the beings of my children.

East Bay Sufi Women, founded by Dr. Nahid Angha, is dedicated to beloved Sufi, Mah Talat Moghadam Etemad Angha, devoted educator and teacher. East Bay Sufi Women acknowledges and preserves the achievement of spiritual literacy. Meditation gatherings are held on select dates and include the study of Sufi poetry and Sufi stories with the serving of tea and sweets. Women and their children are welcome.

The IAS Literacy Program, founded by Dr. Angha, first began for young readers in San Rafael, CA at the community center during a summer program where I was honored to teach children in the primary grades the joy of reading, writing, and illustrating their own stories. The Literacy Program expands to the Greater Bay Area and internationally. Storytelling programs are also presented in libraries and community centers.

Under the guidance of Beloved Sufi Masters, my heart is grateful for the countless ways in which I am granted and afforded the gift of loving service.

You have it. It is with you. God would never create you and then leave you alone.
--Teacher, Sufi Master, Dr. Ali Kianfar

Jalal Brian Heery, Ph.D.

Dr. Heery holds a doctorate in Transpersonal Psychology. He has been exploring the interstices between the body, mind, and spirit since his early career as a world class gymnast and as assistant gymnastics coach at Stanford University. He wrote his dissertation on *Awakening Spirit in the Body* at The Institute of Transpersonal Psychology in 2003. He currently holds the rank of 4th degree black belt in Aikido and is the founder and current head instructor of Rocky Valley Aikido

Dojo in Menlo Park, CA. He is continuing his investigations as a student of Uwaiysi Sufism with Seyyedeh Dr. Nahid Angha and Shah Nazar Seyyed Dr. Ali Kianfar. He frequently gives presentations offering an experiential somatic component at the 40 Days: Alchemy of Tranquility® workshops. He has also presented workshops with Dr. Jamal Granick on the intersection between Sufism and Aikido (A Japanese martial art based on the principle of love). He has also been teaching mathematics to Middle school students for two decades and begins each mathematics class with a few moments of meditation and a student-read teaching story from one of the many wisdom traditions drawing students' hearts and minds into their study of mathematics.

Mary Hendrickson

I was born in 1953. I joined two older siblings, Jack, age twelve, and Barbara age three. I was a precocious toddler, daring and adventurous. If I was momentarily out of my caretaker's site, I likely was to be found trying to climb over or underneath the fence, on a table or piano top, or making mud pies in the garden. My earliest memory is walking down a hospital hallway, my hand being held by my sister Barbara. We found a spot to sit down and Barbara placed her ring, a golden band with a sparkling green gemstone on my finger. I felt loved and safe with Barbara.

Climbing had consequences. At 16 months curiosity led me to climb up into the master bedroom sink and turn on the hot water. My tears and screams for help were not immediately heard by my mother -- she was vacuuming in a distant part of our house. By the time she rescued me I had suffered third degree burns to my legs.

I spent the next five years in and out of hospitals undergoing surgeries to repair my legs. When I was three, my sister died of leukemia. My mother and father were devastated. They decided to sell the family home because it was a constant reminder of my sister's absence.

They bought a new home in a beautiful neighborhood surrounded by trees, near open hills, streams and lakes. My eyes were opened to the majesty and wonder of the natural world. My brother Jack moved away when

I was six years old. It was yet another loss. Jack left one early morning on his motorcycle bound for Mexico and for the next ten years he explored the World. Jack occasionally returned telling tales of adventure, romance and intrigue. He was my hero, and I yearned for his return as soon as he departed on his next journey.

My mother disappeared into her bedroom after my sister's passing. Much of my time was spent alone climbing trees, watching insects, catching butterflies, sitting on sandy creeksides and dipping my feet into the water while staring at the blue sky and watching the clouds pass by. I wondered about my sister and where she had gone.

My mother's Catholic faith became more important to her. She found solace in religion. Mother took me to church with her and enrolled me into Catholic school. I loved the feeling I found in our neighborhood St. Anselm's church. The smell of the incense, light streaming through stained glass windows, statues of Mary, Joseph, Jesus on the cross, the marble font of holy water, golden Eucharistic chalices, Stations of the Cross paintings, flickering prayer candles guarding the statues of saints, parishioners quietly praying their rosaries -- they all created a sense of mystery and captivated my young heart.

I soon felt a disconnection between institutional Church teachings of original, mortal and venial sins, hell, babies relegated to limbo, souls in purgatory and the beautiful notions of the Beatitudes and Jesus' Sermon on the Mount. My questions to priests and nuns were discouraged and my faith was shaken.

My relationship with my mother suffered. She insisted that I attend Mass and remain in Catholic school. My father was a spiritual, but not necessarily a religious man. He taught me concepts of social justice and introduced me to Plato, Aristotle, Emerson, Kant, and Jefferson. We discussed Thoreau, Whitman, T.S. Eliot and Willa Cather. Father encouraged me to memorize the Greek alphabet and the Declaration of Independence. He carefully cultivated a garden filled with fruit trees, roses, vines, and blooming flowers. Father shared his joy of being alive and his appreciation of our mortality. I loved and adored my father.

Much to my mother's sadness, I left the Catholic church at age 14. I still believed in a Divine Spirit. I prayed often and sensed God especially when in nature. I longed for a spiritual community, but doubted that there was a traditional church to nourish me.

Eventually I attended University, became an architect, married and had children. I experienced losses, ecstatic joys and emotional turmoil. Like my mother, through prayer I sought God's solace, sought desired outcomes and expressed my gratefulness to Him.

Life's greatest gifts are my children. As they matured I felt it important to give them a spiritual foundation. I wanted to expose them to the beautiful teachings of Christ and an authentic community of believers. We "church shopped" and found Unity church. Although Unity fell short of my vision of a spiritual community, my children received a positive church experience. I still sought spiritual nourishment.

An Indian family owned a local dry cleaning business. They identified as Sufis. Each time I dropped off or picked up my clothes I felt a magnetic peacefulness in their shop. That peacefulness caused me to linger. One day I picked up one of the magazines on Sufism and browsed through the articles. It was like finding a treasure. I found the spiritual path that my heart longed for.

My quest for a spiritual teacher began -- I visited many *Khaneghahs*. I listened to many teachers. Still, I did not feel the connection and sense of universal truth I sought. I kept searching. I resorted to the phone book and looked under the "Sufism" heading. There I found the International Association of Sufism. I called, Jamal answered, and he agreed to meet me. I spent several hours talking with Jamal. Our discussion was heartfelt and profound, tears streamed down my face. Jamal invited me to a Gathering being held the following weekend. I felt that I found what I was looking for and my life changed forever.

The Sufi path is not an easy one. Sufism is an active endeavor seeking self-awareness and authenticity, universal truth and beauty; it stresses service to others. Fifty years later, I appreciate that my Sufi practice complements my Father's wise words, quoting Shakespeare's Polonius, he often reminded me, "To thine own self be true." [*Hamlet*, Act 1 Scene 3].

Marilyn Kolakowski

Marilyn Kolakowski was born and raised in Ohio and attended Northern Michigan University. She lived in New York City and Dallas, Texas, for several years before permanently settling in the San Francisco Bay Area. She lived for many years in Oakland, California. Marilyn was a successful, self-employed graphic design artist. She worked for several major businesses and was one of

the main graphic designers for the International Association of Sufism for many years. Marilyn's sense of beauty and her peaceful spiritual nature were exhibited in her work in designing several books published by IAS publications, in her design work on numerous IAS fliers, brochures, and newsletters, and her participation in the design and layout of the world-renowned periodical, *Sufism: an Inquiry.*

Marilyn was student of Uwaiysi Sufism under the guidance of Seyyedeh Dr. Nahid Angha and Shah Nazar Seyyed Dr. Ali Kianfar. Marilyn was an active member of Sufi Women Organization and participated in the SWO prison project by visiting women inmates and teaching art at the county jail. In 2001 Marilyn received her Bachelor of Arts degree, graduating with highest honors from Mills College, in Oakland, California. She held a black belt in karate and had many talents and interests including music, yoga, hiking, and photography.

She passed away in 2008 and is greatly missed.

Rahmana Lynn Larkin

"You think you are a small body, yet within you lies the greater Universe"
--Amir al Momenin Ali

Looking back on my life I can see that the search for my true self has been a theme since childhood. This search led me to psychology and spirituality and ultimately to Sufism and the International Association of Sufism (IAS). It was at IAS where I found guidance for my journey with the wise teachings of Shah Nazar Seyyed Dr. Ali Kianfar and Seyyedeh Dr. Nahid Angha.

Growing up in a military family I moved ten times before I reached the age of 18. With each move I stepped into a new environment in which others did not have preconceived notions of who I was. I felt isolated being the new kid and a priority for me was always to figure out how to fit in. I found myself redefining the image I wanted to present in the new school by trying to predict what my peers would find acceptable. This produced a fluctuating sense of self-identity, as I would move from the diverse cultures of Mobile, Alabama to the San Francisco Bay area and then on to the east coast, Washington D.C. area, in a matter of 4 years. I knew these images I was presenting were not me and occasionally had glimpses of a deeper part of myself that was unchangeable and much more peaceful. My search for this part that I now see as my essence, or true self, led me to the world of psychology and to an exploration of a variety of spiritual perspectives.

I went on to become a psychotherapist to help others in their journey but psychology alone could not provide me with the answers to finding my true self. I read widely on spiritual topics and explored a variety of religions but none of them ever felt like the right fit until I met Dr. Kianfar in 1999. Although I could tell immediately this was a man of tremendous wisdom whom I could learn a lot from, I was initially hesitant since Sufism and Islam seemed so foreign to me. I was able to accept Dr. Kianfar as my teacher because in our first meeting he made it clear I did not have to follow any doctrines or accept any beliefs but rather his role was to lead me to myself.

Over the next several years others in the Seattle group and I arranged a series of interfaith talks to help other faiths share in the wisdom of Dr. Kianfar that transcends all faiths. We also arranged retreats so we could immerse ourselves in his wisdom and were able to help arrange two International Sufism Symposia in the Seattle area. Over the years I had the honor of speaking on the Sufism and Psychology Forum at two of these Symposia. In 2007 I was a part of a group of IAS psychotherapists who, under the guidance of Dr. Kianfar, put together a series of workshops (titled 40 Days) for psychotherapists and the general public to help apply principles of Sufism in a practical way to help improve general mental health.

The wisdom of Sufism as taught by Shah Nazar Seyyed Ali Kianfar and Seyyedeh Nahid Angha has helped me personally to achieve a greater state of inner peace and helped me professionally in my work with clients. They have provided accurate guidance as well as spiritual and emotional support. Through them I have learned about unconditional love and that I am much more than this small body. All my life I have sensed that there is a part of me much greater than my images and Sufism provided the specific steps with which to make this discovery.

Salim George Matchette

"And those who persevere in constant remembrance are three groups of people: the thoughtful and reflective ones who are accompanied by self confidence, then those who remember God and are accompanied by sincerity, and finally the insightful who are accompanied by spiritual poverty."[16]

A student of Sufism is fortunate to have any opportunity to serve and it is not up to him or her to make any claim regarding it. The facts are that my first exposure to the International Association of Sufism (IAS) was at the second international symposium held in 1995. I remember I had a serious case of bronchitis, which I seemed then to contract annually. Normally, I would have spent the time at home recovering, but instead I bundled up and made my way to a hotel in San Francisco. By the end of the event, I felt much better and hoped to have the opportunity to learn more.

During the next year and continuing to this day, I was given the opportunity to participate in the Sufi Music Ensemble called Taneen, translated into English as divine melody from Farsi. As a group, we have been permitted to develop melodies from a sampling of the rich poetry that is one of the lasting and ever present legacies of Sufism. We were even more fortunate to have much of this poetry translated by Dr. Nahid Angha, whose sensitivity and intelligence has imported the meaning of Sufi poetry into the English language for the first time. Over the years, Taneen has been given many opportunities to perform this music both in the United States and internationally, but only through the grace of IAS and the help of its Executive Directors and membership.

I have also had the opportunity to participate in the development of the Community Healing Centers (CHC), with psychotherapy offices in Marin and San Francisco, California. Again, we have been rewarded by guidance of the IAS founders in learning how principals of Sufism can assist in the healing of those who come to us for treatment. More importantly, CHC has established a presence in the field of transpersonal psychology, including newsletters, clinical training, and more recently assistance in launching the 40 Days program, a transformational and multi-disciplined effort guided by

200

Dr. Ali Kianfar, Ph.D. I also want to thank Arife Hammerle, who has served as clinical director for CHC for many years, and Amineh Pryor who has developed many of the public programs.

My contributions to the efforts of Taneen and CHC are very modest and I would point you to the teachers and the teachings that have made the many activities of IAS possible. It is my belief that the grace of IAS and the success of its many departments reflect the deep spirituality and full development of Shah Nazar Seyyed Ali Kianfar and Seyyedeh Dr. Nahid Angha who carry forth the light of *la illaha, illHa Allah, Mohammadan rasul-ullah*. From their chest, they constantly are disseminating the truth of what it is to be human and how one can develop to that station. In this regard, I am nothing and know nothing, but hold tight my gratitude and persistence.

Salima Ginny Patton Matchette

Looking back at my life, taking into account all aspects of my mind-body-spirit self, I see that what began and then continued as significant aspirations or callings originated from one seed – a seed planted in my core, at birth. From this one seed seemingly diverse sproutings emerged, developing into increasingly defined branches or aspects of these aspirations: to be a useful servant – having a strong desire to be useful, to use my innate and learned gifts to serve, to be of good purpose; to become an ardent admirer of and active participant in the creative arts; to be a trustworthy friend and partner – wanting meaningful, loving human connection; to be a lover and protector of nature – feeling a profound connection with and responsibility to non-human creation; to continue as a spiritual seeker – seeking to find deeper meaning in the seen and unseen.

The strong but developing desire to be useful in my work has, over time, grown with many twists and turns, often with detours taken in order to support myself financially – but always with the underlying questions: Am I being useful? Is what I am doing serving a useful purpose? Is what I am doing utilizing my abilities wisely and effectively? With these questions as my template, I have managed to serve in increasingly satisfying ways for myself and, God willing, in useful capacities for others. This particular aspiration has no end-point, as long as I am living. The music therapy work that I conduct with the elderly evolves regularly, as does my psychotherapeutic work with folks. Currently, I am extremely fortunate to be part of the 40 Days: Alchemy of Tranquility® Program team of mental-health professionals, created and guided by Seyyed Dr. Ali Kianfar, which provides valuable service to our local communities.

Several connecting limbs representing various aspects of the creative arts grow from a dominant creative branch. I was fortunate to be raised by art lovers – art of all kinds: dance, fine arts, dramatic and performing arts, music, poetry and the written word. My parents not only introduced my siblings and me to the arts but stimulated in us the desire to take part in the creation of it. This creative branch has merged with my inner spiritual seeker and the desire to be useful, most notably when I have had distinct experiences of being used as a vehicle – a vehicle through which a melody, improvisation, song, or creative idea is conveyed, to become a unique artistic expression. I have felt blessed to experience this phenomenon throughout my participation in the Sufi music ensemble, Taneen. The ensemble is continuously inspired by our teachers, Shah Nazar Seyyed Dr. Ali Kianfar and Seyyedeh Dr. Nahid Angha, whose translations of Sufi poetry have been the catalyst for Taneen's music.

Finding meaningful human connection has been the most unpredictable of all my aspirations – like a wild vine winding through rich soil as well as weeds, learning how to recognize and value trustworthy, loving human beings has been quite a journey. Nevertheless, this winding journey has proved to be necessary to discover in myself the ability to allow genuine, trusting human love into my life.

A deep connection with the natural world was nurtured by my parents – a connection that has run parallel and has often merged with my spiritual seeking. What I have learned and continue to learn from silent sittings in woodlands or by waterways or on mountains, from creatures large and small, from trees and plant-life, still informs my inner seeker. I feel a profound responsibility to our non-human neighbors and earthly cohabitants, to somehow help to bring about a healthier ecological balance on this planet.

From a very early age, I have been infused with what I can only describe as a "knowing," that there simply has to be more going on than what is apparent to us in this material world. This innate sense of knowing has grown in strength over time, by various (what seemed like) "other-worldly," unexplainable experiences, as well as forays into religious realms of Christian, Buddhist, and Native American spirituality. I have sought out and have found helpful teachers of religion and spirituality, who have assisted me in my quest to know more, and I am grateful to them for their help. However, I have to say that my thirst for knowledge, for *real* experience has only increased with time and, consequently, throughout my twenties and thirties, I felt a growing emptiness in my inner core, or soul. Thankfully, toward the end of this period, I received the gift of what I had been seeking: wisdom, knowledge, and guidance in the form of true teachers.

I now see that these seemingly disparate sproutings were actually branches from a single tree, grown from one seed. I see how these branches of my aspirations or callings have always intertwined, have always connected. I see that the whole of my being, when truly unified, connected, in harmony, has the *potential* for bringing these aspirations to full fruition. My job is to follow through.

I am deeply grateful for the guidance and teaching I have received. I thank all my helpers and guides, especially my parents, and humbly offer great appreciation and gratitude to true spiritual teachers, caretakers of my heart, Dr. Nahid Angha and Dr. Ali Kianfar.

Jeff McCullough

I was born September 30, 1958 in North Platte, NE. The environment of my youth was simple, good, and wholesome. My parents believed in doing everything themselves, and passed that onto their children. While I lived in towns and not on a farm, the cornfields never felt far away and there was nothing ever blocking the horizon. I learned everything from how to grow a garden to car mechanics and house remodeling. This is quite a contrast to the way my family practiced  their religion, Christianity. I was raised thinking that the only real work was helping others and being a messenger of God either as a pastor or a missionary. The world of my youth was very insular socially with a clear division between things of God and things of the devil. Within me is a strong desire to understand how things work from different points of view, so I felt quite stifled when it came to spirituality and religion.

During my high school years, I found I could no longer stifle what was naturally part of me. My curiosity and wonder caused me to start thinking outside of the imposed religious box. I began reading books on the occult just so I could better understand the other point of view. In the end neither point of view was answering what I felt growing inside me.

Along with my siblings (I'm the youngest of nine), it was assumed that we would learn to play instruments, sing in the church choir, and be good stewards of God. I learned to play the piano and tried out different band instruments (I had a selection of hand me downs from my siblings). The tenor sax was the beginning followed by the trumpet and eventually the French horn.

After high school began the saga of finding my way through college. I attended many different schools with many different majors. During the same time, I started traveling and slowly moving west. My world view began to evolve and expand. The world turned out to be very inviting and exciting. Delight filled me. I loved learning about all the points of view in the cultures where I travelled. I started to explore the many views of the world's religions. I eventually landed in the San Francisco Bay Area, and had a strong sense I was home. The diversity and the natural beauty of the area were natural draws for me. During those years of finding my way in college I also tried out several trades to utilize the talent I developed as a kid of working with my hands (I tried carpentry, electrical work, and furniture building). In the end I found computers seemed pretty cool. I got my first real programming job working for Apple Computer. Eventually I completed a computer science degree at UC Berkeley, and was working there while finishing school. One thing has led to another, and I've been working there ever since in various capacities. I've enjoyed applying my talents there to support research and education. I have also been blessed with two wonderful daughters who are now adults starting their own lives.

In my explorations of the world's religions I started to wonder if I might find a spiritual teacher. One that would inspire a further depth of understanding in the questions I found deeply inside me. My spiritual training began when I had the privilege of meeting two true Sufi Saints, Dr. Angha and Dr. Kianfar, right here in the SF Bay area I call home. Again, I felt that sense of home. Many long time questions were finally answered. Science and spirituality came together.

Following a Sufi tradition of putting mystical poetry to music, I've had the privilege of playing with Taneen Sufi Music Ensemble. The group allowed me to discover the joys of the Persian *ney* and harmonium. More instruments to learn, but that felt good. In a fun kind of way, the music allowed me to come full circle with my upbringing. I was finally able to express the experience of God through music. While I never became a pastor or missionary per se, I've shared my experience.

Along with the richness of playing music I have also had the privilege of serving in the community through work at Phoenix Word and Press, the journal *Sufism: An Inquiry*, and the IAS Sufism Symposium.

Elizabeth Miller

In the name of Love, most gracious and most merciful, I strive to walk every heartbeat and breath in greater wisdom, with the guidance and divine Sufi teachings of Dr. Nahid Angha and Seyyed Dr. Ali Kianfar. Through their pure wisdom and generosity, graciously I am taught that everything I seek resides within my heart, and I learn to value and respect my one true life. I am discovering that with clear intention and exact instruction, it is possible to correct the destination of my life's journey, and in so doing, to discover new levels of aliveness and freedom. Rather than looking all around myself for meaning, validation and identity, I am learning to stand straight and turn inward, and trust the unseen point of unity and love within.

In this process of reorientation, I am tested to return my attention to myself and find balance, no matter the outer conditions. Through greater honesty and self-reflection, I move more fully toward locating strength and stability inside myself, and see newly the potential and majesty of this life. With guidance, I am learning to listen for the way my own stable point, located within my heart, and unrepeated anywhere, provides a direct line to harmony and tranquility. For me, the teachings of Sufism are a bridge, connecting me back to myself, and linking my longstanding love of science with a path of spirituality that provides precise language and practices for directly experiencing connection the whole of Creation.

As I locate this point of stability within myself, I seek to support others in recognizing and cultivating their own inner strength, stability and sense of majesty. I am grateful to do this work in a wide variety of spaces for leaning, including traditional classrooms, and through my participation in projects like Building Bridges of Understanding and *Sufism: An Inquiry*. I bring together graduate and professional research in neurocardiology, eastern and western medical traditions, philosophy, literature, religion, cosmology and ecology. I understand my work as that of a storyteller who weaves science, the arts and spirituality, in service of creating even more beautiful and authentic ways for becoming human in the natural world.

Arthur Mullin III

Arthur attended the graduate Holistic Health Education and Nutrition program at John F. Kennedy University in Pleasant Hill CA. He earned a BS degree in Psychology and Social Action and is has also completed his diploma and certification in personal training and sports nutrition.

Arthur explored many different careers and interests before realizing his passion to become a health educator and holistic nutritionist. In 2008, Arthur decided to leave his long-term marketing job to pursue his ambition to thru-hike the Appalachian Trail, a 2,176 mile long hiking journey on the East Coast of the United States. For six months he lived in the mountains, hiking up to 20 miles per day through bountiful landscapes, learning to depend on himself. Arthur's Appalachian journey was full of personal development, self-realization and spiritual awakening.

While journeying through the Appalachian Trail, Arthur experienced a significant turning point in his life that catalyzed many newfound aspirations and goals. He moved to Northern California with his then girlfriend (now wife) and returned to school at the age of 28 years. He completed his degree at the top of his class.

Throughout his conventional education on the subjects of psychology and sociology, Arthur recognized that traditional schools of thought and scientific theory were not addressing his deeper questions about consciousness, purpose, and spirituality. He also began to be deeply interested in the link between physical, mental and spiritual wellbeing. This led him to pursue his Masters Degree at a University that offered a holistic, integrative perspective on health and healing and also offered an experiential learning model.

Throughout his graduate studies and continued personal quest for truth and meaning Arthur recognized that yet again his deepest longings could not be answered by alternative healing modalities or within intellectual debates. Arthurs wife, a Sufi practitioner, had been involved with International Association of Sufism for several years before Arthur decided to participate in a 40 Days workshop. His initial experience of Dr. Kianfar and Dr. Angha was an awakening to the reality that the answers to his deepest longings are found within.

Currently Arthur is working on developing an integrative model of culture centered workplace wellness. He aspires to introduce the importance of integrating physical health and spiritual wellbeing to the field of workplace wellness. He graduated with his Masters Degree in Holistic Health Education in June of 2014. Arthur will also be sitting for the National Association of Nutrition Professionals board certification exam for holistic nutrition.

Sarah Abbott Hastings Mullin Ph.D.

It is with my greatest appreciation that I have been guided to my teachers Seyyedeh Dr. Nahid Angha and Shah Nazar Seyyed Dr. Ali Kianfar, who through their own self-purification, devotion and love were instructed to teach Sufism and the art of humanity by their Great Master Moulana Shah Maghsoud.

Before meeting my teachers I was scattered in my sense of self, constantly fluctuating in self-esteem and regulation of emotion, almost hopeless to find existential meaning or purpose. When I was 24 years old, I decided to participate in a Vision Quest in Colorado and during my three day fast alone in the desert it became clear that I was to move to California and to become a psychotherapist. Months later, enrolled at the Institute of Transpersonal Psychology, I dove into the depths of the school's philosophy, this philosophy demanding that each student honestly look deeply at oneself and one's psychology in addition to the academic work.

Upon meeting and becoming better friends with my very good friend and classmate, Dr. Jamal Granick and hearing about his Sufi teachers, I recognized that I desperately wanted a teacher and soon began attending 40 Days workshops and other Sufi events. I was 25 years old when I met my teachers. It seems to me that the story of how one meets their teacher and what that experience was like cannot be described, and perhaps is best left unsaid. However, the moments I met Dr. Angha and Dr. Kianfar are burned into my memory as being the beginning of a new life, one full of promise, clarity and love. How extremely lucky am I to have met two people who live only according to Divine rule and principle, whose way of life is constantly attempting to teach wisdom and to heal society, who always promote humanity, who see and help those that no one else recognizes, and who in their spiritual advancement transmit the knowledge of the universe into those practitioners ready to receive such blessings.

In my gratitude, and with the awareness of the honor to be in their presence, and as their teachings increasingly become infused in my being, I progressively feel the calling to also be of service. I long, as the Sufis say, to be "in the world but not of it" and to spend each moment appreciating and putting to action the wisdom of my teachers and their teachers' teachings. It is through their guidance that I have recognized that there is a very distinct goal to spirituality and meditation, and that a practitioner who is determined to experience this goal will experience it. This has made me completely rearrange my life, with the priorities I used to have having faded away as my intention to truly understand and to perfect myself as a human being increasingly becomes the only importance. Instead of looking at the details of life and being attached to all that is changing and temporary, I have been guided to consider and appreciate an everlasting and innate essentiality. Therefore, paradoxically, my life has become simpler while becoming more enriched and less confusing while I have become more aware of life's hidden angles.

I often think about the Sufi teaching instructing the devoted practitioner to become in relationship with his or her teacher like "a dead man in the hands of the one washing the dead." Under the guidance of two people whom I trust completely and whose beings are truly rays of Divine light and love, it has become my greatest desire to remove anything obstructing me from being in alignment with my teachers so that I never feel apart from them. As part of the younger generation trying to bring light into the world, I feel blessed to be guided by the wisdom and direction of these Masters, whom I completely depend on as my constant source of energy, wisdom, devotion and love. Thank you.

Sarah Hastings Mullin is a clinical psychologist in Berkeley, California. Her clinical interests involve working with people with anxiety and depressive disorders, increasing self-esteem and life direction, couples therapy, family systems, the transition into parenthood and co-parenting. Sarah is especially interested in helping client's find their sense of personal meaning and purpose and to help them work through obstacles that prevent intra/interpersonal alignment and balance. Sarah also enjoys practicing the martial art of Aikido and holds a second-degree black belt.

Safa Ali Michael Newman

Since the late 1980's, I have been a practitioner in the study of Sufism under the guidance and supervision of two teachers, Seyyedeh Nahid Angha, Ph.D. and Shah Nazar Seyyed Ali Kianfar, Ph.D., who were students of Moulana Shah Maghsoud Sadegh Angha. I have been a student and researcher in the study of Uwaiysi Sufism for many years. I am currently the President of the Board of Directors of the International Association of Sufism and Chairperson of IAS's Executive Committee of the Institute for Sufi Studies. I have given lectures on Sufism, Islam, and interfaith issues throughout the world including lectures at the Association of Humanistic Psychology Conference and at IAS conferences in Edinburg, Scotland, Barcelona, Spain, and Cairo, Egypt. I have authored a book on Uwaiysi Sufism and Islam entitled *The Gift of the Robe- Uwaiysieh* and co-authored another book on Sufism entitled *Sufi Grace - Sacred Wisdom - Heart to Heart.*

I grew up in a family that had a strong cultural and ethnic sense of the religion to which it belonged, enjoying the religious holidays and traditions that throughout the years were woven into the fabric of family life. But little was spoken of the meaning of the traditions, or of the holidays and their various ceremonies. Being inquisitive, I began to study more and more about religion on my own, reading *The Bible*, particularly the books of *The Torah*, and the stories of Abraham, Moses, and Jesus and others.

Greatly enjoying nature, I also spent many nights camping in the wilderness, looking up at the stars above me, in awe of the magnitude of the universe. Within myself, during my studies or these nights in the darkness, I experienced a strong sense of the divine and an attraction to a divinity that I neither knew nor could comprehend or explain. I felt pulled towards a light, but the light was too far from my grasp. But these experiences only increased the quest within my heart to know more about myself and my being. The religious traditions and ceremonies that I continued to participate in, while rich and beautiful in their own right, did little to satisfy this quest, which intensified as I grew older. I felt like a thirsty man who had been kept from water but knew that it was essential to his survival. I knew that only until I drank a cup of real water — a cup for which I had no name at the time — would I satisfy my thirst.

In time, I found the teachings of Hazrat Moulana Shah Maghsoud Sadegh Angha, a 20th century Sufi. I became a student of two of his students, Seyyedeh Nahid Angha, Hazrat Shah Maghsoud's daughter, and Shah Nazar Seyyed Ali Kianfar, his spiritual son, who had become teachers of his path. Upon meeting these teachers, I now sensed that I was standing before a door behind which was the answer to my quest. I recall vividly that my first "assignment" as a student was to study the *Ayatol Korsi* (the Verses of the Throne), one of *The Holy Koran*'s most exquisite verses (*Sura* II, 255-257). As I look back on this assignment and what led me to the door that I stood before, I now understand that behind everything that had happened to get me to the door, and behind everything that has happened ever since, has been the hand of God and His grace and mercy.

The opportunity to study with two beautiful teachers who wore this Robe was the answer to the lifelong quest of my heart. After meeting these teachers, I strived for many years to be a faithful and loyal student of the Uwaiysi path and do service in the name of the International Association of Sufism, the organization that they founded and direct.

Joe Pace

Joe is a data processing systems architect and engineer for Honda Motor Company, in Torrance, California. He studied computer science and mathematics at the University of California at Davis, with an interest in psychology and philosophy. He grew up not far from Bell Laboratories at Murray Hill, New Jersey, and became a UNIX systems programmer in the early 1980's. Beginning in the mid 1980's he worked with the US Army Corps of Engineers, and served as the liaison between the Army Corps, DARPA, local, state and federal agencies to help develop what has become the Internet. He continues to develop new communications related products for Honda Motor's operations and their customers in the automobile, motorcycle, aviation, and power equipment industry.

In 1985, he had the great fortune to meet the directors of the International Association of Sufism, and has been helping to support the humanitarian mission of this wonderful organization ever since. He credits this moment as a turning point in his life, for which he will be forever grateful for the knowledge and experiences he has attained since this fortuitous meeting.

Mr. Pace has published several poetry transliterations in *Sufism: An Inquiry*, and is fond of poetry, prose, and nature. He enjoys the studies of natural science, cosmology, and history. He currently resides in Los Angeles with his bride, Michelle.

Habib Glenn Pascall

Habib Glenn Pascall has been a student of Dr. Kianfar and Dr. Angha since the year 2000. He is co-compiler (with Sanaa Joy Carey) of *Seasons of the Soul*, a book of daily wisdom from Dr. Kianfar's teachings. Pascall also compiled *Illumination of the Names: Meditation by Sufi Masters on the 99 Beautiful Names of God*, with an introduction based on Dr. Kianfar's teachings. Both books have been published by the International Association of Sufism.

Pascall has served as moderator for numerous panels at the annual Sufism Symposium and as introducer of events at the Sufi Celebration. He joined Soraya Chase Clow and Taher Tony Roybal in a photographic presentation at the 2013 Sufi Celebration.

Pascall's professional and volunteer credits include "best columnist" awards from the American Society of Professional Journalists and the 2013 Conservation Service Award from the Sierra Club Angeles Chapter.

Katherine Preston

Katherine Preston is a student of Uwaiysi Sufism under the guidance of Seyyedeh Dr. Nahid Angha and Shah Nazar Seyyed Dr. Ali Kianfar. As a student, she has been given the opportunity to serve through facilitation and speaking on behalf of the 40 Days: Alchemy of Tranquility® Program, as well as contributing to publications including *Sufism: An Inquiry* and chapters in *Human Self, Volume One: Mind* and *Inspiration on Holy Qur'an*. She considers it a great blessing and honor to assist with the work of the International Association of Sufism.

She was drawn to mysticism from her earliest memory and was supported in her quest for spiritual understanding by her family, most significantly by her mother Betty Hites. She grew up in the woods of Ohio, spending much of her childhood in peaceful rural surroundings, entranced by the beauty in nature, which she considered tangible evidence of the great compassion of God.

She received a bachelor's degree in philosophy having studied philosophy and religion in college in Ohio. She continued her studies in San Francisco and received her M.A. in Social/Clinical Psychology. She began her work as a therapist in 1989 and became licensed as a Marriage and Family Therapist in 1997. Since then she has held many leadership positions teaching and supervising students and clinicians in agencies across the San Francisco Bay Area. Her focus has ranged from gang and domestic violence prevention, to strength-based family therapy to working with individuals with a focus on creative pursuits. She currently maintains a private practice in San Francisco, teaches graduate classes at Sofia University in Palo Alto, and is the mental health specialist at a private school in San Francisco. She has also been volunteering to teach religious education classes for youth and adults at the Unitarian Universalist Church of San Mateo for the past 11 years.

She and her husband Alex Watson have two children, Samuel and Isabelle.

Amineh Amelia Pryor, Ph.D.

Amineh is a student of Uwaiysi Sufism under the guidance of Sufi Masters Seyyedeh Dr. Nahid Angha and Shah Nazar Seyyed Dr. Ali Kianfar. Dr. Pryor is an active member of International Association of Sufism and its many departments, including Sufi Women Organization, founded by Dr. Nahid Angha, and the Sufism and Psychology Forum. Dr. Pryor presents lectures and workshops on psychology and spirituality at conferences, including in Egypt, Scotland, Spain, Canada, and in the United States. She is an accomplished author, having published articles and book chapters on psychology, consciousness, and science, and books entitled: *Psychology in Sufism* and *Sufi Grace* (co-authored with Dr. Arife Ellen Hammerle and Safa Ali Michael Newman). Dr. Pryor is on the faculty of the Institute for Sufi Studies and is a presenter and group facilitator for the 40 Days: Alchemy of Tranquility® program.

Through her work with the International Association of Sufism and as a student of Seyyedeh Dr. Nahid Angha and Shah Nazar Seyyed Dr. Ali Kianfar, Dr. Pryor has had the opportunity to teach meditation and stress management, based on Sufi principles, to women in the Marin County jail, addicts in recovery programs, senior citizens, and youth. She offers a meditation and inspiration group for mothers and offers trainings on trauma, PTSD, and the effects of chronic illness and pain.

Professionally Dr. Pryor is a psychotherapist with over twenty years of experience in community mental health. She has worked at a number of small and large social service agencies as a psychotherapist, clinical manager and supervisor. She specializes in working with individuals in transition, healing traumatic experiences, chronic illness, overcoming addictions, and with people seeking to find balance in life, work, and relationships. She brings a background in business to her psychotherapy practice. She currently sees clients and provides clinical supervision at the Community Healing Centers, a non-profit psychotherapy and training agency in San Francisco and Marin.

Dr. Pryor holds a Bachelor's Degree in Business Administration from San Francisco State University and a Master's Degree in Clinical Psychology from John F. Kennedy University. She earned her Ph.D. in East-West Psychology from the California Institute of Integral Studies. The focus of her dissertation is on Islamic Sufism and Sufi Psychology. She completed her doctoral work with the guidance of Shah Nazar Seyyed Dr. Ali Kianfar and with the encouragement of Seyyedeh Dr. Nahid Angha.

Dr. Pryor relies on the foundation and principles of Uwaiysi Sufism, its lineage and teachings, in her inner practices and in her work in the world. The teachings and examples of Moulana Shah Maghsoud and his wife Mah Talat Etemad-Moghadam Angha inspire her work and her life.

She is a native of the San Francisco Bay Area with family ties in China and the Far East.

Bryan Rich, Ph.D.

Bryan Rich's active spiritual exploration and expression began in the realm of music. That heartfelt practice began with formal study in his home in New York at the age of five, and has been a core practice ever since. He obtained a bachelor's degree in music, and worked in that field for several years.

Bryan was introduced to meditation by a Hindu teacher while in high school, a life-changing event. He continued to practice meditation from that point on, albeit without formal guidance. This changed in another life-changing event when he began studies with the Zen master Eido Shimano Roshi in 1976. At that time, Bryan began a daily practice of meditation. He attended numerous meditation retreats under Eido Roshi and spent several months in residence at his mountain retreat center. Bryan met and began formal Zen studies with

214

Roshi Bernard Glassman in 1979, joining Roshi Glassman's residential center at the Zen Community of New York a few months later. Bryan was ordained as a Zen priest in 1984 and remained in residence at ZCNY for 12 years. During that period, he practiced intensive meditation and study. He attended and participated in managing numerous retreats at ZCNY. He also taught meditation and trained meditation instructors there. A primary element of his practice involved vigorous participation in ZCNY's social action practice. That was expressed in a holistic program of housing development, education and job training and development that was focused on providing opportunities for and working side by side with homeless and economically disadvantaged people. This was very much in keeping with a deep inspiration in Bryan to work with people who may be underprivileged in many different dimensions.

Due in part to the emphasis on interfaith expression at ZCNY, Bryan met the Ramakrishna-Vedanta teacher Swami Aseshananda, a direct disciple of Sarada Devi (Holy Mother) in 1981. He was formally initiated in that tradition by Swami Aseshananda in 1983 and continues to consider that to be an important and cherished spiritual connection. In that same year, in a profoundly important transformational event, he also met Sheikh Muzaffer Ozak al-Jerrahi, the head of the Halveti-Jerrahi Sufi order. Bryan felt a deep spiritual connection with Muzaffer Efendi from that moment, and was initiated by him as a dervish in the Jerrahi order in 1982. Bryan continued to live and work at ZCNY until 1992. From 1987-1992, he also engaged in intensive practice in Tibetan Buddhism under the guidance of Ngakpa Chogyam and Sogyal Rinpoche. He maintained his Sufi practice from the time he met Muzaffer Efendi, participating in weekly gatherings and spending a considerable amount of time with Efendi during his frequent extended visits to New York until his passing in 1985. Bryan continued to practice under the guidance of Sefer Dal al-Jerrahi, the succeeding leader of the Jerrahi order.

In 1992, Bryan left ZCNY, feeling drawn to a more heart-oriented practice. After a 100-day retreat led by Sogyal Rinpoche in France, he journeyed to visit the home center of the Jerrahi order in Istanbul, Turkey—and remained there for four years. He attended gatherings at the Jerrahi tekke three times a week and engaged with the Jerrahi community on a daily basis. He had the opportunity to study Qur'anic recitation with senior teachers.

Also throughout that time, he studied *tasawwuf* music in the Turkish tradition under master musicians. He had the priceless blessing of making the *Hajj* pilgrimage in 1993, and also made *Umrah* visits to the holy cities of Mecca and Medinah in 1994 and 1996.

While in Istanbul, he met Sheikh Ragip Robert Frager, Ph.D., the leader of a local Jerrahi group in the Bay area in California practicing under the guidance of the head sheikh in Istanbul. After four years in Istanbul, Bryan came to feel that the appropriate place to pursue his longtime, heartfelt calling to serve was in his home culture, where he could fully utilize whatever abilities he had been given. Ragip Baba invited him to attend the Institute of Transpersonal Psychology, the graduate institute in a whole-person, spiritually-oriented approach to psychology that he himself had founded. Bryan gratefully accepted that invitation in order to further explore the psychological dimensions of spiritual practice. He received a Master's degree in counseling psychology there in 1999, and a Ph.D. in transpersonal psychology with certificates in clinical psychology and spiritual guidance in 2005. Also beginning in his study at ITP, Bryan began practicing Aikido as a direct and powerful whole-person engagement with spiritual realities, a practice which he continues to this day.

At the same time that he began study at ITP in 1996, Bryan also began working full-time in community-based mental health. He worked for over five years in a residential psychiatric crisis program, working with individuals with severe mental illnesses in crisis states. From 2002-2012, he worked at a nonprofit organization providing a variety of mental health services to children and families. Beginning in late 2012, he began working as a therapist in a county mental health agency providing services to adults with a wide range of mental and emotional problems, many of which are based in the experience of severe trauma. Bryan's awareness of the spiritual journey of human beings has been continually deepened by this experience of working closely and deeply with people in these real-life situations. This work has also provided a deeply cherished opportunity to pursue the calling to service.

In 2010, Bryan experienced another life-changing event, a meeting with Shah Nazar Seyyed Ali Kianfar and Seyyedeh Nahid Angha. Dr. Kianfar and Dr. Angha are teachers in the Uwaiysi Sufi order and intimate successors of the extraordinary teacher Moulana Shah Maghsoud. Ongoing practice with Dr. Kianfar and Dr. Angha opened previously unimagined vistas in spiritual practice and awareness. This manifests most essentially in providing essential guidance in fulfilling Bryan's core, God-given wish, to open his heart and allow him to return to his true spiritual home, from whence he hopes to truly worship and to serve. He looks forward to a lifetime of study with his teachers, of service, and of singing the song of worship and praise.

Hamed Blake Ross

Hamed is a member of the International Association of Sufism and has attended *khaneghah* and contributed efforts to the non-profit for more than twenty years.

He writes, "I have found that I am a stranger to myself. Careful, patient reflection on various, pivotal experiences in my past have proven this to me. Formal and spiritual education have been an important part of my quest to understand the purpose of my life, if there is, indeed, any purpose at all."

Hamed was born and raised in the Bay Area. His family has deep roots in California going back five generations. He was brought up in a secular/Catholic home. He developed an interest in religion early in life and studied both Christian mysticism and Eastern religion in his teen years before eventually settling on the Sufi path in his early twenties. He began attending International Association of Sufism gatherings in the late 1980s. He continues to develop interests that intersect the space between religion, mysticism, philosophy, psychology and science. He sees the Uwaiysi Sufi school of Seyyedeh Dr. Nahid Angha and Shah Nazar Seyyed Dr. Ali Kianfar as a solid foundation to develop these interests for both personal growth and a broad world view. Hamed believes that the intersection between science and spirituality is an essential area of study for humanity. Western and Eastern cultures are often at odds and suffer many mutual misunderstandings. There has never been a greater need to resolve the disparate world views of East & West. He believes all people and cultures should be respected and all have an individual truth while sharing one common truth. The search for that common truth, which ties the individual to the Whole, has been the persistent passion of his life.

Through the activities of the IAS, Hamed has had the opportunity to travel through Europe, North Africa and the Middle East to meet people of different cultures and share common appreciation of Sufi wisdom and celebrate our united human family. The experiences have left deep and rewarding impressions on his personality.

Dr. Nahid Angha and Shah Nazar Seyyed Dr. Ali Kianfar's Uwaiysi teachings addresses Hamed's concerns and desires for a more rich and full experience of life. The philosophical gnosis of Sufism combined with the direct, spiritual gnosis allows him to develop greater self-awareness, more compassion for others and a better understanding of his and humanity's place in the universe. The result has been more peace and confidence in his life. A persistent feeling of emptiness and futility has been replaced by a sense of purpose and direction that is not fulfilled by any other aspect of his life.

Hamed has been a contributor to IAS activities in various capacities from grassroots marketing to social network media marketing. He contributes articles on Sufism, philosophy and science to the IAS journal, *Sufism: An Inquiry*. He participates in fundraising efforts and he also contributes video production to the recording and publishing of IAS events.

Hamed has a background in software engineering, a B.A. in Cognitive Science and he is completing a Master's Degree in Humanities with a focus in Big History from Dominican University. He plans to continue formal studies in the areas of Big Data, Big History and Complexity.

Anthony Taher Roybal

In the name of Allah, the most gracious, the most merciful.

I was born Anthony David Roybal in San Rafael, California on July 13, 1953. My father, Anthony Joseph Roybal, was a staff sergeant at Hamilton Field in nearby Novato. My mother, Lucille Adelida Roybal, was a homemaker and house cleaner. A few years later my sister Deborah was born. When I was in first grade, my father was transferred to Elmendorf Air Force Base near Anchorage, Alaska. A few months after the Kennedy assassination and shortly before the Great Alaskan Earthquake in the spring of 1964, we were transferred to Castle Air Force Base near Merced, California. My dad retired at Castle and I grew up in Merced.

We were raised Roman Catholic, but my sister and I always attended public schools. My exposure to my religion was through attending mass with my mom and sister plus a few years of catechism instruction after school. When I was a kid, the mass was something to endure, as I sat squirming on the hard benches while the mass was said in Latin. Catholicism was mysterious but distant from me and my life. Always curious, it was in high school that a deep desire to know (really know) became my primary focus. First I explored the religions of my friends: Presbyterians, Mormons, and Jesus freaks. Unsatisfied, in college I turned my attention to comparative  religions and then philosophy. My intellectual journey continued through philosophy of the mind, physics and philosophy of science, and ended with linguistic philosophy. I was looking for pure, unassailable truth. It was a journey of the mind, and for me it was unsatisfactory. I learned how to see both sides of a position and how to support either side. But it wasn't what I was looking for and I became disillusioned and I dropped out of school shortly before graduation.

While in college I had started working outdoor jobs to support my education. Among these were: fire crew for the forest service, field technician for an erosion study in Redwood National Park, and road crew in the southern Sierra. I moved to Colorado and for the next several years I worked Cadastral surveys for the Bureau of Land Management throughout the state. In all these jobs I always had my camera near; my love and appreciation of the American West and photography grew hand in hand.

A career-ending leg injury led to my return to college at the University of California. At Berkeley I met Jeff McCullough, the manager of the campus computer lab where I had a class. We became friends and after I graduated he offered me a job in the lab and I started my new career. It was Jeff who told me about Sufism and introduced me to my teachers Shah Nazar Seyyed Dr. Ali Kianfar and Seyyedeh Dr. Nahid Angha. My first meeting was at a public class led by Dr. Kianfar, and few days later I was able to meet with him individually. Later that year I attended the Second Annual Sufism Symposium, working as the staff photographer. I have continued to photograph and videotape many IAS events over the intervening years.

My career in Information Technology (IT) at Berkeley gave me the skills to provide computer and technical support for a variety of IAS projects and services, most importantly, the IAS web sites and I continue to serve as the IAS IT administrator. It has also been my privilege and honor to sit at Dr. Kianfar's side as he worked at his business, Phoenix Word & Press, helping out where I could, but really listening and learning. PWP published many important IAS publications, mostly notably our journal, *Sufism: An Inquiry*. I was humbled to witness Dr. Kianfar standing by his press working late in the evening, night after night.

With my teacher's encouragement I joined Taneen, Sufi Music Ensemble. In spite of my life-long love and appreciation of music, I had never before performed music, and this was another gift from my teacher, as well as a great responsibility. As a member of Taneen I have played before audiences throughout California, the Northwest, and Northern and Southern Europe. In Taneen we present the sacred poetry of Sufi masters, such as Rumi, Hafez and Moulana Shah Magshoud. Most of the poetry has been translated by Dr. Nahid Angha. Our music is drawn from our experience of western music, influenced by Persian and Middle Eastern music and instruments. We have released four recordings of our music, working with our amazing producer David Rosenthal. And Gillian Lovejoy provided essential encouragement, vocal training and love to all of us in the group.

My life has been profoundly changed by my teachers, Dr. Angha and Dr. Kianfar, students of our master, Moulana Shah Maghsoud. In my experience, their wisdom has only been exceeded by their patience and love. My blessings include: my name, Taher, or "pure" bestowed on me by my teachers; my colleagues and friends in Taneen; my fellow students; and my partner in life and Sufism, my beloved, Nancy Carroll. I greatly appreciate the opportunity to serve in whatever way I've been able to contribute. Whatever I have given has come back to me tenfold. No matter how many times I stubbornly look outward from myself, my teachers always guide me back to my heart.

Sheida Safarisamani

I was born on noon of May 3rd, 1967 in a Muslim family. But I was never forced to practice my ancestors' religion or faith.

In my life of praying I always asked: "Allah, guide me to right action and give me the knowledge, and let me be with those who are pure in the path." When I was preparing to come to the United States in October of

1999, I was questioning "Allah" about why I was going to the US, where the majority of people are Christian. Little did I know that I would find my Holy Teacher on the other side of world; a man with profound knowledge who is teaching the purity of Islam.

I was blessed that I met my teachers only three months after I came to the US and that I received my white clothing in six months. Since then I have had the blessing to be in their presence and to receive their teaching, and guidance. And I think this was the answer to my praying. As Dr. Kianfar has told me, "I have not brought you all the way from Dubai to here for nothing."

Words cannot describe my feelings and the blessing that I have received through my teachers. I am so grateful for having my teachers in this universe.

Arthur Scott

Arthur Scott has taught history/cultural studies for many decades centering on Dominican University of California, Contra Costa College and University of California at Berkeley Extension. His specialty has been in Islam and Native American Studies, offering courses on Islam in the early nineties at Dominican University. Realizing that Islam had a deeper philosophy, spirituality and aesthetic that could not be learned from books, he sought a mentor and it was this desire that led him to the office of Dr. Ali Kianfar, a renowned Sufi practitioner. When Professor Scott encountered Dr. Kianfar, he immediately had a heart connection with him similar to the relationship between Rumi and Shems. He knew that he was spiritually home. Since then, Professor Scott has been a devoted student and has incorporated the 'Tasawuf' teachings into his life.

Dr. Kianfar, along with Dr. Nahid Angha, invited Professor Scott to become a member of the International Association of Sufism and to participate in *zekr* (*zikr, dhikr*) prayer gatherings first at their home and later at the *Khanegah*. For over twenty years Professor Scott has given presentations and has moderated at IAS Sufism Symposia. The Symposia are an experience as they draw Sufis, intellectuals, artists from all over the world, who are bound in love by the Sufi commitment to peace, service and surrender. At these

Conferences, many miracles have occurred to those attending. In one session the panelists were talking about Prophet Muhammed, 'peace/blessings be upon him,' when a sudden waft of exotic perfume embraced the speakers and we all acknowledged the presence. Conference themes run the gamut of human experiences from "The Beauty of Gnosis," "Practicing Harmony," to "Rumi /Modernity."

In addition, Professor Scott walked the talk by incorporating Dr. Kianfar's teachings into the classroom and into his writings. Core points being "to know thy self is to know thy Lord," "what you are looking for is within," "silence the mind and learn to listen to the heart," "return to the center of your existence," "you thought yourself small but within you is the entire universe," and "be not confused by the ramblings of mind." These powerful themes were conveyed to 'Pathway Students,' returning adults at Dominican, who were struggling with their issues of identity and seeking a personal understanding of spirituality for their lives and existence. To bring students to themselves each class began with a 'heart meditation' in which listening to one's heart beat became the core focus. This was supplemented by readings from Dr. Kianfar's *Seasons of the Soul* and Rumi's *Where Two Oceans Meet* which most often generated soulful classroom discussions.

To be in Dr. Kianfar's energy has been a privilege and a miraculous experience in personal growth, wisdom, knowledge and love. Hardly a day goes by in which his 'voice' is not present encouraging me/us to clean up, to practice, to be quiet, and to listen to the deeper poetry of existence. There is no way in which I can repay him for this love except to follow his example and to cherish his teachings. I conclude with this Sufi verse which captures best his blessed essence: "I saw my Lord with the eye of the heart and asked, 'Who Art Thou;' the Lord replied, 'You.'"

Ashley Elizabeth Werner, Esq.

Ashley Elizabeth Werner was born to her parents, Mary Josephine Hendrickson and Christopher Arthur Werner, in the early morning of December 2, 1985 in Greenbrae, California. Ashley was raised by her parents in Marin County,

222

California, initially in Sausalito and then for most of her childhood in San Anselmo.

Growing up surrounded by the abundant open space of Marin, Ashley gained a life-long appreciation for nature. Ashley's parents taught her by example to appreciate the magic and beauty of life, to respect herself and others, to fulfill her responsibilities in all realms of life and to work hard to make the most of the opportunities given to her and achieve her human potential.

Ashley attended St. Ignatius College Preparatory in San Francisco for high school. During this time, Ashley played piano, practiced gymnastics and ran competitively and benefited from exposure to Jesuit dedication to learning, self-reflection, and service rooted in human solidarity. She participated in immersive service-learning experiences, co-coordinated a weekly food distribution program for the poor in San Francisco's Tenderloin District and served on the St. Anthony Foundation Youth Advisory Council.

During her sophomore year of high school, Ashley met her spiritual teachers, Dr. Ali Kianfar and Dr. Nahid Angha, Sufi Masters of the Uwaiysi Tarighat. The words of these teachers turned a key in her heart to a truth that resided within of the unity of humanity and of the perfection, value, and divine origins of our human identity. Through the teachings of Sufism and her experiences during high school, Ashley recognized a calling within herself to gain knowledge of her own identity and to work for the creation of a society in which all people have the opportunity to flourish and to fulfill their potential.

Following high school, Ashley attended Swarthmore College in Pennsylvania, where she majored in Economics and Religion and took courses in Arabic, Sociology and Anthropology, Political Science, Mathematics, Literature and History. As an Economics Major, Ashley sought to gain practical tools to apply towards the resolution of social issues relating to poverty and inequality. As a Religion Major, Ashley studied contemplative and meditative traditions of the world's major religions and their catalytic role in movements for social change. Ashley spent part of her junior year in Thailand studying the impacts of large-scale economic development initiatives and globalization on poor rural and urban communities as well as Buddhist thought, practice, and social activism.

Upon the recommendation of her Sufi teachers, Ashley applied to and attended law school. She graduated from Boston College Law School with a Certificate in Human Rights and International Justice in 2011. During and immediately following law school, Ashley worked in Peru with several Peruvian and international non-profits providing legal assistance with cases pending before the Inter-American Commission on Human Rights and the Inter-American Court of Human Rights and supporting initiatives of rural women for the advancement of rural development and women's human rights. Ashley had the opportunity to travel in Peru's highlands, jungle, and desert coast and gained an appreciation for the rich diversity of its people, cultures and geographies.

In March 2012, Ashley moved to Fresno, California to begin work as an attorney with California Rural Legal Assistance's Community Equity Initiative and to return closer to home and her teachers and Sufi community. As an attorney at CRLA, Ashley worked with community residents to increase government investment in and responsiveness to the needs of disadvantaged communities in California's Central Valley. In September 2013, she took a position as an attorney at the newly-formed non-profit, Leadership Counsel for Justice and Accountability, where she continues her work on behalf of disadvantaged communities to secure access to opportunity for all. Ashley regularly travels to the Bay Area to participate in gatherings and events of the International Association of Sufism.

The Rev. Shari Maruska Young

I have been ordained an Episcopal priest for almost 26 years. During this time I have been the Chaplain at Cathedral School for Boys in San Francisco; Associate Priest at Grace Cathedral; Vicar of St. Aidan's in Bolinas; and Associate Rector at both St. James, San Francisco and St. Stephen's, Belvedere where I currently serve.

Prior to my commitment to the Episcopal Church, I was a student of Joshu Sasaki, Rinzai Zen Master and served at Cimarron Zen Center in Los Angeles as Shoji, Leader of the Students. This began when I was 19 years old.

There have been several predominant threads through all posts: My love of ritual (liturgy), preaching, and teaching; a commitment to justice and

224

mercy for the poor;

an emphasis on the earth as our source and sustenance; and a great joy in facilitating the spiritual education of children. I have been a retreat leader, activist, event planner, and parish priest with a variety of faith communities, organizations, and venues.

Compassion, kindness, beauty and love have been my guideposts. I am grateful that my path has led to Dr. Kianfar and Dr. Angha who emphasize all four. The Sufi teaching has led me into a deeper realization of the truth of being, and given me a new point of view for both living and leading.

My son Matt is the joy of my life and will be graduating from high school this year and going to college.

The International Association of Sufism: A Brief History

The International Association of Sufism (IAS), a California non-profit, charitable and humanitarian organization, a United Nations NGO/DPI, was founded in 1983 by Dr. Nahid Angha and Dr. Ali Kianfar in order to create and provide a global forum for a continuing dialogue amongst Sufis, scholars, interfaith leaders, poets and artists from diverse cultures, nations and schools; to bring together Sufi principles and scientific understanding; to preserve and advance the study and goals of Sufism; and to promote equality and human rights.

Through the efforts of many Sufi masters, the contributions of Sufi orders and schools, and with the help of scholars, educators, translators, and artists interested in the discipline of Sufism, the Association has successfully accomplished its founding goals. To our knowledge, this is the first association to be formed to enable Sufis and scholars from around the world, from many nations and traditions, to establish relations and come together in the spirit of unity and harmony.

Publications

One way that the International Association of Sufism has worked to achieve these goals is through an extensive publication program, which has brought Sufi Masters together with writers, translators, editors, and other members of the English speaking intellectual community. Among its many publications and productions are: *Sufism: An Inquiry*, a quarterly journal, and newsletters including: *Insight, Sufism Psychology Forum, Al-Hadi, Sufi Women, Voices for Justice*. Working both separately and together, members of the Association have written many articles and essays, translated important Sufi works into English and contributed to *Sufism, An Inquiry* as well as IAS Newsletters. The quarterly journal introduces readers to the Sufis of the past and present – their schools, biographies, words of wisdom, instructions, poetry, and principles.

Scholars and Translators

Sufism is a universal discipline, a multinational practice-yet often has been obscured by difficulties of language and traditions. We have been greatly honored to be able to take on this important task, and make available to the English speaking world accurate translations of Sufi philosophy, poems, and teachings, most of which were never previously translated into English. International Association of Sufism has a network of translators and scholars fluent in English, Persian, Arabic, French, Spanish, and German. These Sufi scholars are dedicated to the accurate translation of the complex and often elusive Sufi texts.

Production

IAS has a library of over 300 recording productions of presentations and teachings of Sufi Masters, interfaith leaders, scholars, artists, poets, musicians, and zikr from many Sufi Schools.

Sufism Symposium

One of the most significant IAS achievements is the annual celebration of Sufism: Sufism Symposium. This international, multicultural festival has brought prominent Sufi masters from around the world to the USA, as well as Spain, Egypt and Scotland to celebrate this most influential school of civilization and to share their wisdom with a wide range of English-speaking audience. Sufism Symposium is an annual IAS springtime event.

IAS Departments and Projects

Since its conception in 1983, IAS gradually included human rights advocacy, scientific inquiries, art and music, global peace efforts to its mission, and over time developed eleven Departments and many Programs.

IAS Departments and Programs

Sufi Women Organization

The Sufi Women Organization (SWO) was founded in 1993 by Dr. Nahid Angha, a world-renowned Sufi teacher and author. SWO has over seventeen Chapters and many representations around the globe. SWO is a non-profit, non-political, humanitarian organization whose mission is to support, protect and educate for the human rights, with focus on women's and children's rights.

Serving as a forum for all women, SWO has been extremely successful in bringing together women from diverse cultural backgrounds across the globe who seek to share knowledge and improve the quality of life for women everywhere. SWO's primary humanitarian goals include protecting women's rights, providing and encouraging education for women, and increasing social awareness of women's needs. The devotion of all who have volunteered their time, energy and expertise has led to substantial achievements.

One of the motivations for the founding of SWO was to protect, support and acknowledge Sufi women's voice, opening lines of communication among Sufi women from many different schools in many different countries. The organization also promotes Sufi women's literary and artistic work, provides support for Sufi women in their endeavors, offers opportunities for dialogue with other women of faith and provides volunteer service to the various communities in which women live.

Breaking New Ground in Women's Leadership
In 1993, at the invitation of Dr. Angha, a group of women, from many different social and cultural backgrounds and various Sufi and spiritual affiliations joined together and became the foundation of the Sufi Women Organization with headquarters in Northern California. These women established themselves as an organization of strong and knowledgeable women. In 1994, SWO founder, Dr. Nahid Angha sat in the inner circle of zikr side by side with her Islamic and Sufi brothers, leaders from around the world, from Kuwait to Ghana, from Turkey to Canada, from India to Algeria, and many lands in between, and led a zikr. This inner circle is usually reserved for male Sufi masters, and Dr. Angha was the first woman to sit in that inner circle of leaders at the IAS Sufism Symposium – a truly revolutionary accomplishment.

Inspiration to Action
In 1995, Second Annual Sufism Symposium, many Sufi women stood side by side with their brothers, took parts in panel presentations before a packed conference hall, and even with many attendees waited in the hall to hear what the women of SWO had to say. SWO has maintained active participation and leadership in the IAS Symposia and Festivals each year since.

In 1997, SWO established the online Sufi Women Dialogue, and SWO became a close family, with sisters around the world. Through this effort, people who had never met came together and developed trust, respect and friendship. The Dialogue provides information and support for women and addresses women's issues.

Soon, SWO chapters and representations were established around the world, and in 1998, SWO held its first fund raising event – an Art Show in Marin County. In the fall, SWO held a working retreat at Walker Creek Ranch in Marin County to make plans for the future of SWO. This banner year also saw the publication of the book, *Sufi Women: The Journey toward the Beloved,* containing the stories of eleven Sufi women from six different Sufi schools and four different cultures.

SWO chapters used their voices to protest injustices to women. Following the riots in Indonesia in 1998, the SWO Indonesian chapter assisted by all the members of SWO, in protesting against the rapes and murders of Chinese women in Indonesia and in urging that the perpetrators be brought to justice. SWO members met with the Minister of Women's Affairs to bring the facts to the attention of those at the highest level of government and urge that action be taken. SWO has also written letters to officials regarding injustices toward women in the Sudan and other countries.

Another notable chapter active in providing assistance to the needy is in Egypt. SWO has also provided health supplies, clothing and educational materials for children living in Haiti and, in connection with Project Amigo, in the state of Colima, Mexico. Working with other humanitarian organizations, SWO has also been able to provide immunization, after school supplies, clean water, medical need, and clothing for children and refugees, around the world and in areas in need for such services. SWO has hosted numerous conferences and symposia in the US and abroad. In 1999, SWO sponsored a two-day, interfaith "Women's Wisdom, Women in Action" conference at Dominican University of California in San Rafael, bringing together a multitude of women of many faith traditions from the local community and around the world.

SWO also began to develop specific projects, including Prison Project and Literacy Project. The Prison Project developed and maintains correspondence with women prisoners throughout the United States. In California, it works within women's jails to provide education, health awareness, cancer prevention and stress reduction services. The SWO Prison Project has received an award for its work from the Marin County Sheriff's Office, and because of its work, members were invited to participate in a Women in Prison conference in California in 2000. SWO Literacy Project collects and contributes books in English and Spanish for low-income children at child-care centers in northern California.

SWO publishes a newsletter that is distributed nationally and internationally, and has published four books written by its members: *Sufi Women: The Journey toward the Beloved, The Veil, Women's Wisdom*, and *The SWO Cookbook*.

Lecture Series

Since 1997, SWO has hosted regular luncheon lecture series in the greater San Francisco Bay Area, and invited many outstanding women leaders to share their wisdom with each other and the public. 2006, SWO had the distinct honor of welcoming Nobel Peace Prize laureate, The Honorable Dr. Shirin Ebadi from Iran, who presented a lecture in San Rafael, California, sponsored by IAS and Dominican University. Much of SWO's work in the area of public education and advocacy is directed toward peace-making and has presented talks at numerous United Nations events including the NGO Conference in New York in 2000, the UN Millennium Peace Summit and the 50th Anniversary of the Declaration of Human Rights.

The Code of Ethics

SWO has also created a code of ethics with the help and active participations of over one hundred women from around the world working for eight months. SWO members have adopted this Code of Ethics as a guide. Upon the completion of this significant achievement, the SWO Code of Ethics and Declaration of Principles was presented at the 1998 IAS Sufism Symposium and read to the audience by Dr. Hamaseh Kianfar. This document of profound beauty, clarity and power is sure to endure for generation to come.

Preamble: The Sufi Women Organization, a humanitarian, non-political, non-sectarian organization, has been created to introduce, disseminate, honor and acknowledge, with Divine Guidance, the contribution and service of Sufi women to the world civilization.

The mission of this organization is to come together free from human prejudice to share the knowledge, wisdom, experience, and concerns of Sufi Women of the past and present with our societies and time, remembering that the essence of the human being, regardless of gender or color, time or place, has been regarded as reverent, dignified, and respectful by teachers of humanity. Such magnificence is the gift of the Being and recognizing such magnificence is learned.

Sufi Women Organization was organized to support, protect and educate for such learning. It is important that the Sufi teaching be protected; such teaching is not to be used for selfish gain or corruption of any kind. True Sufism requires great vigilance and sustained continuous self-improvement efforts. We, as a group of honorable and responsible women, have come together to serve as educators, guides, advisors and friends.

The Code of Ethics continues with thirteen principles to emphasize recognizing and honoring the value of human beings; accepting responsibility for one's well-being and action; to improve one's own education, skills; that all human beings, regardless of gender, race, age, social and economic status, have the right to educate themselves to their full potential and to advance on the spiritual path and attain spiritual leadership; respect the rights of others to hold values, attitudes and opinions that differ from one's own as long as those values, attitudes and opinions treat all people with dignity, honor and respect; dedicate ourselves to supporting those who suffer or are oppressed in communities and shall encourage the oppressed to speak and be heard by denouncing unethical conduct and manipulation within communities and in the larger society; support human rights and humanitarian peace efforts through other organizations; support and protect the rights of children; and will take active roles in support of equality of genders in both spiritual and secular domains.

Since it's founding in 1993, SWO has accomplished so much, but nothing has been as magnificent as creating a global sisterhood.

Sufism and Psychology Department and Programs

The Sufism and Psychology Forum, a continuing dialogue between the people of mind and soul, was established in 1993 through the efforts and vision of Dr. Ali Kianfar. SPF was founded to bring together the application of principles and practices of Sufism and the study of psychology through research, translation and discussion. SPF publishes and distributes the newsletter *Psychology: Traditional, Spiritual, Contemporary*, publishes books on Sufi Psychology, sponsors lectures and seminars presented by Sufi psychologists, and has created a forum and line of communication between Sufi psychologists, including an online dialogue. From this original set of goals, other institutes, programs, and centers developed including Institute for Sufi Psychology and Community Healing Centers.

Institute for Sufi Psychology

The Institute for Sufi Psychology was created to further explore the relationship between the study of Sufism and psychology. Members from around the world bring together the application of Sufi principles and practices and the study of psychology. The ISP has been successful in opening and maintaining an international dialogue among spiritual practitioners who work in the field of psychology, and in facilitating the integration of Sufi principles into the practice of psychology. The Institute for Sufi Psychology works collaboratively with the Community Healing Centers.

Community Healing Centers

The Community Healing Centers is a non-profit counseling organization that has been serving San Francisco, Marin, Novato, and surrounding areas in the California Bay Area since 1997. The Community Healing Centers provide counseling and psychological services, classes, support groups, workshops, educational and stress management programs. CHC provides continuing education classes for psychotherapists and offers a comprehensive training program for registered interns. Licensed psychotherapists and supervised interns offer an integrative approach to psychotherapy for adults, children, couples, and families.

The Community Healing Centers were founded to provide essential services to the community. The individualized and client-centered counseling and psychological services are designed to meet a variety of needs and integrate Western psychology with ancient wisdom to bring balance and harmony to the whole person. The clinical staff is comprised of highly trained and qualified licensed psychotherapists and interns with backgrounds and training in Western and Eastern psychologies who specialize in a broad spectrum of clinical issues.

Classes, groups, and workshops are offered by the Community Education

Program on a variety of topics including navigating transitions, stress-reduction, parenting, meditation, and continuing education classes for therapists. Educational and stress-management programs may be custom designed to meet specific needs and are offered on-site to corporate and non-profit organizations. Therapists from the Community Healing Centers offer and participate in local and international seminars and conferences on Western and spiritual psychology. More information may be found at: www.community-healingcenters.org

Institute for Sufi Studies (ISS)

The Institute for Sufi Studies offers educational programs and invites the public from around the world with the common interest of Sufism to join together for research, dialogue and study. The Institute offers a broad range of classes, workshops, retreats, and community educational events directly through its center in Northern California, online, and at other educational institutions. Subjects cover a wide-range of topics and have included: Qur'an, Hadith, Islamic Studies, Islamic Law, Principles of Sufism, Meditation, and poetry. The faculty members of ISS are practitioners of Sufism and teachers in many diverse disciplines including religion, literature, language, psychology, philosophy, sociology, humanities, law, and physics. ISS has been currently creating a library of Sufi books, with a great range of publications

The Institute for Sufi Studies hosts an annual Humanitarian Award Dinner to honor and celebrate outstanding individuals for their contribution in elevating the level of humanity in our society. https://ias.org/sufism/

Taneen Sufi Music Ensemble

Formed in 1996 under the guidance of Sufi Masters Shah Nazar Seyyed Dr. Ali Kianfar and Dr. Nahid Angha, Taneen Sufi Music Ensemble is based in the San Francisco Bay Area of California, U.S.A.

The music of Taneen (Divine melody) springs from the heart of prayer, inner practice, and spiritual discipline and is a celebration of the heart's longing to feel connected to the source of mystery behind this reality and the source of peace within us all. Their music is an offering and a service intended to increase tranquility in the world.

With an authentic fusion of Middle Eastern and Western influences, Taneen Sufi Music Ensemble creates new, original melodies, although their

234

music is deeply rooted in the Sufi tradition in its intention and inspiration. The ensemble primarily sings ecstatic love poetry of the great Sufi masters (such as Rumi, Hafiz, Omar Khayyam and Shah Maghsoud), translated into English by Dr. Nahid Angha, making the profound message of love that the Sufis profess very accessible to all audiences. Taneen's recordings include: *Divine Breath*, 1997; *Into Ecstasy*, 2000; *Awaken*, 2005; and *Ocean Of Love*, 2012. Members include: Sheikh Salman Baruti, Soraya Chase Clow, Salim George Matchette, Salima Ginny Matchette, Jeff McCullough, and Taher Anthony Roybal. In addition, David Rosenthal, who produced, engineered, and mixed Taneen's music, was a guest performer during numerous public performances, as well as recordings.

Taneen Sufi Music Ensemble has performed locally and internationally at events that focus on peace-building, human rights, and interfaith understanding and cooperation, including such events as: the annual IAS Sufism Symposium and IAS Songs Of The Soul Festivals; Women's Partnership for Peace in the Middle East Conference, Oslo, Norway; Parliament of the World's Religions, Barcelona, Spain; Sufi Music, Poetry and Shared Chanting, Edinburgh, Scotland; United Nations 50th Anniversary Celebration, San Francisco, CA; Earth Day Celebration, Grace Cathedral, San Francisco, CA; Building Bridges of Understanding Series, Dominican University, San Rafael, CA; and Healing the World Conference, Asilomar, CA. {Please refer to http://www.taneen.org for a more complete performance listing.}

Voices for Justice (VFJ)

Voices for Justice, founded by Dr. Hamaseh Kianfar and with heartfelt works of Emily Hedges, Neda Tejada, and Samiramis Behjat was established in 2005 as a department of the Sufi Women Organization. Voices for Justice (VFJ), is an organization of youth leaders advocating for the rights of children by providing a forum for public awareness through: education, community service, events and programs so that every child has the opportunity to fulfill his or her highest potential. VFJ has partnered with several non-profit organizations both locally and internationally to ensure that children have access to quality education, shelter, clean food and water, and health care. VFJ strives to give a voice to members of our society who have historically been underprivileged.

VFJ has been invited to make presentations at various luncheons, speaker's series, and symposia about youth activism, human and children's rights, cross-cultural identity, and social awareness. The organization has been nominated and received awards for volunteer excellence, international service, fund raising, and community contributions. In 2007, Voices for Justice attained the distinguished honor of being named Ambassadors for UNICEF by contributing and collaborating with the *trick-or-treat* for UNICEF program.

Food Banks and UNICEF

Voices for Justice is dedicated to providing resources to those in need both locally and globally, and has contributed towards annual food drive to support low-income families and shelter programs in Marin, San Francisco, and Alameda counties; created a calendar that its proceeds from sales were donated to UNICEF. Calendar was the outcome of the art works of children, ranging in age and experience, who were asked to reflect on children's access to the basic needs of shelter, water, health care and nutritional food. In turn, these children created beautiful pieces of art for the calendar, raising awareness about the basic needs that every child deserves to have filled.

Domestic Violence Outreach

VFJ created a domestic violence resource card for women and children to carry in their wallets. The resource card included contact information for local shelters, transitional housing, crisis and support hotlines, and community food banks. The resource cards were donated to domestic violence shelters in Marin County.

VFJ also participated in the following international work and advocacy:

Baby Knit Cap Project: Malawi, Africa

Voices for Justice knit and donated over one hundred wool caps for infants and young children in Malawi, Africa. Through our collaboration with The Global Aids Interfaith Alliance, knit caps were donated to orphanages, hospitals, clinics and schools. Malawi is one of the 11 poorest countries in Africa and there are 550, 000 orphaned children currently living in Malawi.

Adopt a Classroom in Central America
Voices for Justice collected supplies, assembled school kits and backpacks and donated over 50 backpacks to underprivileged school children in El Salvador. The backpacks included art and school supplies and educational materials.

Women and Families
The Executive Director of VFJ, traveled to Burma and Tibet to work in a clinic in the northern part of Burma that provided services to HIV positive Muslim women. Voices for Justice provided services and supplies.

Ambassadors to UNICEF
VFJ has supported the work of UNICEF by donating to the *trick-or-treat* for UNICEF program annually. Voices for Justice support has helped to immunize young children and infants in Darfur, create safe afterschool programs for children and families in Lebanon, and provide clean drinking water and mosquito nets to children in Africa.
Founding Members: Dr. Hamaseh Kianfar, Founder and Executive Director; Neda Ana Tejada, Finance Director; Samira Behjat, Secretary; Emily Hedges, Public Relations

Sufism: An Inquiry

Sufism: An Inquiry is the world's longest running journal on Sufism. Published regularly by the International Association of Sufism (IAS) since 1987, the scholarly journal has provided an international space for the many voices of Sufis from around the globe, and for the voices of spiritual seekers of all faiths and traditions.

Since its first issue in 1987, with Dr. Nahid Angha as Executive Editor and Shah Nazar Seyyed Dr. Ali Kianfar as its Editor-in-Chief, the *Journal* has been an essential representation of every aspect of the IAS' mission. It is a living reflection of the dynamic energy and growing global community of people living from the heart. The *Journal* aims to foster the study and advancement of the meaning of religion, the interrelation between the principles of religion and the principles of science, and inner practices that foster equanimity, the expression of love, and the wisdom of peace.

In more than 60 issues to date, the pages of *Sufism: An Inquiry* have championed women's rights and the work of the Sufi Women Organization; published scientific inquiries ranging from the physiology of HeartMath to the latest findings of astronomers; shared new scholarly translations of classic works of Sufi literature and poetry, and many stories of Sufi saints previously unavailable in English; offered essays by noted scholars on literature written through the centuries by and about Sufis, and presented articles by leading psychologists on human development and the spiritual path. The *Journal* has also reported on human rights and other diplomatic movements ranging from the work of the United Nations to interfaith organizations such as the United Religions Initiative; explored the cultural gifts of world religions diversely embodied around the planet; and provided insight into a wide variety of effective practices for spiritual development.

Since the time the IAS first began publishing *Sufism: An Inquiry*, the world has experienced an amazing transformation full of new opportunities and challenges. One notable dimension in which the world has changed significantly is in terms of media with the advent of the Internet and advanced technologies. Just as the IAS has been at the forefront of leadership efforts for reducing conflict and enabling peace, human rights and equality, religious freedom and international cooperation, in 2013 the IAS re-launched the journal *Sufism: An Inquiry* in an online dynamic digital format more accessible to a worldwide population, with plans to develop video, audio, and interactive social media content online as well as to offer each issue of the journal in print in downloadable format and in other formats readable on e-readers.

The tradition at *Sufism: An Inquiry* of promoting peace by featuring the work of great teachers, scholars and scientists from a broad range of global perspectives, historical contexts, and fields of specialization runs deep and strong throughout the journal's history and will continue to grow far into the future.

Sufism Symposium

From the very beginning, in March of 1994, it was clear that something special was happening. By the end of the peaceful and enlightening weekend of the First Annual Sufism Symposium, the strength of the common bond uniting all Sufis was apparent. It was clear, too, that the combined energy of Sufis can revitalize society with the breath of life - in the words of one participant, the Symposium marked "…the beginning of the healing of this world."

In 1994, presenters and audience alike came from across the United

States and around the world - the first time ever so many different groups have gathered to introduce Sufism in all its varied forms and practices. An audience of about 500 came to share in the presentations of more than 39 Sufis and scholars. Each of the presenters brought a special experience. From the opening prayer led by Sheikh Ahmed Tijani of the Tijaniyya Order of Ghana to the final presentation of turning, music and poetry of Rumi by the Mevlevi Order of America, the variety of talks and workshops held something new for everyone.

Among the highlights of the first Symposium was the *zekr* Saturday night, which included all participating Sufi Orders. Dr. Nahid Angha became the first woman ever to sit in the inner circle with Muslim leaders from around the world. Never before have the *zekr* from all of these groups been blended in one circle, and the result was a powerful experience that no one will soon forget.

From the very first year, the Annual Sufism Symposium has begun with the *azan*, or call to prayer, usually delivered by the melodious voice of Sheikh Ahmed Tijani. The presenters and audience are welcomed, the theme introduced and the tone set in the opening statement of Dr. Nahid Angha, co-founder and co-director of the IAS. Dr. Angha has pointed to the significance of the Symposium in the history of Sufism, and acknowledged the various viewpoints presented throughout the Symposia, noting that: "beneath this great diversity of individuals, schools, and customs is the deeper unity illuminated from one source - the Divine. The message of the Divine is expressed by the Prophet who brought the news of that unity: *la illaha illa Allah*—all that is, is but the Divine."

Dr. Ali Kianfar, co-founder and co-director of the IAS, has given closing statements at the conclusion of each of the Symposia, offering reflections and expressing gratitude for all participants: the presenters and exhibitors, many of whom had traveled long distances; all of the attendees; and the crowd of IAS members whose volunteer efforts facilitated the beautiful flow of events. On one such occasion he said: "Throughout these two days, we have witnessed a diverse group of individuals who have come to express their spirituality in different forms. Yet we were all tied together by a common message that: human being is a magnificent creation - a hidden treasure – so search for this treasure not in any place other than within."

The Symposia have included talks, panel discussions, workshops, sacred music and poetry, centered on themes such as: the History of Sufism, Principles and Practices of Sufism, Sufism and Self-Discovery, Expressions of Beauty, Global Ethics, and Old Traditions for a New World. Presentations have focused on Women in Islam, the connections between spirituality and health, ecology and responsible stewardship of the Earth, the sharing of different spiritual practices, and the meaning of spirituality in modern times, moving to increasingly deeper levels of understanding and wisdom over the years. An extraordinary diversity of Sufi schools and orders have been represented, some of whom have attended nearly every year since the beginning, while each year has witnessed new members in the ever-growing family of friendship among Sufis, interfaith leaders, artists, writers, poets, scientists, and many more.

During the Symposium weekend, the Sufi Women Organization (SWO) has held its annual luncheon meeting, the only opportunity for regular members and guests from around the world to sit together to renew friendships and address vital issues concerning the status and condition of women and children in all parts of the world. During the 2004 SWO meeting, signatures were collected on the Campaign Letter, a petition asking heads of government to acknowledge rape during war, whether civil or international, as a war crime, punishable by law, and copies of the petition were given to the audience to distribute at home. The SWO luncheon has been one of the most popular and well-attended events on the Symposium schedule, and many of the men were eager to join in this center of energy and activity; they were often the highest bidders for items in the fund-raising fashion shows and auctions!

The Sufism and Psychology Forum panel, during these many years of Sufism Symposia, has provided another high point, has featured a wide variety of psychologists, practitioners of Sufism and other spiritual traditions, who have spoken with both deep knowledge and experience regarding the inner-connection of psychology and spirituality.

Sufi Youth also gather during Symposia, presenting panels and roundtable discussions focused on issues of particular interest to young people. A special one-day workshop, "Global Arts for Global Hearts," was part of the 2002 Symposium. This workshop provided a hands-on opportunity for participants to notice the role of perception in developing self-knowledge and express their spirituality in the form of tangible artwork; it led to discoveries of a surprising range of talents.

Very early in the history of the Sufism Symposium, the longing of attendees to gather early and share the melodies and lyrics of Sufi poetry before the opening of formal presentations evolved into the tradition of beginning the Symposium with an evening concert, featuring Taneen: Sufi Music Ensemble, as well as guest musicians of Sufi and other spiritual traditions. Many who are drawn to the beauty of the poetry and music became interested in its underlying wisdom, deciding to stay for presentations and informal discussion during the weekend.

Alongside the presentations, the exhibit area has provided a spiritual marketplace for such items as books, music, artwork, calligraphy, jewelry, clothing, handcrafts and more. Its festive atmosphere, colorful traditional dress, and many cultures and languages were fertile ground for exchange and conversation, and enduring friendships have developed.

As multi-religious and multi-cultural events, the IAS Sufism Symposia have included presenters from many faith traditions, including: Buddhist, Hinduism, Catholic, Jewish, Native American, and Protestant. They have drawn people from Afghanistan, Bangladesh, Canada, Costa Rica, Denmark, Egypt, England, France, Germany, Ghana, Hong Kong, India, Iran, Italy, Jordon, Kuwait, Morocco, Nigeria, Scotland, Senegal, South Africa, Syria, Turkey, and across the United States. The Symposium has also traveled to the people: expanding outwards from the IAS home base in Marin County, California, Symposia have been held throughout the San Francisco Bay Area, as well as Seattle and Philadelphia in the US; Cairo, Egypt (co-sponsored by Egyptian Society for Spiritual and Cultural Research); Edinburgh, Scotland (co-sponsored by Edinburgh Institute for Advanced Learning and the Edinburgh International Centre for World Spiritualties); and Barcelona, Spain (in cooperation with The Parliament of the World's Religions).

Symposium presenters have included scholars from many colleges and universities, among them: Amherst College, California Institute of Integral Studies, Dominican University of California, Duke University, Harvard University, Indiana University, Institute of Transpersonal Psychology, John F. Kennedy University, Louisiana State University, Sonoma State University, University of California at Davis, University of California at Irvine, University of California at Riverside, University of Georgia, and University of San Francisco. The Sufism Symposium has made its mark on civic life as well – in 1996 San Francisco Mayor Willie Brown declared March 29 as "The

International Association of Sufism Day" in San Francisco.

Music, poetry, movement, and artwork from Sufi and other traditions have been key elements in Sufism Symposia. The enchanting and broadbased appeal of these forms of expression often reaches directly to the heart, bypassing mental and logical processes. Based on participant response, the IAS developed *Songs of the Soul Poetry and Sacred Music Festival* in 2012, featuring even more poetry and music in conjunction with presentations on principles and practices. The Songs of the Soul Festivals have continued annually, generating a new energy and reaching a wide audience.

For more than 20 years, IAS members have volunteered to work tirelessly under the guidance and direction of Dr. Angha and Dr. Kianfar to provide this service for humanity. Scores of presenters have volunteered their time and knowledge, and hundreds of attendees have shared in the richness of these offerings. Each year, the hotel hosting the Symposium has commented on the peace and beauty of the weekend, and asked IAS to return.

Sufism Symposia have introduced Sufism as a path of direct connection with the Divine, beyond labels, and open to all who seek wisdom and achieving self-knowledge. It is a practical path to living as a reflection of the Divine wisdom that is contained in each one of us. Full reports of each Symposium are on the IAS website at www.ias.org. Recordings of Symposium presentations are also available.

Songs of the Soul: Poetry and Sacred Music Festival

The International Association of Sufism's production of the *Songs of the Soul* Poetry and Sacred Music Festival has quickly established itself as one of the premier gatherings in the world for artists, religious scholars, and enthusiasts from many faith traditions, cultures and generations to come together in celebration and exploration of our humanity. The festival was designed for people of all backgrounds and spiritual traditions to come together in a shared appreciation for aesthetic beauty and wonder, especially through poetry and sacred music.

Among the highlights of the festival were the poetry contests in 2012 and 2013. Poets from all cultures and traditions were invited to submit their works (work) on themes of *The Natural Rhythm of Wisdom* and *Love's Eternal Melody*. The range of their lives and experience was reflected in the variety of beautiful works submitted, and the distinguished poets, scholars, writers and editors who participated as judges were challenged to select among the inspired poems. The winners were announced during the Festival, and introduced as they recited their winning entries.

In the 2014 festival, *Cosmology and Spirituality: Universe and Human Being*, the attendees were offered a celebration of the harmonious spirit that connects us and the inward journey of the heart. There were wonderful presentations by cosmologists and spiritual leaders about cosmology, spirituality and the universe, and on the topics of the human being and future potential for humanity. Festival participants have been mesmerized by the poetry of Sufis from the past and present and enchanted by Sufi music and zikr from Persian, Moroccan, Turkish, Indian, Bangladeshi, Sri Lankan and Pakistani origins, among others. Consistent with its intent to be inclusive, the Festival has also featured poetry and sacred music from other cultural and faith traditions, including Native American, Jewish, Christian, Japanese, African and Yemenite. The festivals have also featured a truly innovative Poetry Slam Collective, *Avay-i-Janaan*: Echoes of the Unseen, combining elements of sacred poetry and music with contemporary rap, to the delight of the audience.

Many Sufis, poets and scholars addressed topics concerning poetry and healing while others focused on poetry in relation to awakening, prayer, and the stations of the heart and the power of sound and listening.

Festivals have been held in 2012, 2013, and 2014.

Sufi Youth International

Sufi Youth International, a department of the International Association of Sufism, was created to develop and expand an international support network for youth that encourage youth to explore the spiritual and value questions of life. SYI was led by Sahar Kianfar who invited many of Sufi youth to create a forum designed to support youth who seek to incorporate spirituality into their everyday lives and are dedicated to creating an ethical society for humanity.

Sufi Youth International founded in 1999 at the Women's Wisdom: Women in Action conference organized by the Sufi Women Organization. A group of youth from both the Sufi and Interfaith community sponsored the Encouraging Wisdom: Youth and Leadership forum at the conference.

The youth-led action panel was a great success, which led the development of two strong community projects: Community Service with an Interfaith Reflection and Youth-led Support Groups. Although both programs were based in Northern California, USA, the core group of Sufi youths were very interested in fostering an international network of supporters with a desire to create the same type community programs in their communities. From this evolved the Sufi Youth International, which has recently gained new momentum through the college groups, online dialogue, and research groups.

Avay-i-Janaan Echoes of the Unseen

A program of the IAS, Avay-i-Janaan Echoes of the Unseen is a poetry slam collective originating through the Echoes of the Unseen. The members represent the journey of a human being from and into the heart and creation of the universe within themselves. Through poetry, movement, rhythm, and song, the audience is invited to seek your own origin in the light that emerges from the stillness of inner peace and unity.

40 Days – Alchemy of Tranquility®

The 40 Days program is based on the ancient recognition that psychology, physiology, and spiritual experience are interrelated and interconnected dimensions of the whole self. The program is comprised of co-leaders and Sufi Masters Dr. Nahid Angha and Shah Nazar Seyyed Dr. Ali Kianfar and a team of experienced psychotherapists and educators. The intention of the program is to offer each participant a well-developed style of personal practice for how to understand the self—this style of practice is rooted in ancient mysticism and influenced by psychology.

The 40 Days Alchemy of Tranquility Program was conceived of and introduced to the public by Shah Nazar Seyyed Dr. Ali Kianfar, who has been teaching spiritual practices and techniques for over forty years. This is the first time in history that the introduction to and preparation for *chelleh* (forty-day practice) has been offered publicly, as Dr. Kianfar has been directed. The practice itself remains individualized and private and is available only to those who qualify themselves. It is also the first time that this highly spiritual practice of purification has been combined with psychological training, recognizing that many people carry psychological wounds that first must be healed before they can progress on their spiritual journey. Dr. Angha and Dr.

Kianfar provide spiritual wisdom and deep knowledge of the psychology of the human being so participants have the opportunity to gain full awareness of themselves and learn to act in ways that reduce conflict and foster wisdom and love. Dr. Kianfar has trained a group of seasoned therapists, musicians, and martial artists who hold advanced degrees in their individual fields and bring experience and spiritual awareness as facilitators of the programs, workshops, and retreats.

In the 40 Days program, awareness is developed through knowledge gained in ongoing practice. The 40 Days program offers practices that are based on psychology, spirituality, science, meditation, poetry and music, and the martial arts. Practice and increased awareness of self foster emotional balance and a deeper understanding of attitudes, behavior, and spiritual development. Those who practice seriously and consistently experience awareness and transformation. This transformation is known as the Alchemy of Tranquility.

Many people ask why the program is called 40 Days. With clear intention and wise guidance, transformation is possible in 40 days, as has been discovered in many traditions and spiritual paths. The message of 40 Days has been repeated over generations, across the human family in all traditions, and at this time, we have the opportunity to access the secrets of the mystery of the forty days.

The program and practices and are helpful for individuals of any religious/spiritual background and for those interested in a practical approach to psycho-spiritual development. 40 Days publications include the book: *Human Self, Volume 1: Body.* For more information go to: https://ias.org/programs/fortydays/ or email forty-days@live.com

The Building Bridges of Understanding Series

The Building Bridges of Understanding Series is an educational program of the International Association of Sufism and Dominican University of California Humanities Department, in cooperation with Marin faith communities.

First conceived by Dr. Nahid Angha, in 2001, and was highly supported by Dr. Harlan Stelmach who has chaired and taught courses at Dominican University Humanities Department, the Building Bridges series began with an interfaith forum to investigate shared spiritual values that could help the community respond to and heal from the crises of September 11, 2001. As

Dr. Angha said in her closing address at the first forum, "communities ensure the well being of their members through shared information, concerns, resolutions, awareness, active participation, appreciation and creation of common ground, and beneficial goals and hope for the future of our community."

The Building Bridges of Understanding Series is ongoing, intended people of various faith traditions, students, educators, psychologists, physicians, community activists, artists, families and seekers of all ages and backgrounds. Themes for this Series have included: Expressions, the contributions of lyrics and songs towards social and global movements towards human rights, equality, freedom and civil rights. The Program has also created a scholarship; Women's Leadership: Navigating the Language of Power, Self Awareness and Leadership, Leadership and Global Awareness; Enlightenment and Ethical Conducts; Tolerance; Youth Realities; Compassion; Stewardship: Care for the Earth; Service; Understanding Judaism and Social Justices; Understanding native American Spirituality; Understanding Hinduism; Understanding Buddhism; Understanding Islam; Hosting Shirin Ebadi: the Noble Peace Prize Laureate; Waking Up in a New Religious America; the Many Faces of Violence; Bridging the Shared values; Experiencing Peace through Arts, and many more. http://ias.org/buildingbridges/

Bridging the Cultural Gap: a Muslim non Muslim Dialogue

Another program of the IAS is: Bridging the Cultural Gap: a Muslim non Muslim Dialogue, developed in cooperation with Campus Ministry of Dominican University. The program has created a forum for a continuous dialogue, round table discussions amongst Dominican University's Muslim and non Muslim students in hope of promoting mutual and multicultural understanding. The program aims to bridge the cultural gap between young Muslim/non Muslim citizens/immigrants university students through presentations, dialogue and discussions.

This project has served a diverse group: immigrants, multi-ethic minorities, whites, and African American participants aged 20 to 30 years old. Our young citizens remain the greatest assets of our nation as well as the globe. The wealth of our society's diversities and a great range of cultural identity have enriched our nation. These qualities enhance a community, and if respectful, educational and peaceful forums of dialogues are created, offered and provided, then every voice will be given the opportunity to be heard, and concerns will be addressed. Such forums will help individual(s) to be actively engaged in decision making, taking informative and educational steps towards possible solutions, and experiencing the world through each other's eyes.

In Conclusion:

Here, we conclude the history and contribution of the International Association of Sufism, its members, volunteers, departments, programs, and all those who have embodied such magnificent service, an unprecedented movement. Our work will continue, we will develop new programs suitable for the need of the time, and we are honored to have been given the opportunity to serve Sufism, its Masters, and its friends, in this short moment of time.

May the story of love continue to be told, through its people, during times, in languages, in cultures, in every breath, and may this moment of our existing be saturated by such magnificent gift of everlasting beauty.

Sufism Symposium

presented by:
The International Association of Sufism

1994

Endnotes

[1]From the introduction to the human growth program, "The True Me: Focused, Free, Fulfilled" (under publication).

[2]An idea about these two books is accessible in the biography of Assayyed Ali Rafea.

[3]Presented to the International Association of Sufism and published in *Women of Sufism: A Hidden Treasure*, edited by Camille Adams Helminski, and available at: http://www.amazon.com/Women-Sufism-Camille-Adams-Helminski/dp/1570629676/ref=sr_1_1?ie=UTF8&s=books&qid=1246276874&sr=1-1

[4]Presented at the International Association of Sufism Symposium, Seattle, Washington, USA, 2000.

[5]Presented at the Barcelona Interfaith Conference, 2004.

[6]Presented at the International Coalition for Humanism Conference, Petersburg, 2006.
http://forhumanism.org/en/materials/sharpening_rafea.htm

[7]Published in A Road Home e-magazine: http://www.aroadhome.org/c6a26_en.html

[8]Presented at the Women's Islamic Initiative in Spirituality and Equity (WISE), a conference held in New York, NY, Nov. 17-19, 2006, and arranged by the American Society for Muslim Advancement (ASMA).

[9]Presented at the International Association of Sufism Symposium, Edinburgh, Scotland, 2005.

[10]Presented to Threshold Society (Garrison, New York, 2006).

[11]This is the name common among the family and the spiritual circle. The official name is Dr. Ahamad Rafea.

[12]Ali Aliaa Rafea, and Aisha Rafea, *Beyond Diversities: Reflections on Revelation*, Dar Sadek, Alexandria, Egypt, 2000, Nahidt Misr Publication, 2005.

[13]Aliaa Rafea and Aisha Rafea, *Islam from Adam to Muhammad and Beyond*, or *The Book Of Essential Islam*, The Book Foundation, Watsonville, California Bath England, 2004.

[14]Ali Rafea, '*Islam: Living In Harmony with the Laws of Life*,' Anthology, Sadek Publications, Alexandria, 2007.

Sufism
Symposium

INTERNATIONAL
ASSOCIATION OF SUFISM